IMAGES
of America

CAMDEN AND ROCKPORT REVISITED

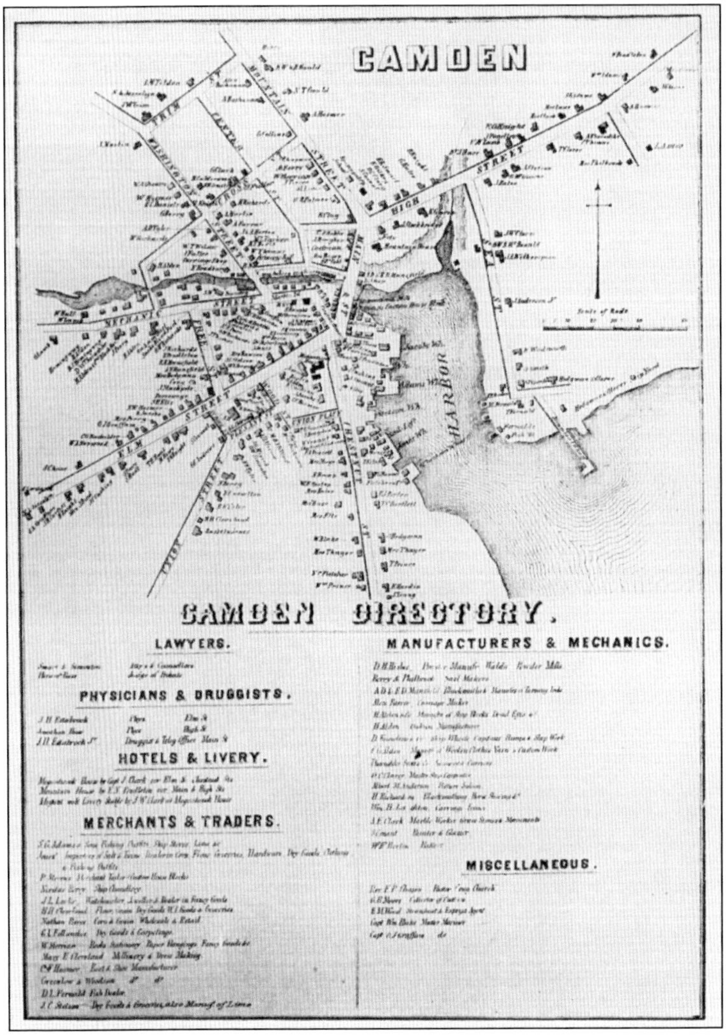

This map of Camden was drawn in 1859 and illustrates the remarkable growth of the village since the early settlers arrived in the mid-1700s. The Megunticook River and Camden Harbor were the center of industry throughout the 19th century. Today, the beauty of the area attracts thousands of visitors throughout the seasons. (Courtesy of the Camden-Rockport Historical Society.)

On the Cover: Stephen Ritterbush (at far right in hat) was one of the area's busiest builders. Here, he is with his large crew, taking a break from working on Timbercliffe, the cottage of Chauncey Keep on High Street in Camden. Ritterbush employed more than 100 men, and his crew built many of the large estates in the Camden and Rockport area, including Chauncey Borland's Grey Rocks on High Street and the Sneath cottage on Beauchamp Point. His crew also built the Mount Battie Woolen Mill in 1892 and the Camden YMCA on Chestnut Street in 1916. Ritterbush had the honor of sending the first parcel post from the Camden Post Office, which contained samples of dirt from the post office lot on Chestnut Street. The samples were sent to the architect supervising the plans for the new post office. (Courtesy of the Camden-Rockport Historical Society.)

IMAGES
of America

CAMDEN AND ROCKPORT REVISITED

Heather E. Moran for the
Camden-Rockport Historical Society

ARCADIA
PUBLISHING

ISBN 978-1-4671-2314-3

Published by Arcadia Publishing
Charleston, South Carolina

Printed in the United States of America

Library of Congress Control Number: 2014949904

For all general information, please contact Arcadia Publishing:
Telephone 843-853-2070
Fax 843-853-0044
E-mail sales@arcadiapublishing.com
For customer service and orders:
Toll-Free 1-888-313-2665

Visit us on the Internet at www.arcadiapublishing.com

This book is dedicated to all the past and present members of the Camden-Rockport Historical Society and to the generous people of the mid-coast area who are committed to helping preserve our shared history.

Contents

Acknowledgments

All images used in this book come from the collections given to the Camden-Rockport Historical Society since its inception in the 1930s. The author gratefully acknowledges and thanks all those members of the communities of Camden and Rockport for the donation and use of these images. The author also wishes to thank local historians and historical society supporters Jack Williams, Barbara Dyer, and Paul Putnam, for this book would not have been possible without their detailed recordings of our communities' history.

Introduction

In 1605, Capt. George Weymouth of the ship *Archangel* first sighted the Camden Hills on his voyage to Maine. He sailed up Penobscot Bay, anchored on June 12, 1605, and described the land as "abreast the mountains since called Penobscot Hills." In 1614, Capt. John Smith evocatively described the Camden hills as "the high mountains of Penobscot, against whose feet doth beat the sea." It is the only area on the whole East Coast of the United States except for Acadia National Park where the "mountains meet the sea." It was not until 1769 that James Richards, the first settler, arrived following the completion of a survey of the Waldo Patent by the Twenty Associates in 1768. In 1791, the town was named for Charles Pratt, first Earl of Camden, a judge and nobleman who sympathized with the colonists during the American Revolution.

Rockport, then known as Goose River, was settled in 1769 by Robert Thorndike, who built a small cabin near the mouth of the harbor. By the early 1800s, there were more than 18 homes in Goose River Village and a small saltworks on Beauchamp Point. The granite building at the curve of Central Street housed a general store and post office. By 1840, William Carleton moved his business ventures from Camden to Goose River and established shipbuilding, lime manufacturing, and ice harvesting operations.

During Camden's early years, the town had a steady growth in population and a prosperous economy. The 1870 census recorded a population of 4,512 and a valuation of $1,497,631. Numerous industries supported the population, including shipbuilding, an anchor factory, and the lime industry.

Beginning in the late 1880s, Camden's natural beauty began to attract wealthy "summer folk." These families built large summer cottages to rival those in Bar Harbor. Families such as the Curtises, Boks, Keeps, Gribbels, Dillinghams, and Borlands built beautiful estates, and their generosity to the community resulted in the elegant public library and graceful open spaces such as the Amphitheatre, Harbor Park, and the Village Green in Camden. The Bok family hired nationally known landscape architects Fletcher Steele, for the Amphitheatre, and the Olmsted Brothers, for Harbor Park and the Village Green. Magnificent private yachts such as Cyrus Curtis's *Lyndonia* filled the harbors. Many of the summer visitors arrived by the "Boston Boat," the steamboats of the Eastern Steamship Co. that made trips from Boston, Massachusetts, to Bangor, Maine, with stops at Rockland, Camden, and Belfast. The first run was in 1823, and the last was in 1937.

Goose River separated from Camden in 1891, almost 100 years to the day after Camden's incorporation in 1791. The village of Goose River became the town of Rockport. This split not only deprived Camden of three-quarters of the town's territory and half of its population but also the profitable lime and ice harvesting industries. In 1892, a fire destroyed nearly all of Camden's business district. However, town citizens quickly rebuilt the downtown area using brick instead of wood, leaving a legacy of permanence and grace that exists to this day.

As the 19th century came to an end, Camden's H.M. Bean shipyard launched the first six-masted schooner ever built—the *George W. Wells*. Shipbuilding continued in the Bean Yard throughout the 20th century, with the high point being the building of minesweepers and transport barges for the Navy during World War II. During that time, employees totaled over 1,500 men and women. After the war, many beautiful private yachts were built, and Camden Harbor was the scene of many yacht launchings. Other important employers for Camden's and Rockport's citizens were the several woolen mills along the Megunticook River that prospered well into the 20th century. The Knox Woolen Company made the world's first endless papermaking felt and was one of Camden's largest employers.

Yachting continued throughout the 20th century with the unique HAJ Boat racing fleet at the Camden Yacht Club. In the 1940s, the old, working schooners were converted to cruise vessels by Capt. Frank Swift, and the windjammer fleet continues to this day. In 1965, a new road was built up to the top of Mount Battie through the Camden Hills State Park, enabling thousands of people to enjoy an expansive view of Penobscot Bay as well as Megunticook Lake. Part of the natural beauty of Camden and Rockport is the Megunticook Lake area bordered by Turnpike Drive and shadowed by Maiden's Cliff. A popular recreational area for residents and visitors alike, its shores are dotted with summer cottages.

Music and cultural interests flourished with the establishment of the internationally renowned Salzedo Harp Colony and the founding of Bay Chamber Concerts. Theater productions at the Opera House and Shakespeare in the Amphitheatre enriched the lives of residents and summer visitors. Edna St. Vincent Millay, who grew up in Camden, was the third woman to win the Pulitzer Prize for Poetry. In Rockport, the Curtis Institute of Music Summer Colony brought world-famous musicians to the area.

In the 21st century, Camden and Rockport have succeeded in preserving their natural beauty, providing diverse educational and cultural opportunities, and fostering a strong sense of community for nearly 10,000 year-round residents.

One

A Place Called Home

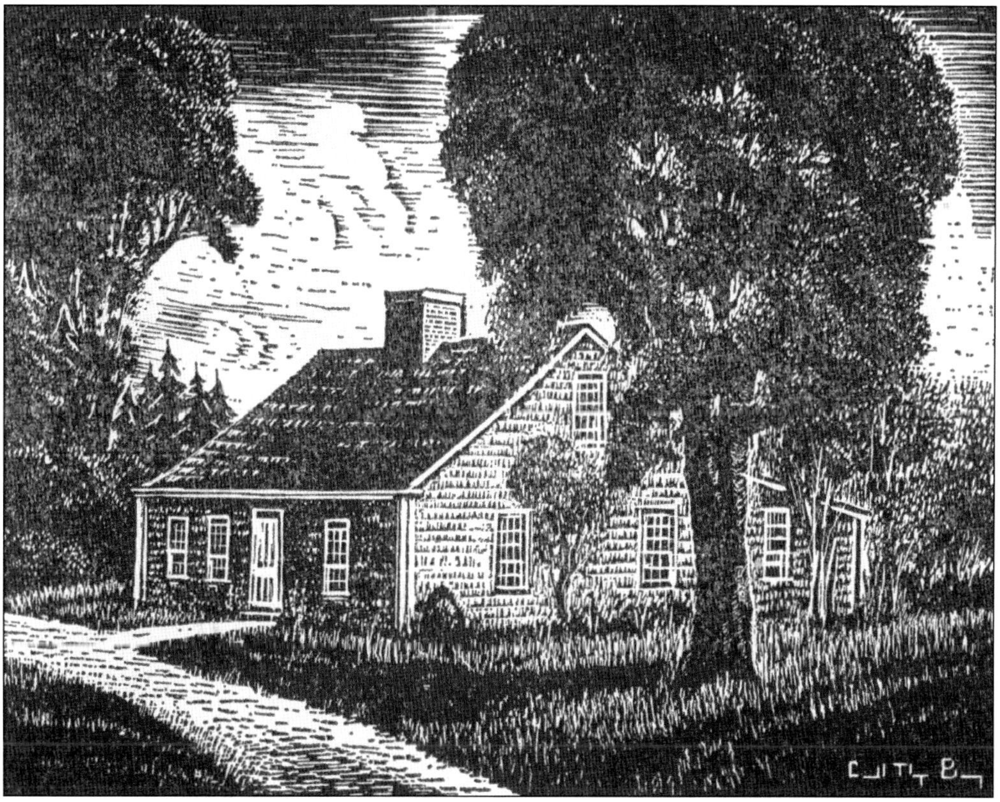

This beautiful wood-block print of the Conway homestead was created in the 1950s by renowned local artist Carroll Thayer Berry, a founding member of Maine Coast Artists in Rockport. The homestead was built around 1780 and at one point in its history belonged to relatives of Camden's Civil War hero William Conway. The homestead, barn, blacksmith shop, museum, and maple sugar shack form the Camden-Rockport Historical Society complex.

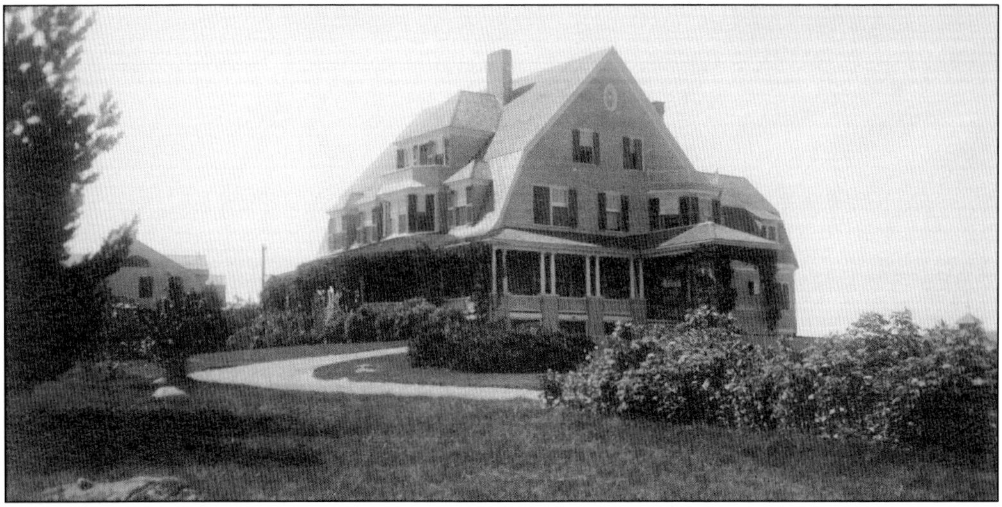

These photographs show examples of the magnificent summer homes to be found in the area. The first image is the Shingle Style summer estate of Parker Morse Hooper, Hill Acres, located on upper Chestnut Street in Camden. Hooper was a descendant of the Morse shipbuilding family in Bath, Maine, and resided in Fall River, Massachusetts. Along with Mary Louise Curtis Bok and Rev. Ralph Hayden, Hooper was one of the primary forces behind the construction of the Camden Public Library during the Great Depression. Having worked on several projects in Massachusetts, he and his partner Charles Loring donated their expertise as architects to design the new Camden Public Library in 1928. Sadly, this beautiful home was lost to arson in the mid-1980s and never rebuilt. The second image is of Spite House, located on Beauchamp Point in Rockport. Built around 1806 in Phippsburg, Maine, by Thomas McCobb, this lovely Federal mansion was loaded onto a barge in 1925 and towed up the coast by tugboat. It was bought by Donald Dodge of Philadelphia, Pennsylvania, who wanted it moved to Beauchamp Point in Rockport, where he planned to reside in the summers. Even the foundation was taken down and marked for resetting in Rockport.

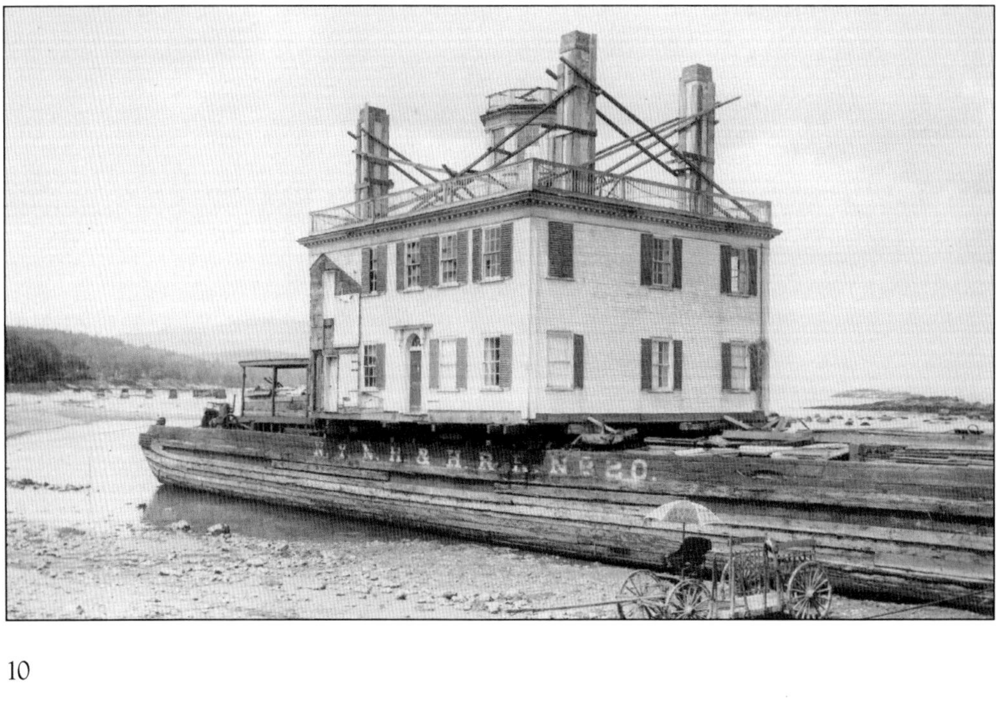

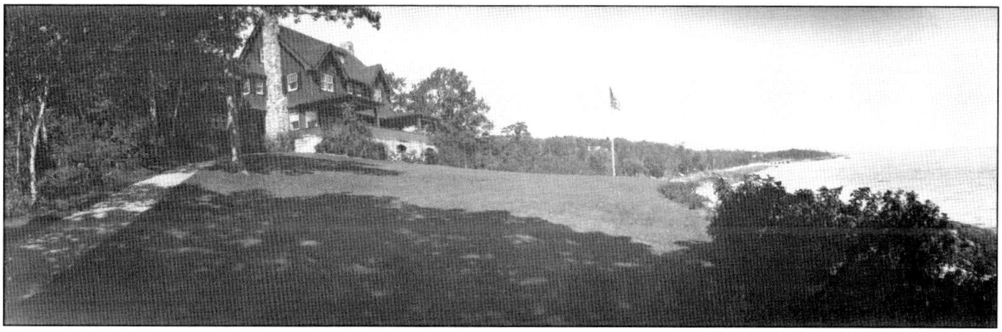

These photographs from the early 20th century show the large cottages built by wealthy summer residents. The image above shows Lyndonwood, the summer home of publisher Cyrus H.K. Curtis of Philadelphia. The house in the photograph below is Weatherend, at the tip of Beauchamp Point in Rockport, owned by John Gribbel, president of Curtis Publishing. While the first summer people came from cities in Maine such as Bangor, the Eastern Steamship Line quickly established routes that brought Bostonians seeking to escape the city. The building boom started in earnest in 1886, when industrialist Joseph Stearns built his stone castle known as Norumbega on High Street in Camden, and soon wealthy Americans began arriving from cities like Philadelphia, Chicago, and New York to establish their own summer estates.

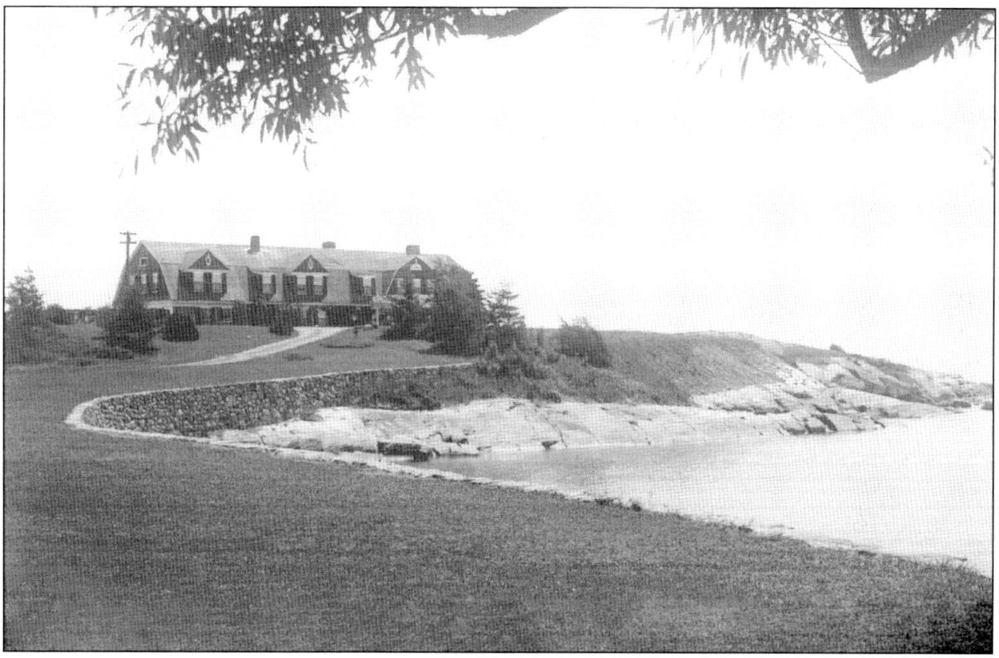

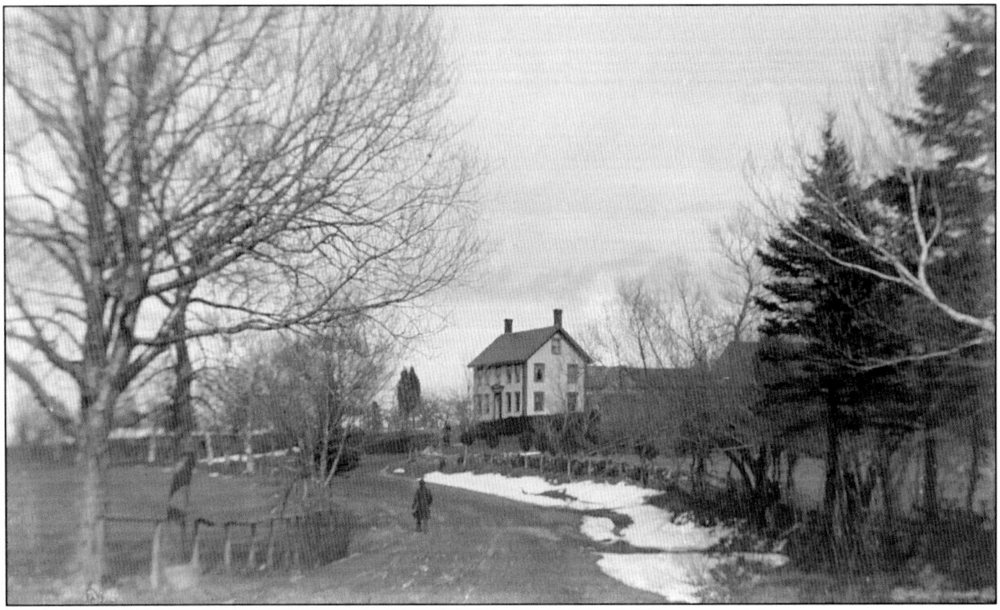

A lone figure ambles down a snowy path toward a large home on Russell Avenue near Calderwood Lane in Rockport. At the time this photograph was taken around 1888, the villages of Camden and Rockport had not yet split into separate towns. This home now houses the offices of Aldermere Farm, home of the beloved Belted Galloway cattle herd brought to Rockport by Albert Chatfield.

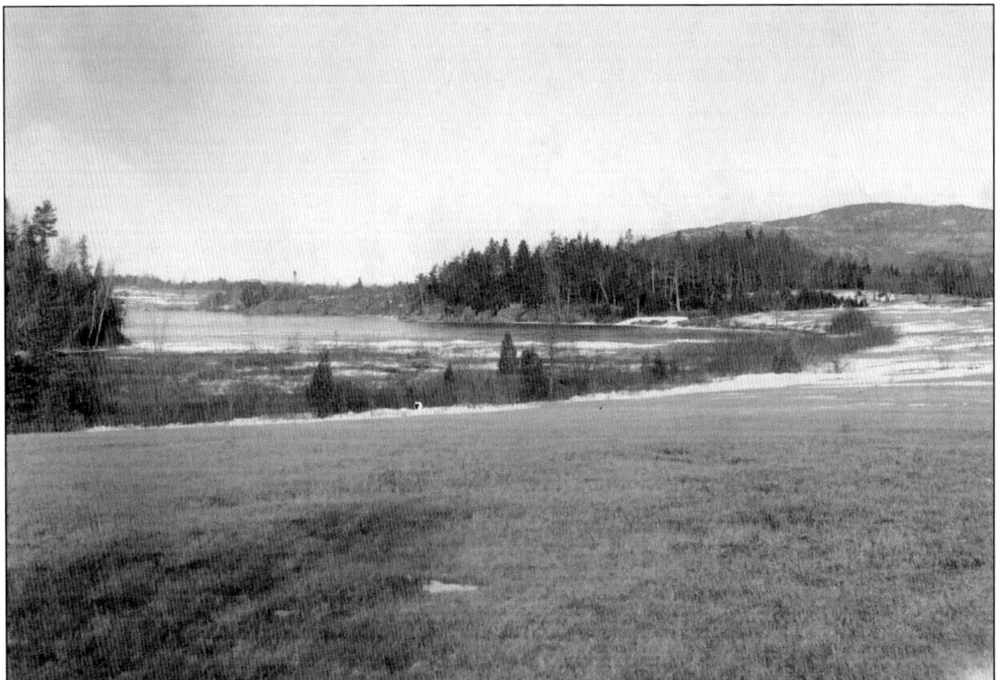

This is a view of the Lily Pond near Aldermere Farm in Rockport. The pond was known for the purity of its ice, a major industry in the area from about 1850 to the 1920s. At onetime, as much as 50,000 tons of ice were cut here, worth $4 per ton. It was packed in sawdust in the large icehouses along Rockport Harbor and could be shipped as far away as the Caribbean.

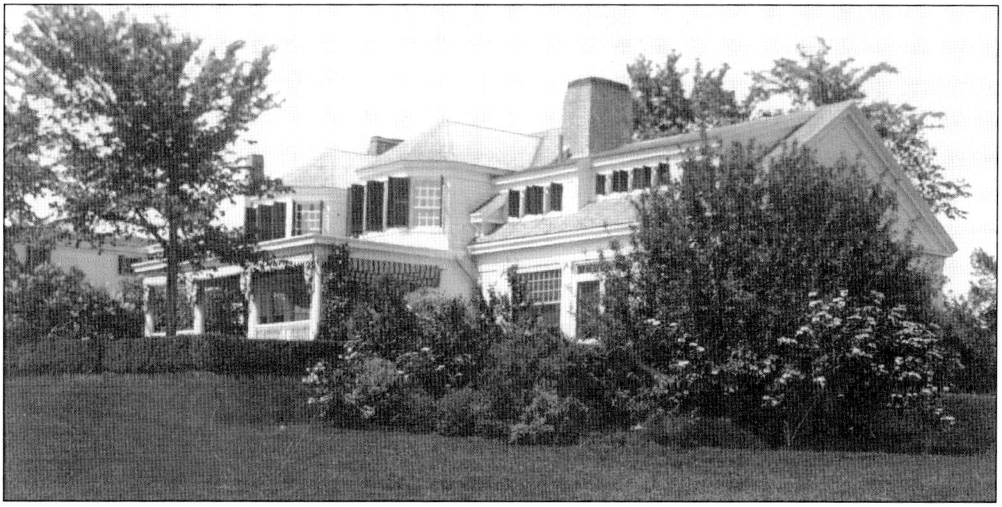

Pictured here is Aldermere Farm, the summer estate of the Chatfield family, as it appeared about 1920. Albert Chatfield Jr. and his wife, Marion, originally from Cincinnati, Ohio, retired to the estate in the 1950s and established the Scottish breed of hardy beef cattle known as Belted Galloways at the farm that would become a beloved attraction on tree-lined Russell Avenue winding through Rockport.

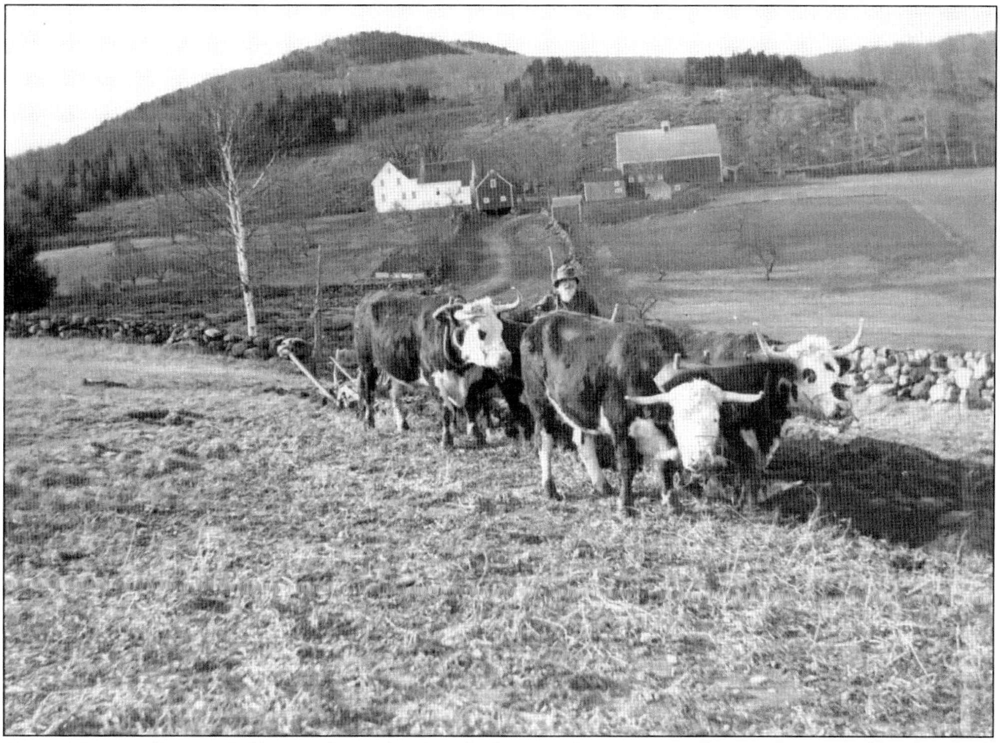

Oscar Howe of Howe Hill is working the family farm with his team of oxen. Oscar and his brother, Walter, both bachelors, lived on the farm their entire lives and were well known for their frugal lifestyle. One year, they spent only $50, growing all their own food and working the land. Walter used to tell how Oscar would "buy overalls three sizes too large so he could cut the bottoms off the pants to make a hat."

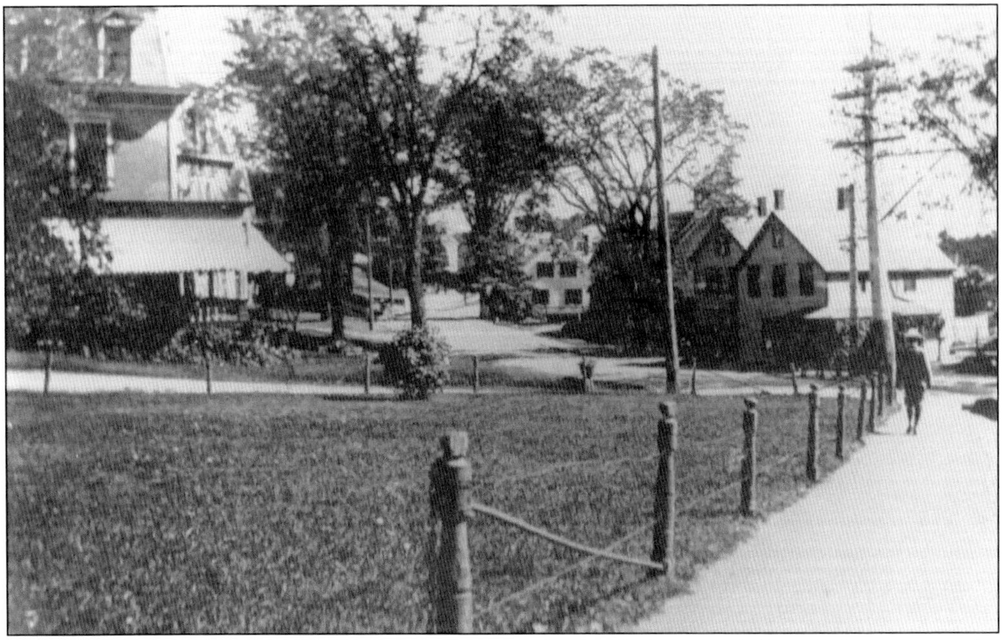

This image, taken in the early 1900s, shows the corner of Union and Russell Avenues in the center of Rockport village. The Carleton House stands at the left. It was a huge hotel owned by the Carletons, a prosperous family with a long history in Rockport. The Rockport Public Library now occupies the site.

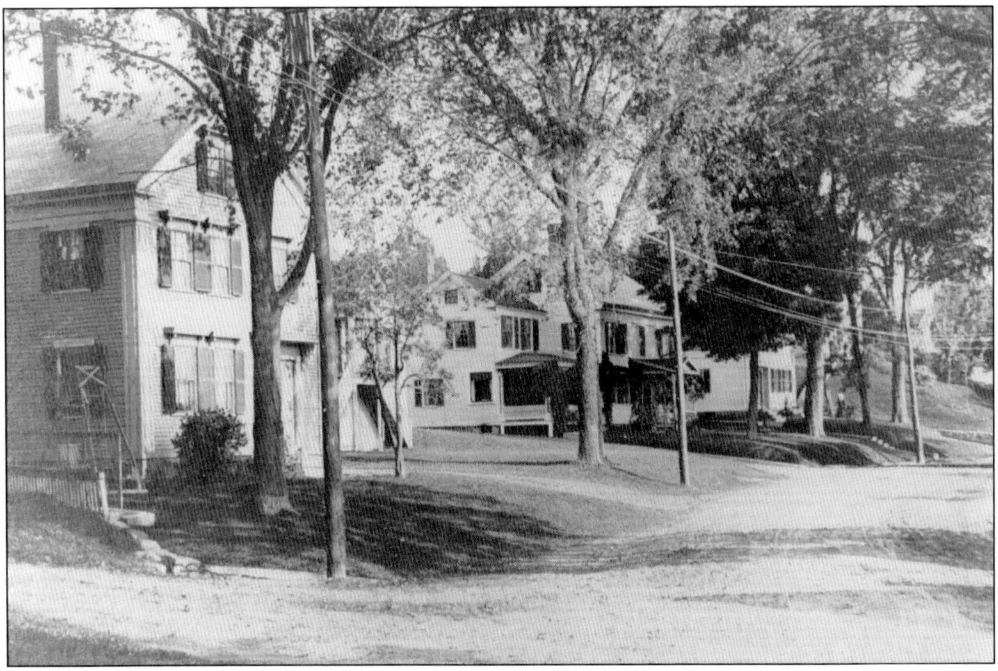

This is a late 1800s or early 1900s view of the north side of Russell Avenue in Rockport opposite Maine Coast Artists, which is now known as the Center for Maine Contemporary Art. Maine Coast Artists was founded in the 1950s by Carroll Thayer Berry, William and Stell Shevis, Denny Winters, and Peg Shea.

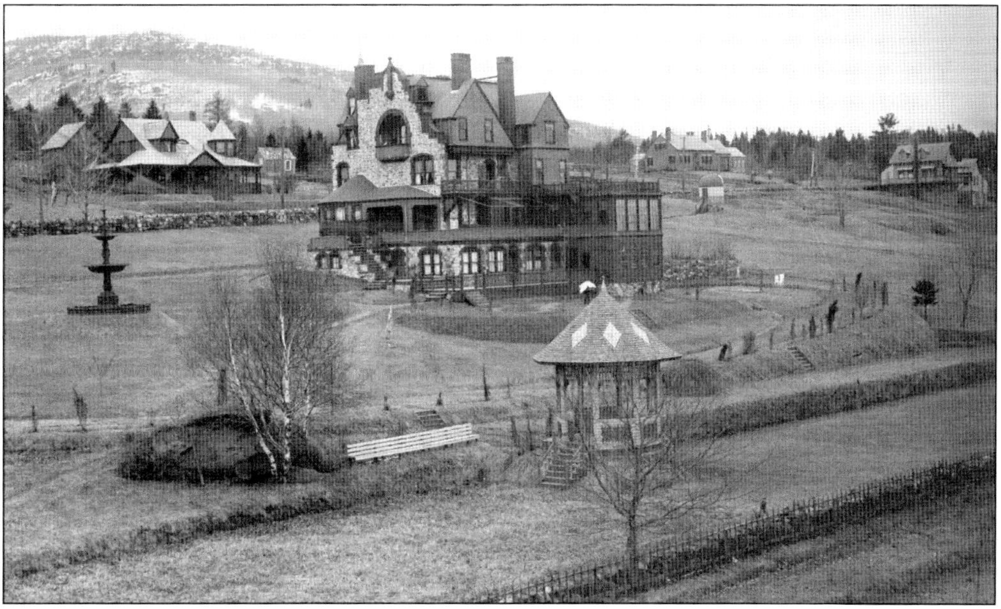

Built in 1886 by wealthy industrialist Joseph B. Stearns, Norumbega is Camden's beautiful castle located on High Street. Stearns was born into poverty in Weld, Maine, in 1831. He studied telegraphy, and by 1867, he was elected president of the Franklin Telegraph Company. He invented the duplex system, in which two messages could be sent over the telegraph at the same time, which revolutionized communications at that time. Stearns fell in love with Camden and settled there for the rest of his life.

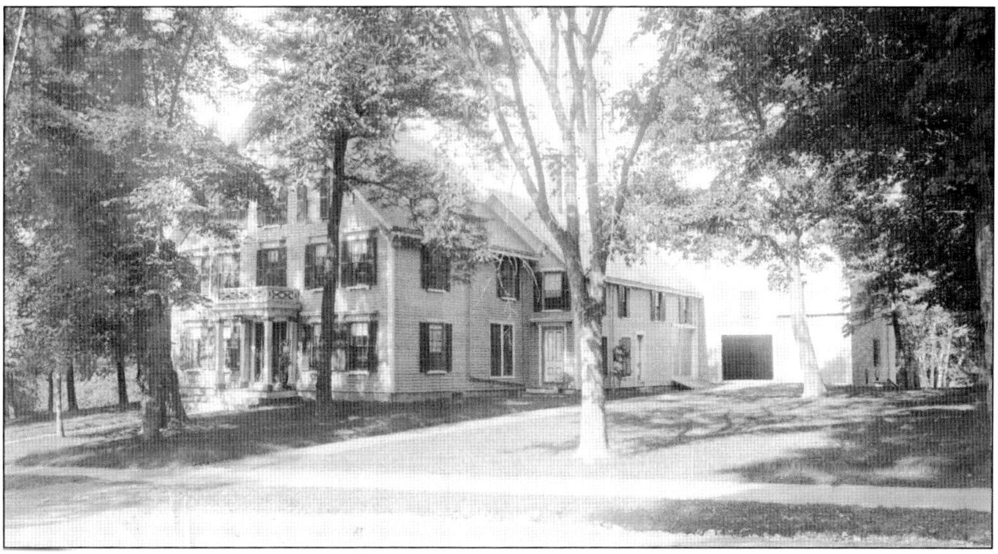

This home at 22 High Street now known as the Maine Stay Inn is located on land sold by Gen. Henry Knox to William and Joseph Eaton. The house was built in 1800 by Alden Bass and owned by William Carleton, a prominent Rockport businessman, who sold it to his cousin Joseph Hall. Hall commanded 30 men during the War of 1812 and supervised the building of forts in Camden on Eaton's Point and Jacob's Point. His daughter Mary married Dr. Jonathan Huse, and they lived in this house through the 1800s. The three-story home is known for its ornate cornices and moldings.

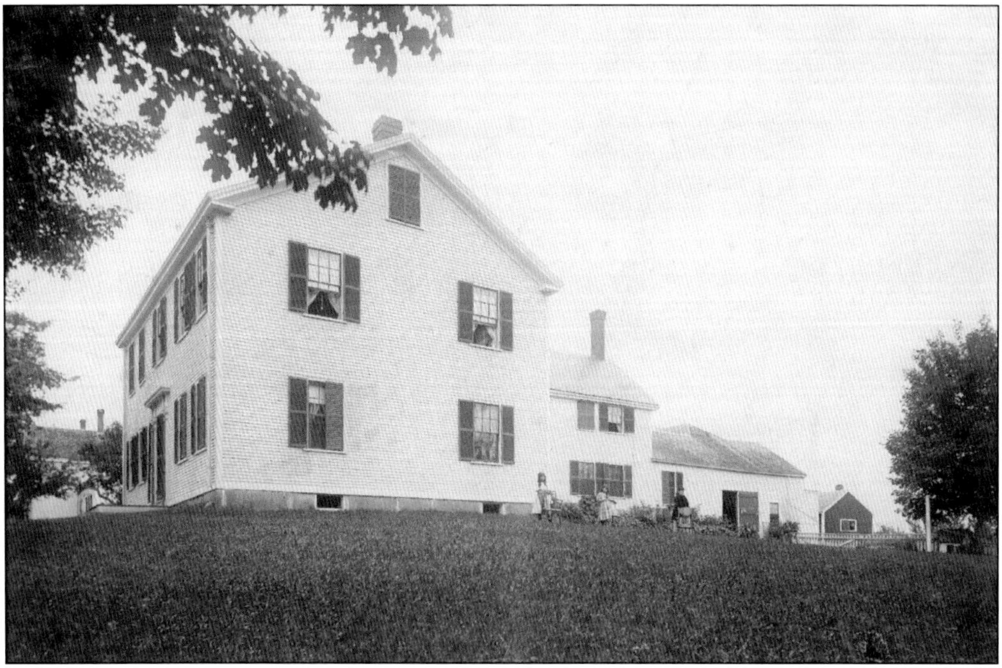

The Eaton home at the corner of High Street and Sea Street in Camden as it appeared about 1880. One of the oldest farmhouses in town, it was built around 1800 and appears on some of the earliest maps of the area, which show the property stretching all the way to the harbor.

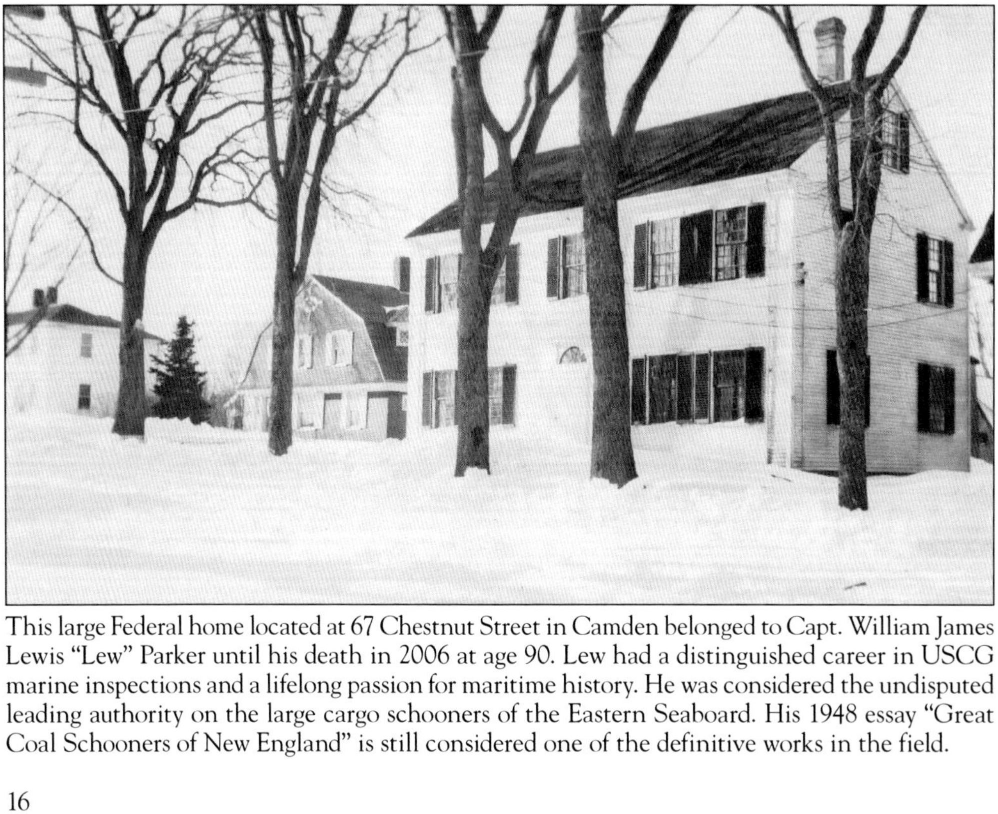

This large Federal home located at 67 Chestnut Street in Camden belonged to Capt. William James Lewis "Lew" Parker until his death in 2006 at age 90. Lew had a distinguished career in USCG marine inspections and a lifelong passion for maritime history. He was considered the undisputed leading authority on the large cargo schooners of the Eastern Seaboard. His 1948 essay "Great Coal Schooners of New England" is still considered one of the definitive works in the field.

Two

OPEN SPACES

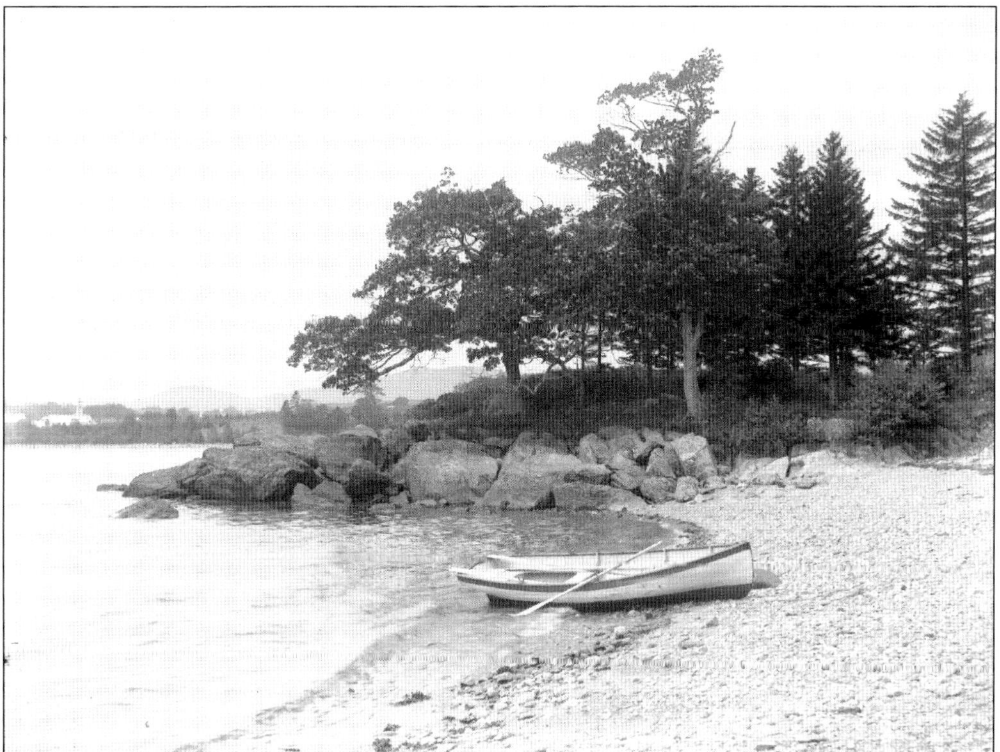

The coast of Maine is known for its rocky outcrops and coves. Sheltered spots such as Sherman's Cove in Camden and Beauchamp Point in Rockport help protect the harbors from seasonal gales and provide lovely areas for picnicking or taking in the beautiful vistas of the surrounding hills.

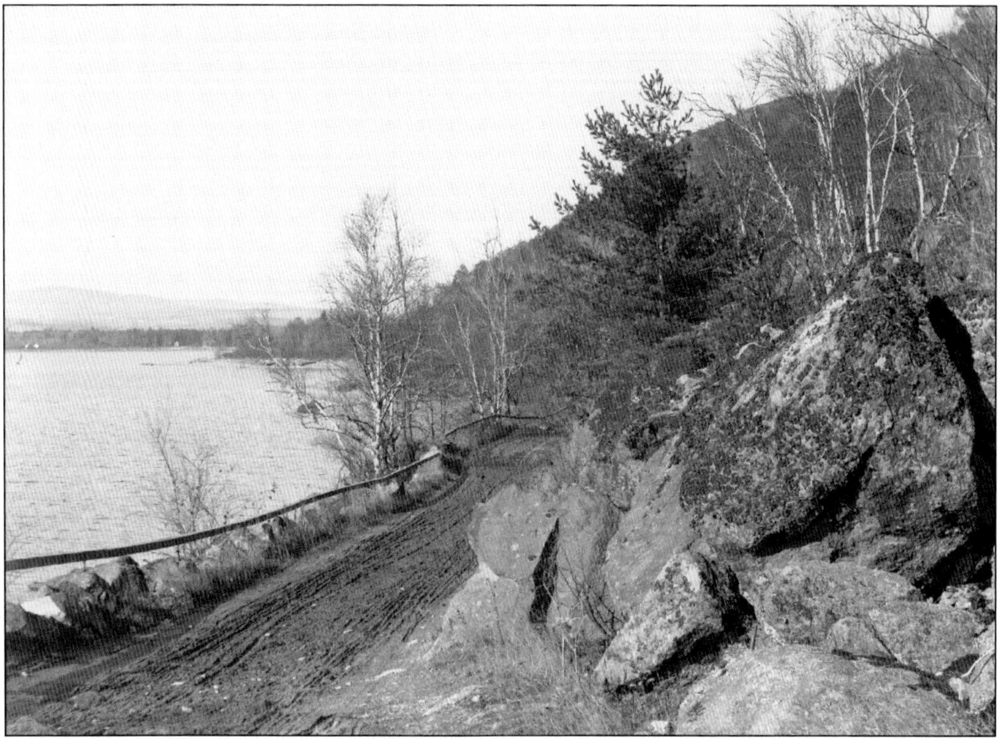

Turnpike Drive winds toward Lincolnville along the edge of Megunticook Lake. At the time this photograph was taken, the way was little more than a rough dirt road with just a fence standing between riders and a steep tumble into the lake. Part of Mount Megunticook is visible in the background as are some of the massive granite boulders that have slid down the mountain.

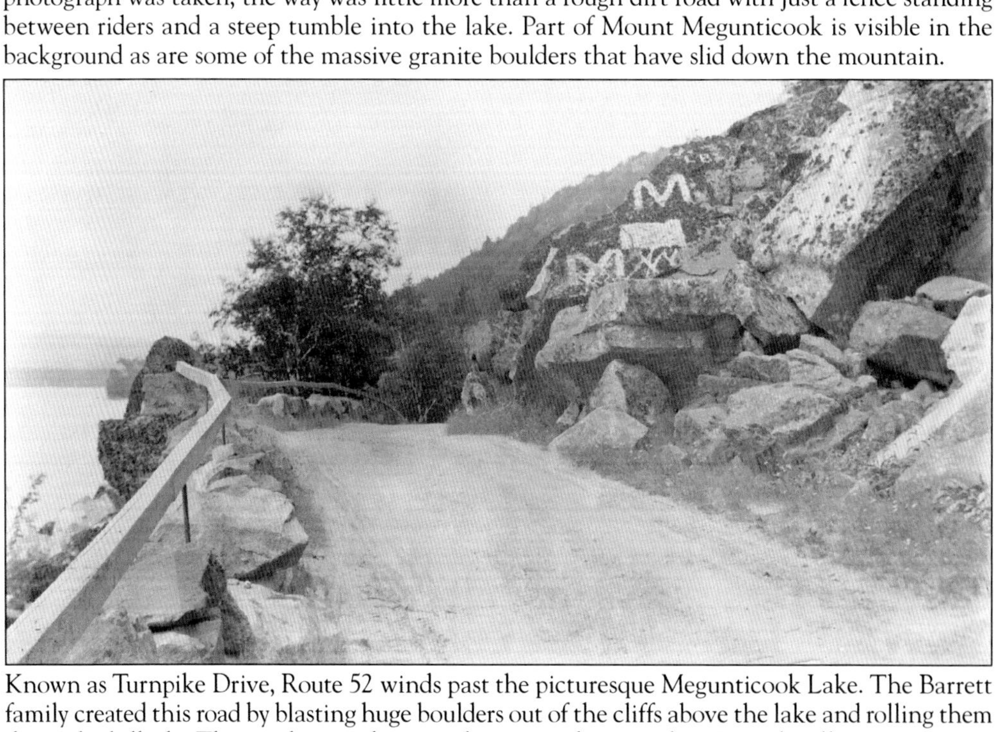

Known as Turnpike Drive, Route 52 winds past the picturesque Megunticook Lake. The Barrett family created this road by blasting huge boulders out of the cliffs above the lake and rolling them down the hillside. This road opened up another, more direct path to Lincolnville.

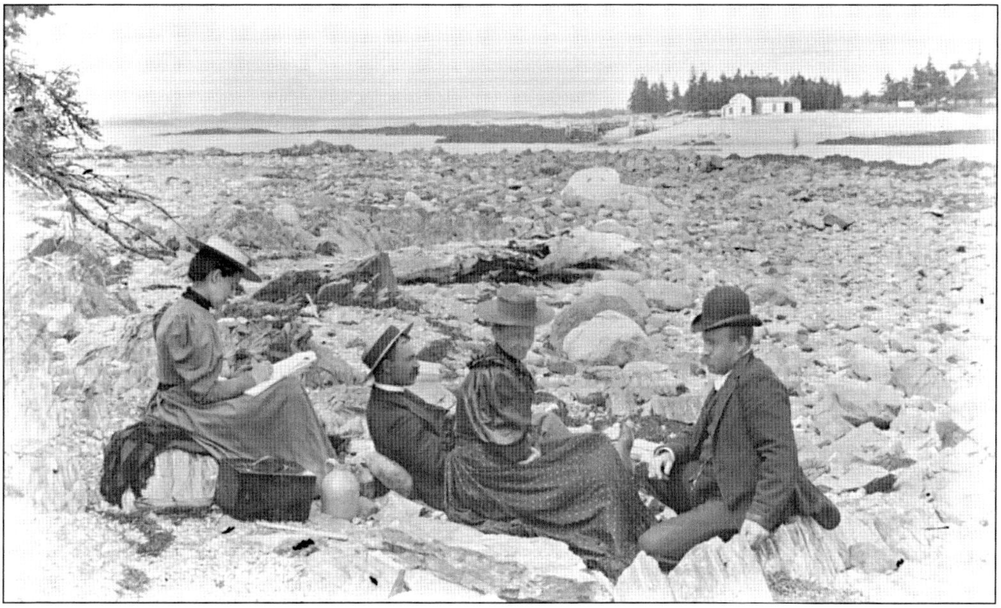

The abundant coastline of mid-coast Maine offered locals and tourists alike a place to go to escape the summer heat. Relaxing on the rocky shore and perhaps enjoying a cool sea breeze, these couples are stylishly attired in their dresses, hats, and three-piece suits. The young woman at the left is perhaps sketching the seaside view.

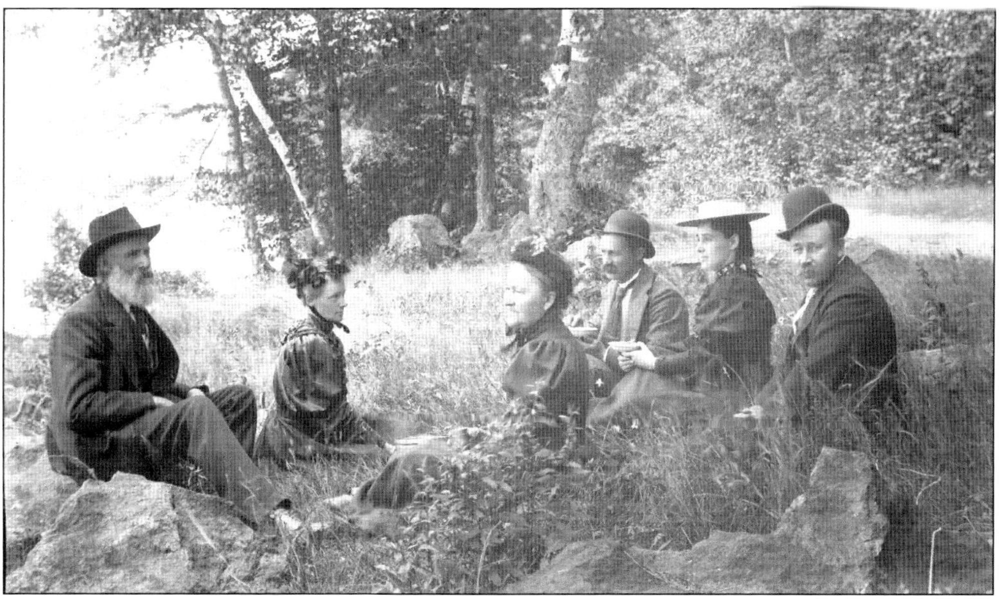

In this second photograph from the same collection, the man in the bowler hat is picnicking with family and friends in a shady spot near the shore. Although the people in the photograph are unidentified, the man in the beard could be William Barrett, a local character with a booming voice who was a descendant of one of the first settlers of Camden.

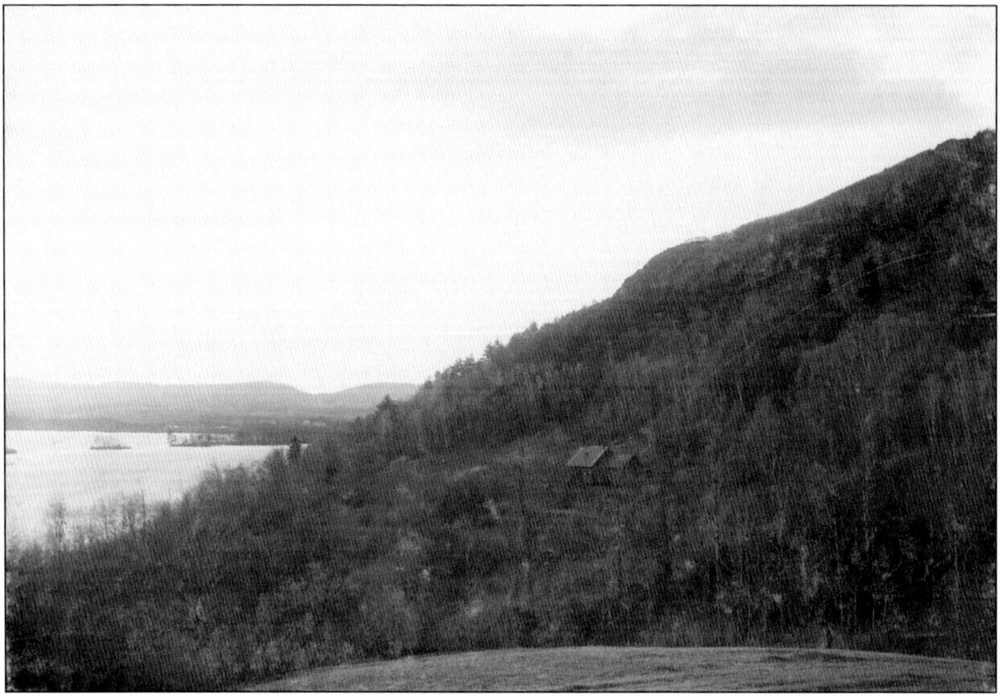

The image above is a rare view of the roof of the Barrett homestead, on the hill overlooking Megunticook Lake. The Barrett family were among the earliest settlers of Camden, and Daniel Barrett was granted a charter to build the Turnpike Road along the base of the mountain toward Lincolnville. He did this by rolling large boulders down the mountain to form a wall and then filled in with debris and dirt to make a road. It took nearly six years to build, at a cost of up to $6,000. Up to 50 men labored to build the toll road in exchange for a perpetual free pass. The toll rate until 1834 was 3¢ per passenger on foot, 8¢ for horseback riders, and 17¢ for a carriage. The view below looks across to Maiden's Cliff from the opposite side of Megunticook Lake.

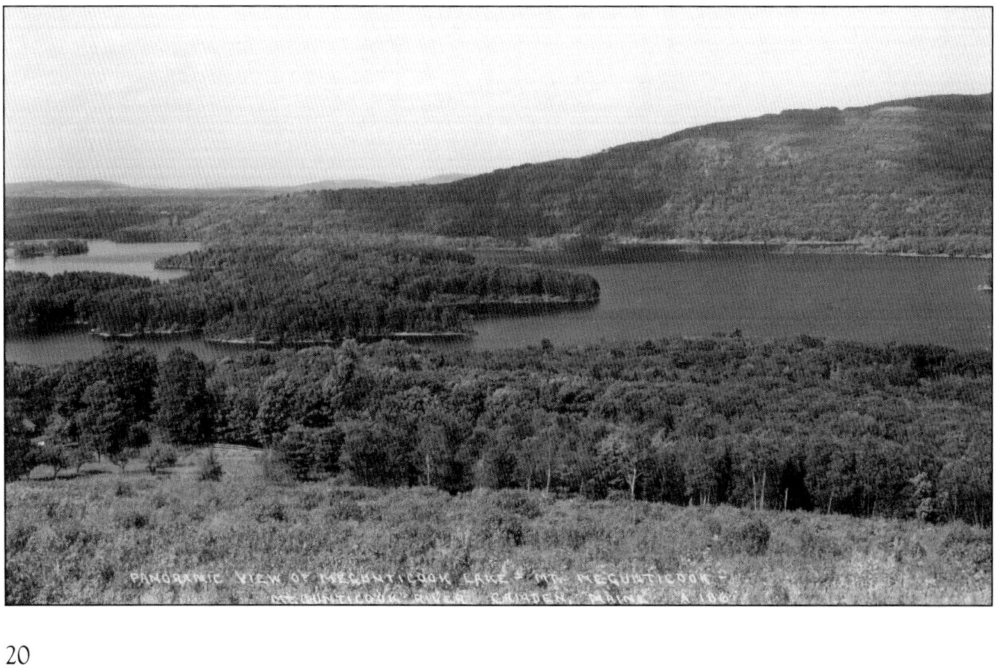

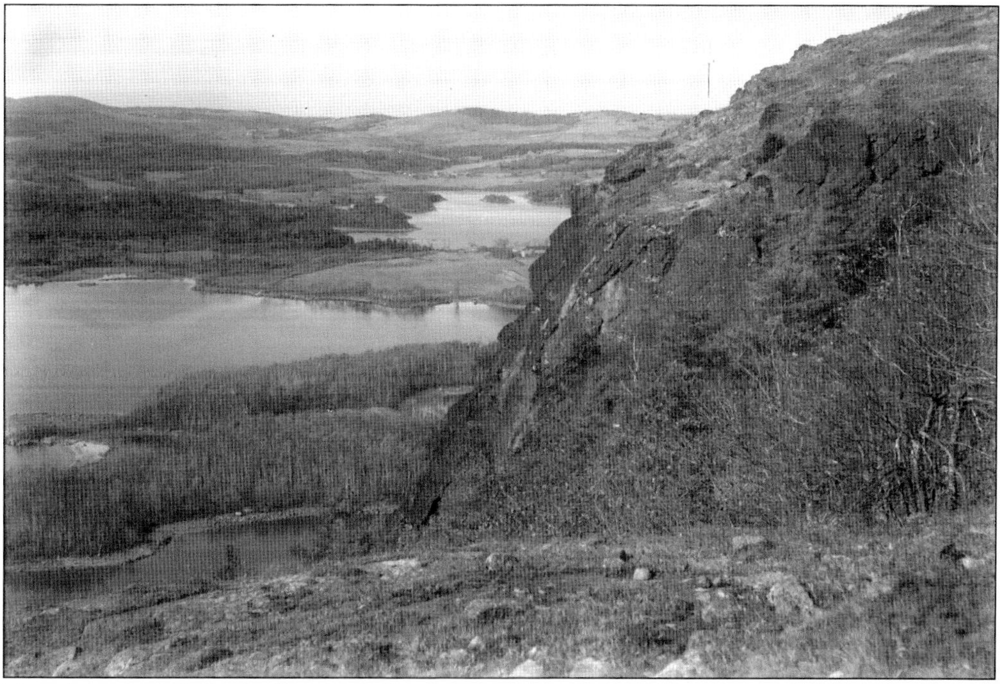

This photograph from the late 1890s shows an expansive view of Megunticook Lake and Maiden's Cliff. The white cross at the edge of the cliff marks the spot where, on May 6, 1862, eleven-year-old Eleanora French was on an outing with friends when the wind caught her hat. When she tried to catch it, she plunged 300 feet to her death.

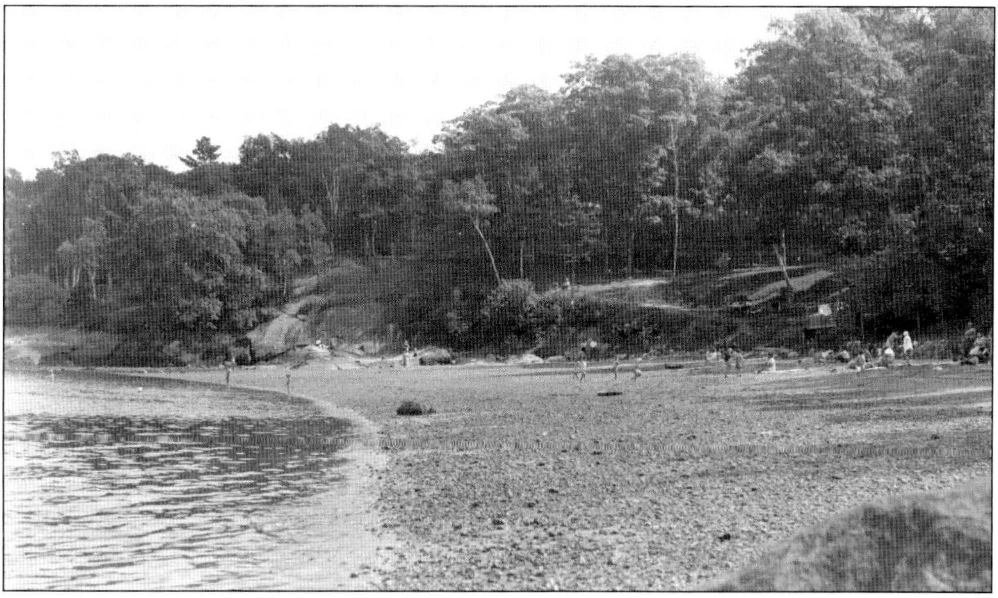

One of the area's favored getaways to cool off during a hot summer day is Barrett's Cove at Megunticook Lake. There have been many improvements to the area over the years. The changing area and restrooms have been upgraded, as has a picnic area with new picnic tables, fire pits, and footbridges, to name a few. This location has been the site of many triathlons and training lanes during the summer for the local swim team.

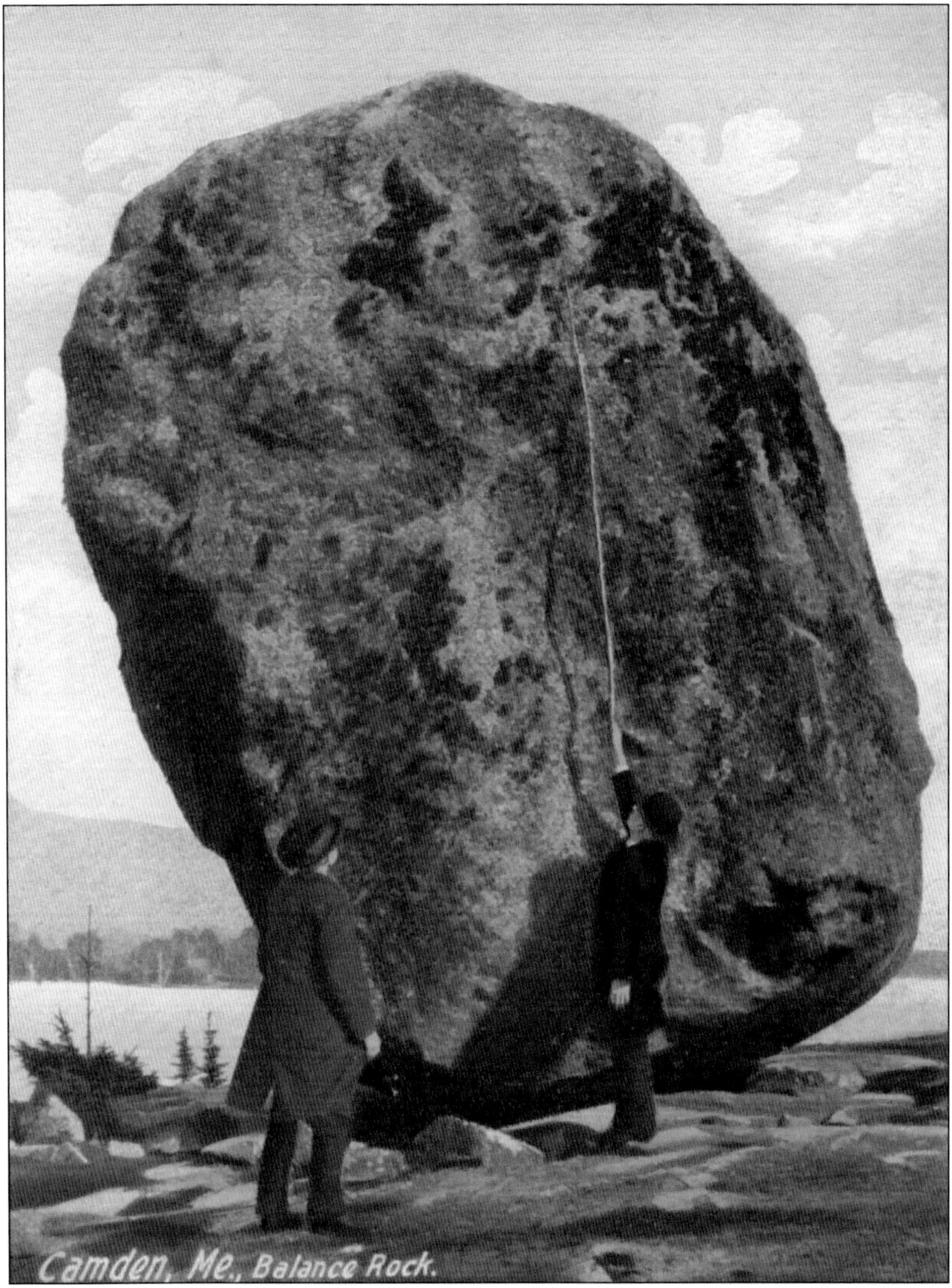

Balance Rock is a unique formation left behind by glaciers during the last glacial period. It can be found on Fernald's Neck, which is now part of the Coastal Mountains Land Trust on Megunticook Lake. It is a familiar sight to natives and summer residents who enjoy sharing it with newcomers to the area.

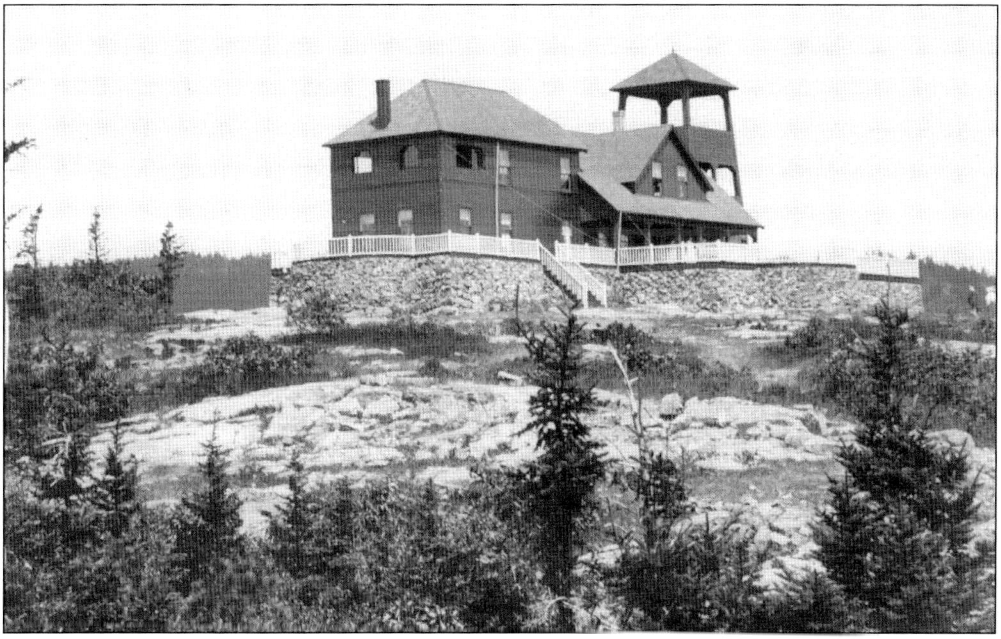

The image above is of the Summit House (later known as the Mt. Battie Club House), which was located on the top of Mount Battie and offered a panoramic view of the surrounding hills and Penobscot Bay as seen in the image below. The bird's-eye view of Camden, Curtis Island, and looking farther south toward Beauchamp Point in Rockport is as breathtaking now as it was in the 19th century. In 1897, Columbus Buswell, a Camden resident, built a carriage road to the top of the mountain, and in 1898, the Summit House was opened to the public as a hotel. The Mt. Battie Association, a group of Camden's wealthy summer residents, bought and renovated the building in 1899. Many notable people visited the Summit House during the heyday of carriage travel.

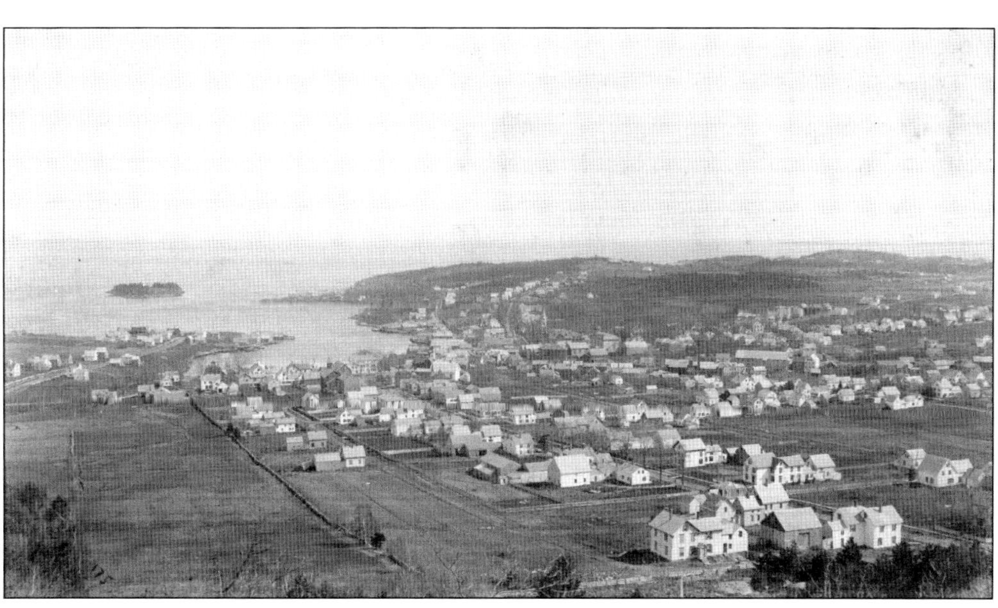

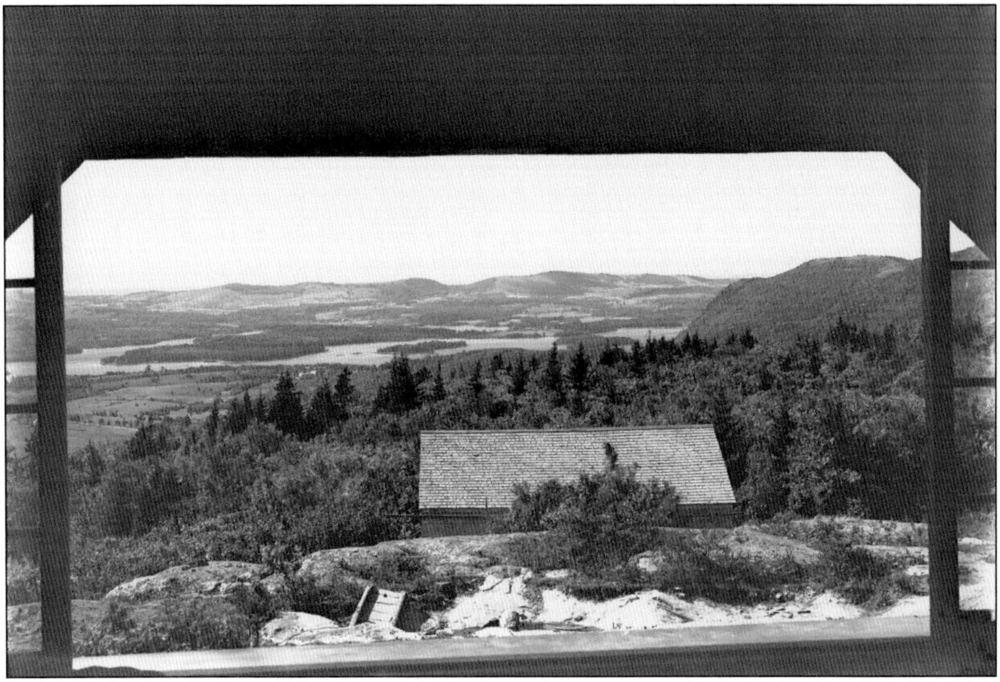

These two images are from glass negatives found in the historical society collection. The unknown photographer framed both shots through the windows of the Summit House on the top of Mount Battie. The Summit House (known after 1899 as the Mt. Battie Club House) was a popular destination for travelers by carriage. In the image above, the photographer points his lens out toward Megunticook Lake and the hills of Lincolnville and Hope. Maiden's Cliff is at the right of the frame. In the photograph below, Camden Harbor, Curtis Island, and Sherman's Cove are featured. The islands of Penobscot Bay are just visible in the background. Upon closer inspection, one can see the large steamship wharf just beyond Eaton's Field at the mouth of the harbor.

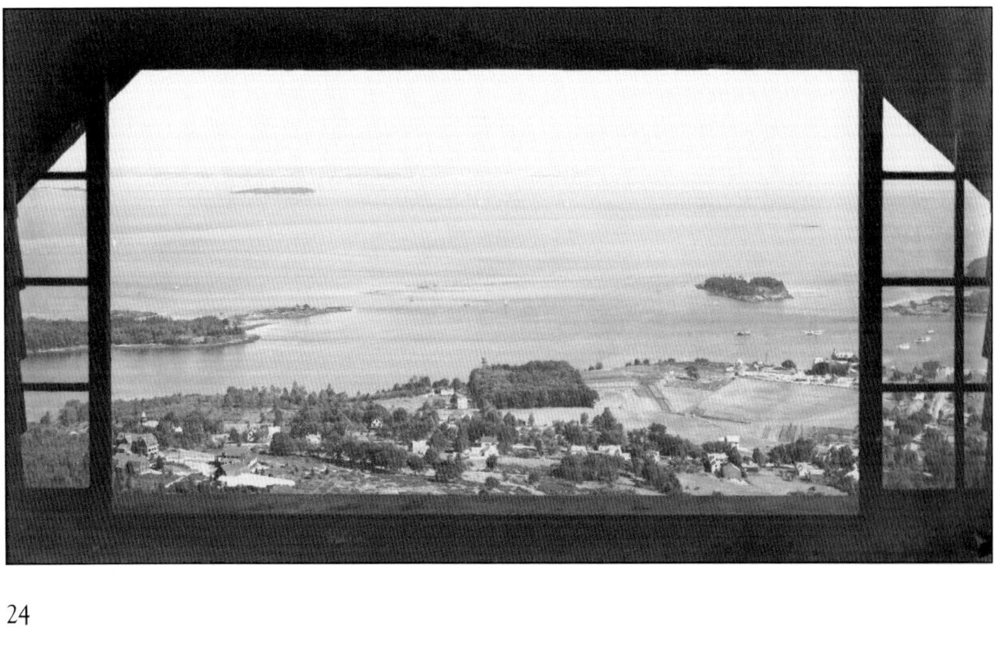

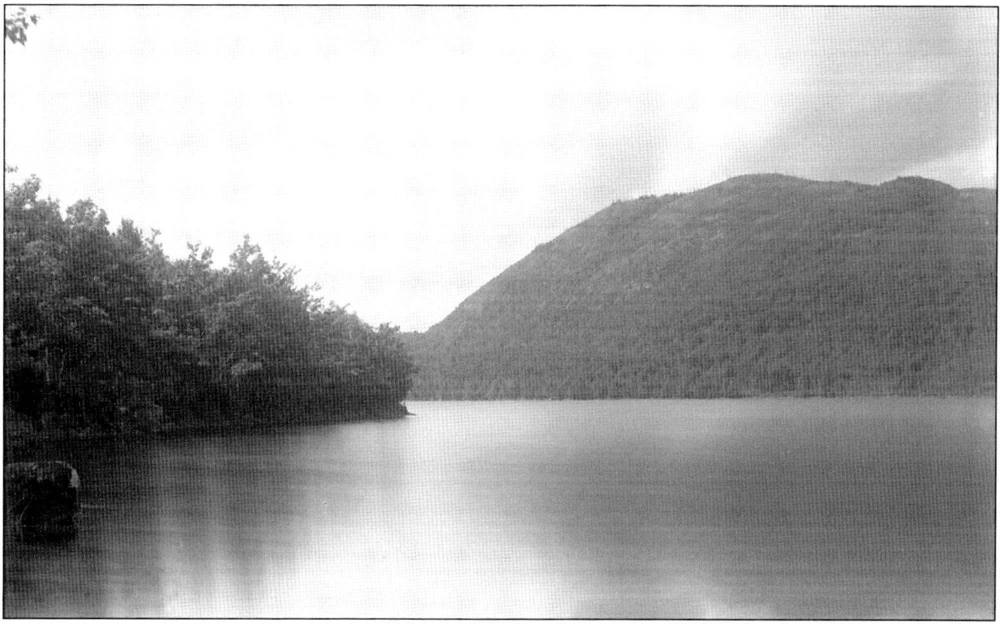

Rockport's Mirror Lake is located approximately 350 feet above sea level, and it is the spring-fed source of drinking water for the towns of Camden and Rockport. In the early part of the 20th century, boating was allowed on the lake, but no activity is permitted today.

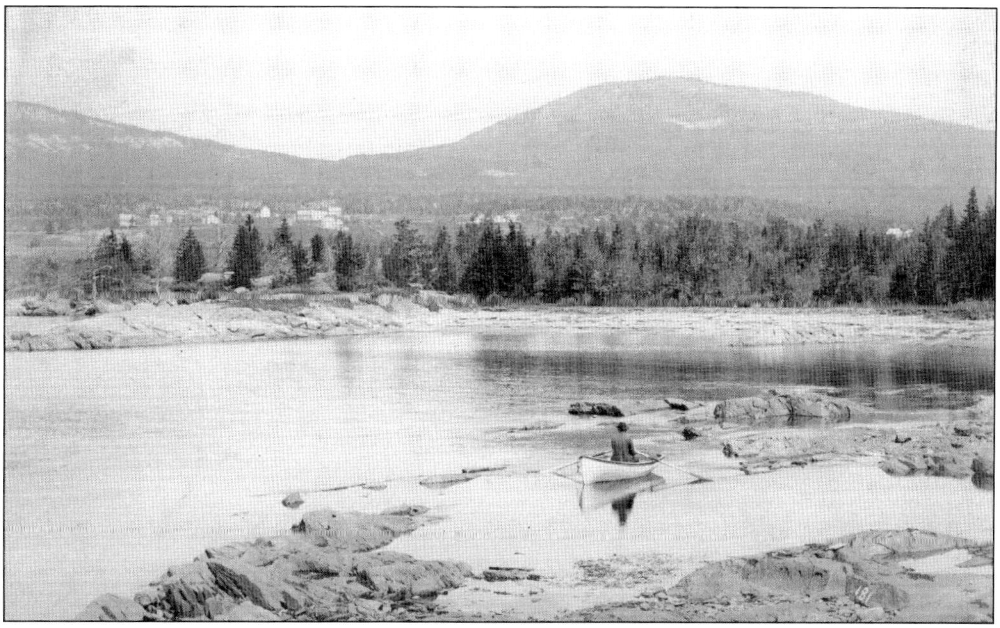

A lone boater meanders through the tidal pools in Sherman's Cove, which form part of the protective curve of the outer harbor in Camden. The Camden hills (Mount Battie, Mount Megunticook, and Bald Rock) rising in the background show why the area is still referred to as "where the mountains meet the sea." Sherman's Point was sold by Ignatius Sherman's heirs to George Wilson of Philadelphia in 1901. Wilson built a macadamized road connecting the Point to Route 1 but managed to sell only two lots by 1916. The area was abandoned and used as a picnic area until it was sold by the Town of Camden at auction in 1940.

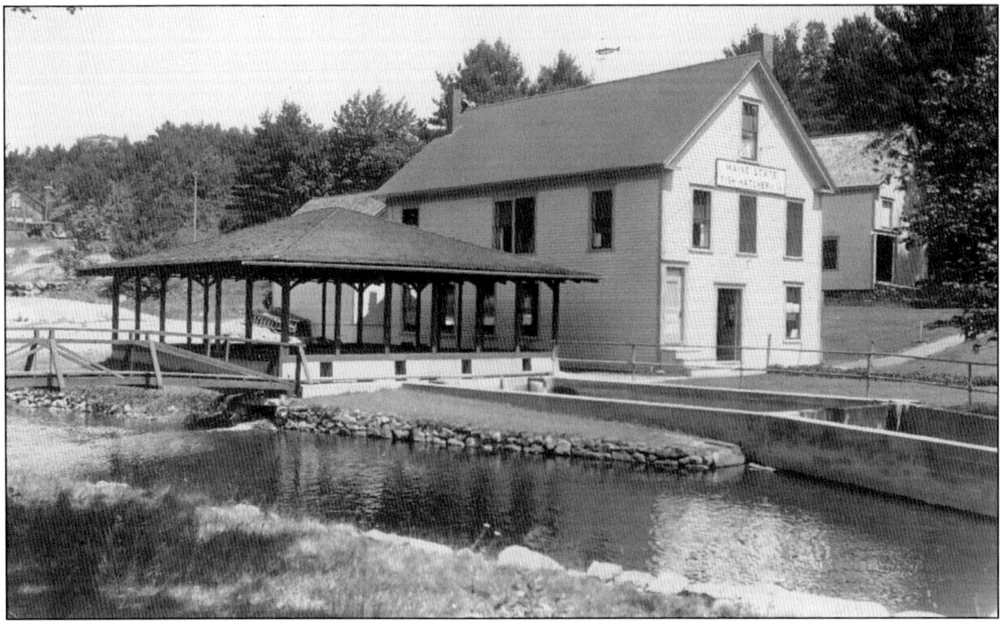

In the heart of the Molyneaux Privilege, a venture sprang forth little known to outsiders. The Camden Fish and Game Company, with the support of the Megunticook Dam Company, established a thriving fish hatchery. Opening in the spring of 1910, this was a state-funded venture that the association was granted for the sum of $5,000. During its operation, it required 125 pounds of liver a week, as well as a ton of ice.

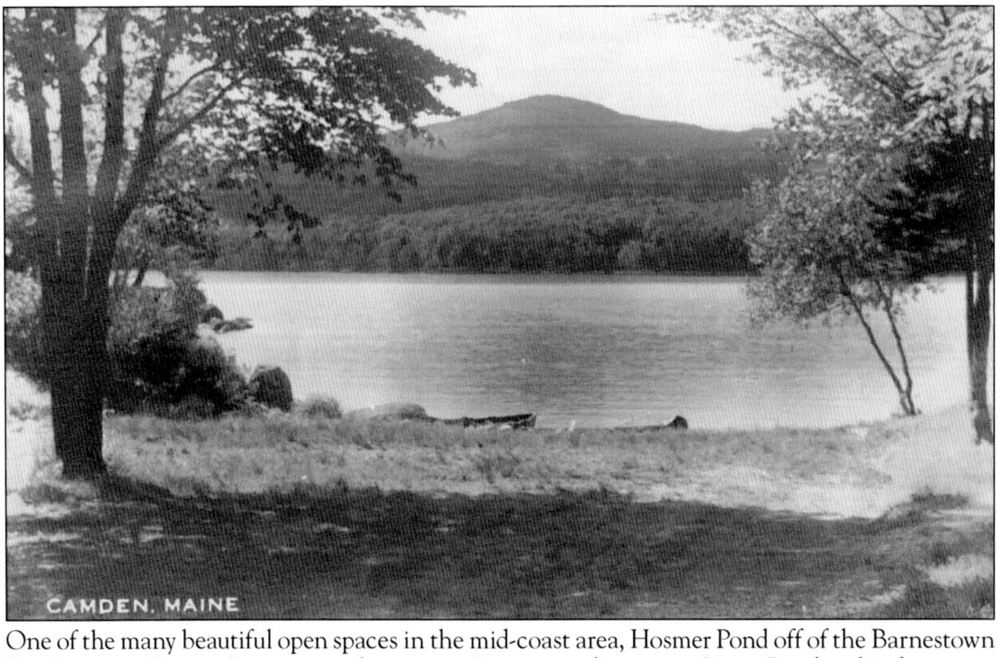

One of the many beautiful open spaces in the mid-coast area, Hosmer Pond off of the Barnestown Road is a popular site for year-round activities. It was once known as Goose Pond and is the source of the Goose River, which terminates at Rockport Harbor. The Snow Bowl recreation area is next to the pond and offers skiing and skating in the winter and mountain biking and other outdoor fun in the off-season.

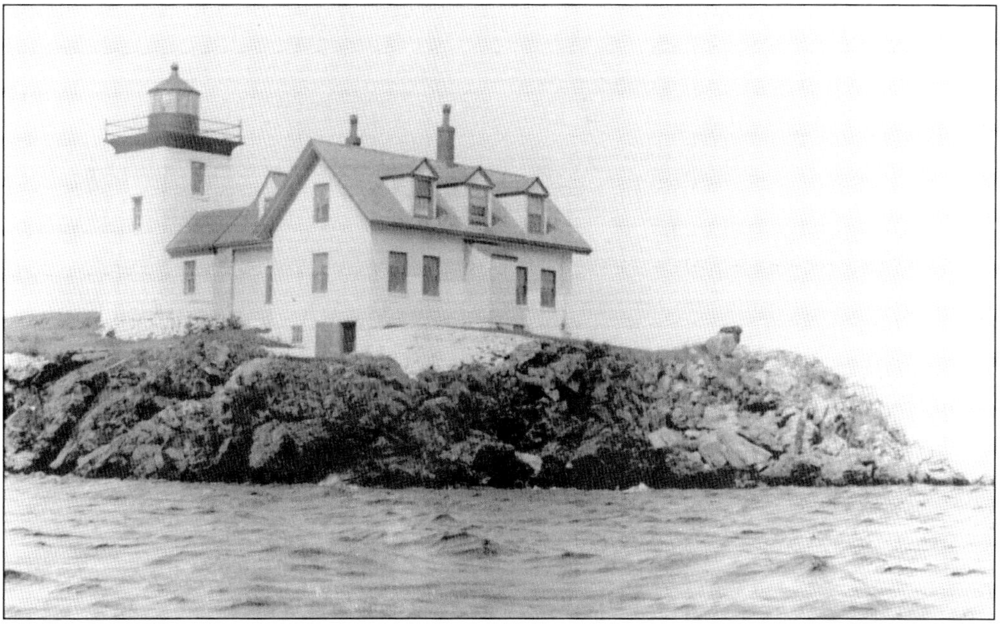

These two postcards show views of Indian Island Lighthouse in outer Rockport Harbor. There are differing stories about how Indian Island earned its name. According to local lore, the island was used by Native Americans as a rendezvous or camping place. An alternative legend says that a Captain Blaisdell of Newburyport pursued Native American settlers off the island and into the forests of Beauchamp Point during the French and Indian War. An act of Congress on March 5, 1849, approved $3,500 for the construction of a lighthouse, due in large part to the efforts of the Honorable Ephraim K. Smart, a member of Congress from Camden. Originally called Beauchamp Point Light, according to the town history, the island is connected with the mainland by a sandbar passable at low tide. The earliest lighthouse keeper was Silas Piper.

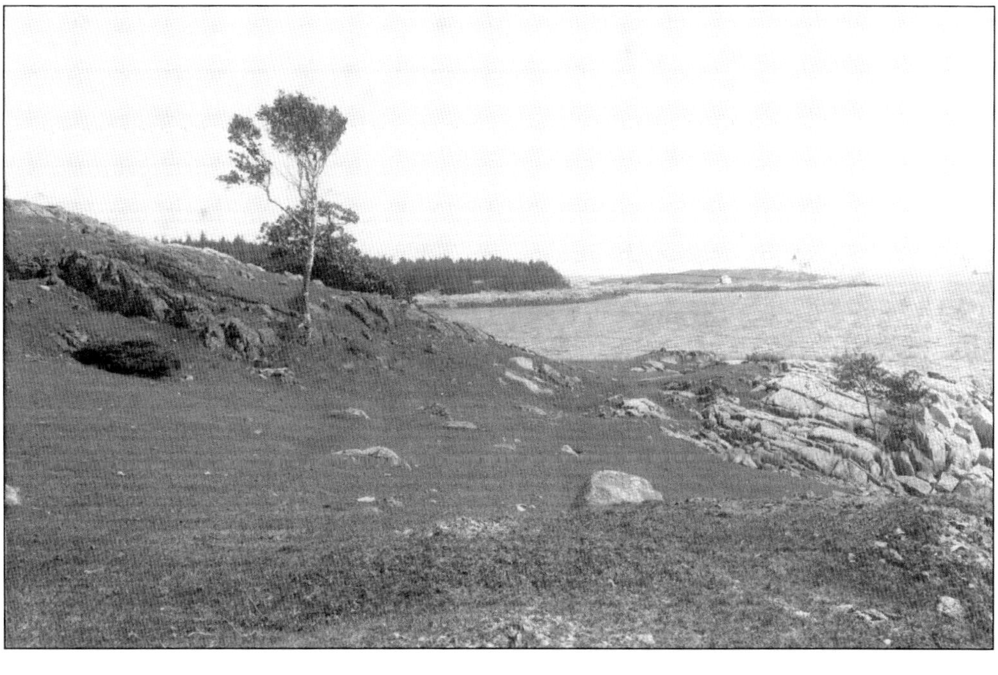

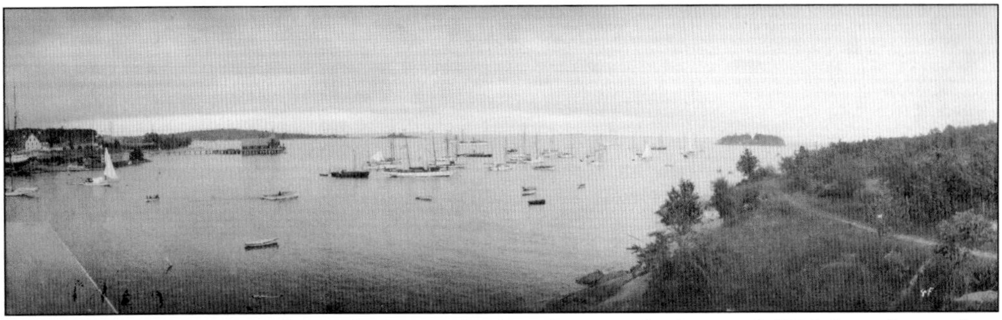

This is a panoramic view of Camden's outer harbor photographed around 1900 from the rooftop of a building on Bayview Street. Development of Bayview Street did not begin until around 1866, and in this later image, outer Bayview Street appears to be little more than a bridle path along the shore. The steamboat landing is visible in the left background, and Negro Island is at the right.

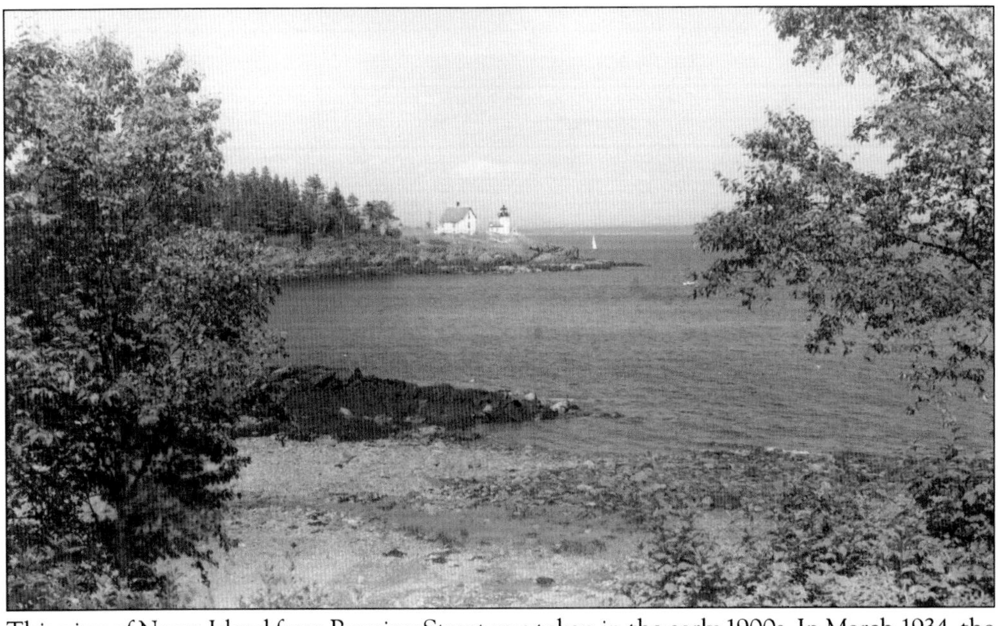

This view of Negro Island from Bayview Street was taken in the early 1900s. In March 1934, the name was changed to Curtis Island in honor of publishing magnate and town benefactor Cyrus H.K. Curtis. The lighthouse was built by George Galt in 1835, and the first lightkeeper to arrive was H.K.M. Bowers in 1836. The island was officially turned over to the town in September 1973.

Three

School Days

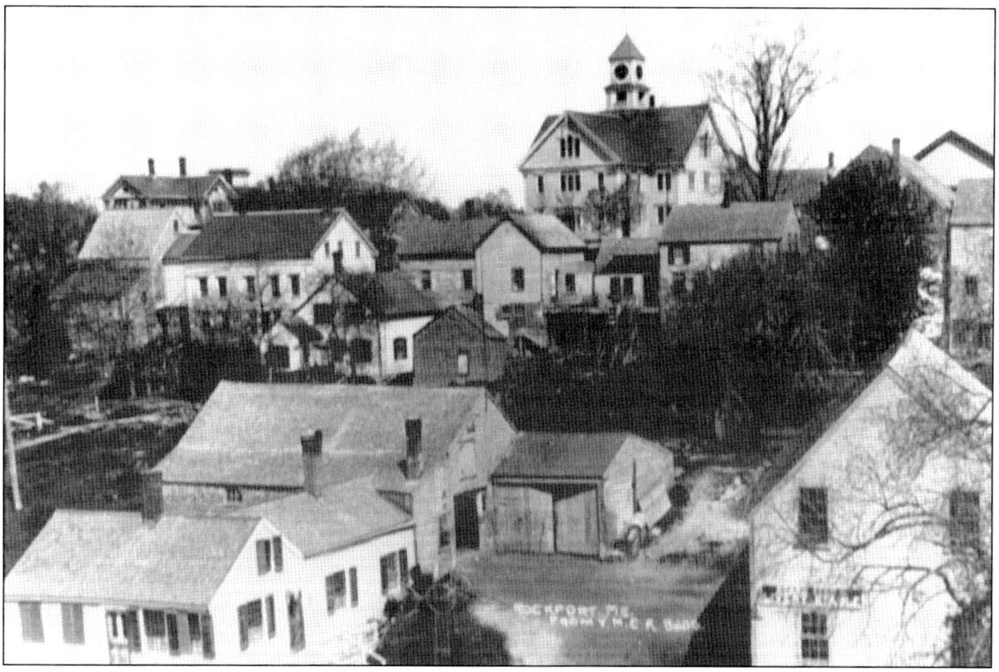

The view in this image looks north toward the Rockport schoolhouse with its large bell tower. The school, located on School Street, was built in 1891 at a cost of $10,000. The high school here would eventually close in the mid-1960s to merge with Camden's high school on Knowlton Street.

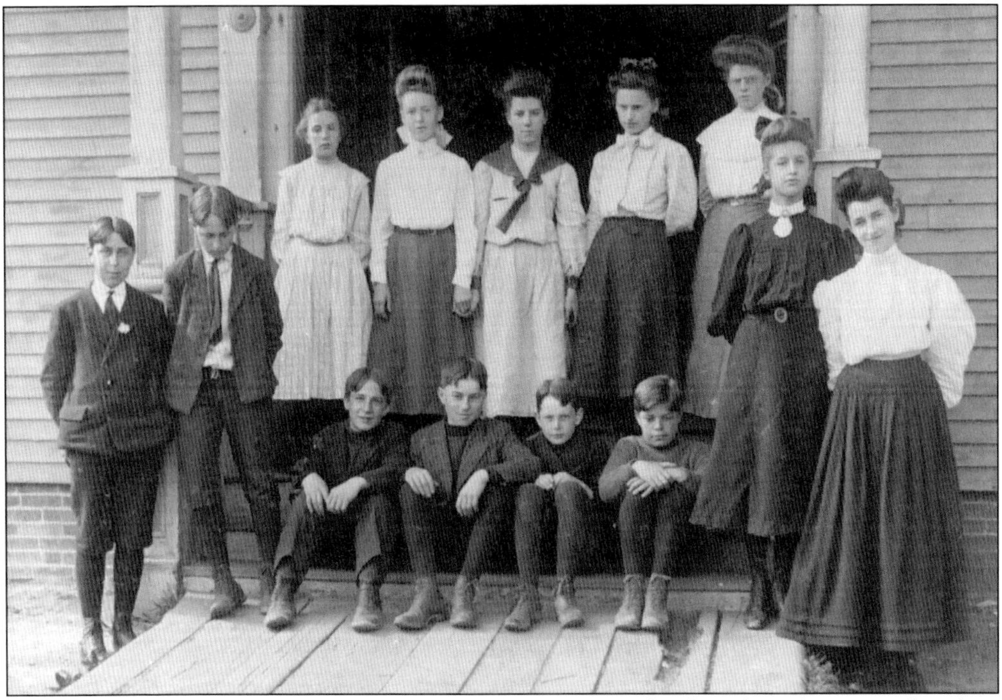

This is a photograph of one of the classes attending an area school, with student attired in their best clothes for picture day. The lovely young woman at the far right is likely the teacher. In addition to smaller schools scattered throughout the two towns, Rockport built a new high school in 1891. In 1869, Camden built the iconic Elm Street School, which housed all grades until a new high school was constructed on Knowlton Street in 1904.

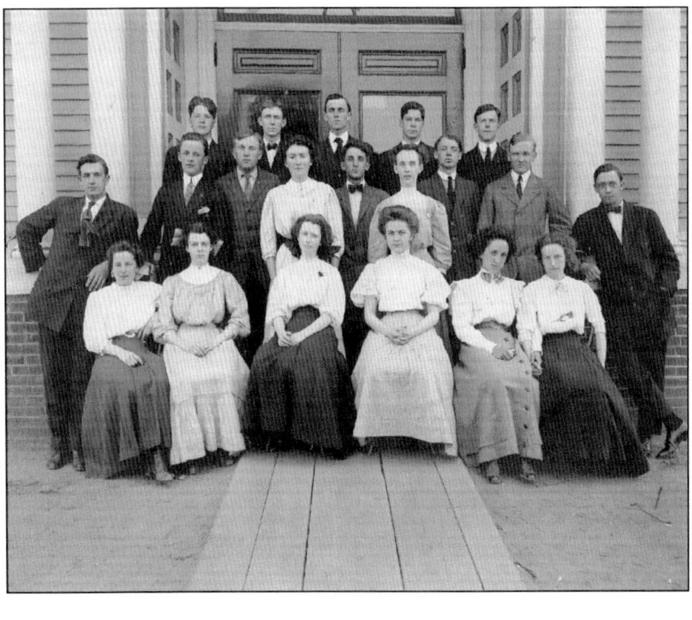

This image is of the Camden High School graduating class of 1909. Wearing a dark skirt and seated third from the left in the front row is Edna St. Vincent Millay. Millay went on to international acclaim as the third woman to win the Pulitzer Prize for Poetry. She is seated with her close friend Corinne Sawyer (second from left), who became librarian at the Camden Public Library and collected volumes of newspaper clippings, photographs, and letters from her famous friend.

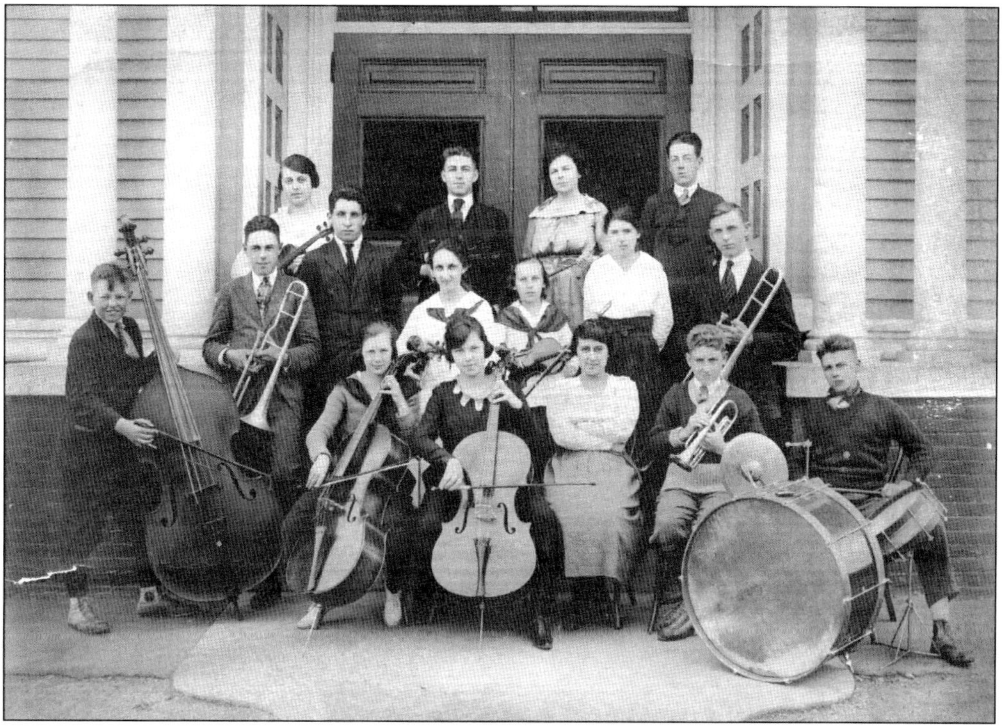

Maria Tibbett's band class poses outside the Camden High School around 1910. Pictured, from left to right, are (first row) ? Berry, Rita Young, Kathleen Walker, Adelia Morse, Clifton Conary, and Waleter Thurston; (second row) Burt Stevenson, ? Pendleton, Margaret Crockett, Lucie Bowden, Katie McDonald, and Arnold Calahan; (third row) Esther Morse, Louis Longman, Maria Tibbetts, and Bob Bean.

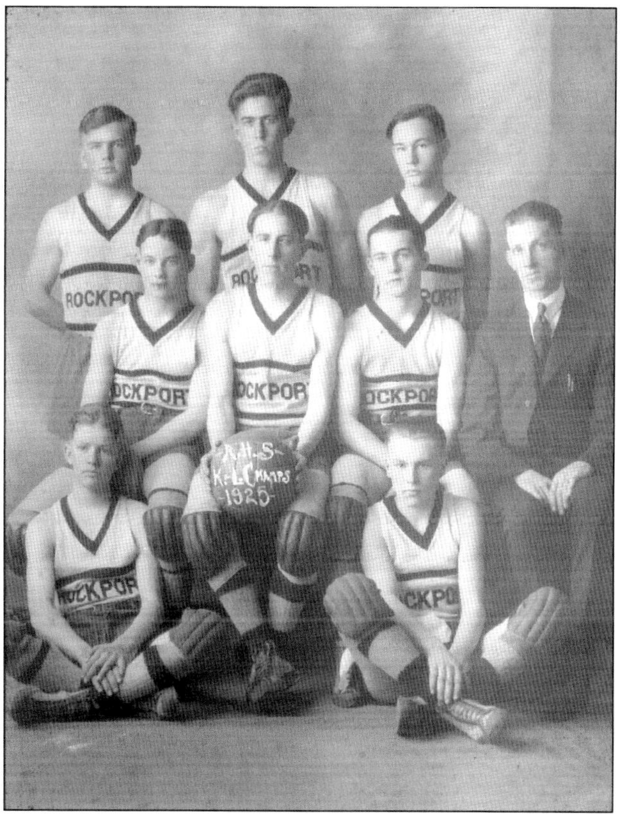

This photograph of the Rockport High School championship boys' basketball team and its coach dates to 1925. Camden and Rockport had separate high schools until 1965, when the Rockport school on the School Street hill closed to merge with Camden's high school on Knowlton Street in the heart of Camden's village.

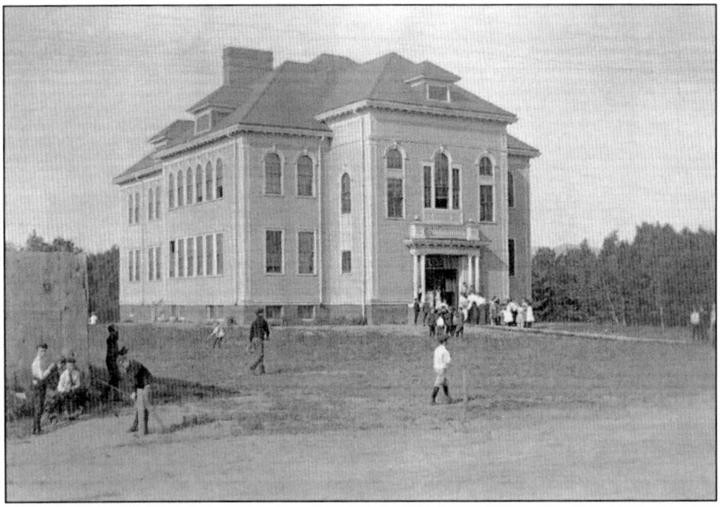

The new Camden High School was constructed in 1904 next to the Bean Trotting Park at a cost of about $20,000. In the early 1900s, if a student graduated from high school, he or she was able to take a teaching job anywhere in Maine. By 1925, the brick Knowlton Street school was built next to the high school, which was renamed the Mary E. Taylor School in 1956.

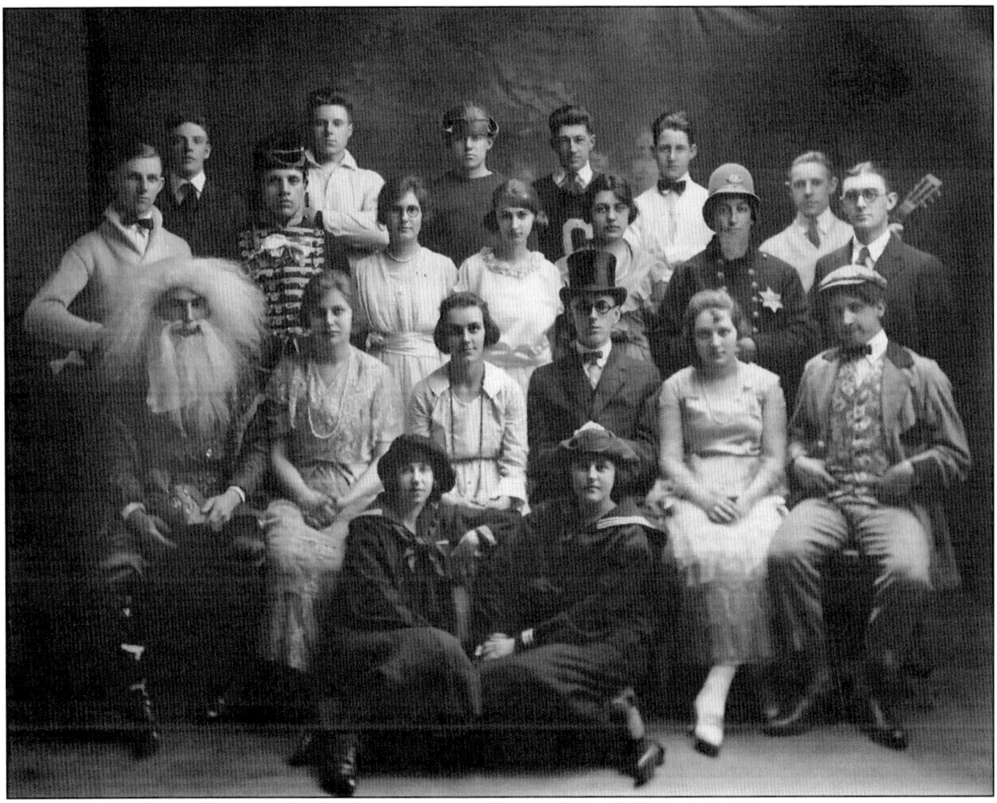

This photograph shows members of the Camden High School class of 1922 in costume for one of Stephen Gushee's Follies shows. Pictured here, from left to right, are (first row) Patty Cole and Gladys Fernald (Young); (second row) Win Richards, Phyllis Littlefield, Hazel Kidder, Steve Gushee, Lucille Hall, and Ephraim Pendleton; (third row) Arnold Calahan, M. Bowers, Etta Lunt, Josephine Thomas, Dot Gross, Phil Raynes, and Gleason Perry; (fourth row) C. Gross, two unidentified boys, H. Joy, and Bob Smith.

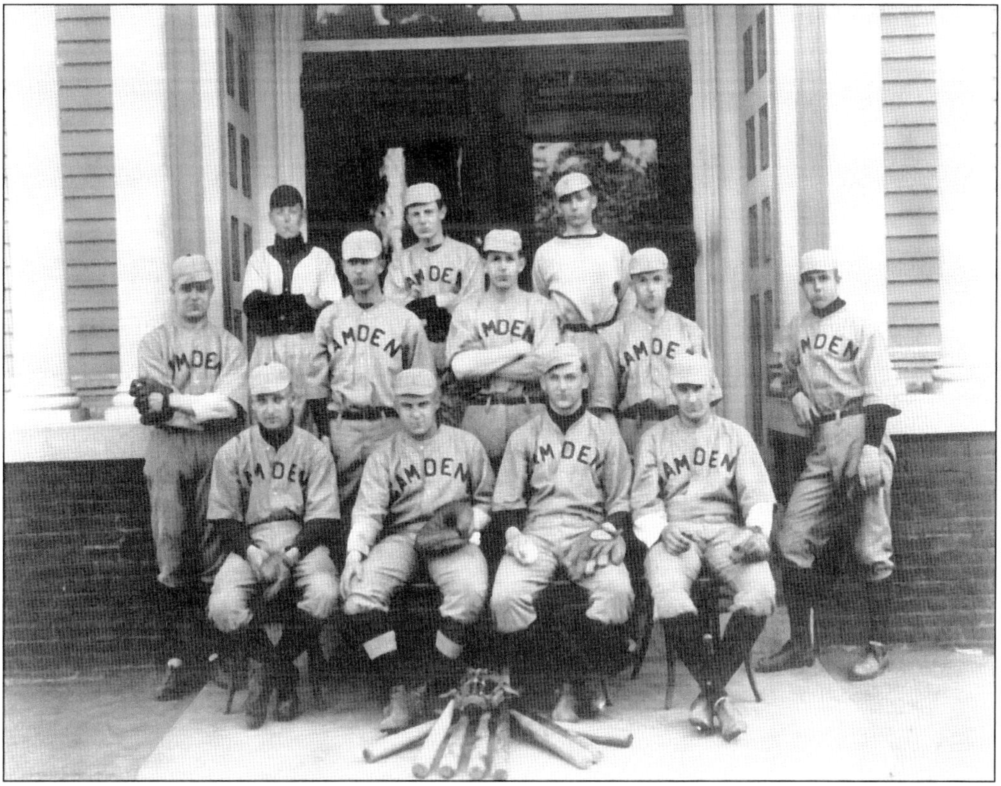

This is an early photograph of a Camden High School baseball team, taken probably around 1906. Camden is known for its strong sports teams even today.

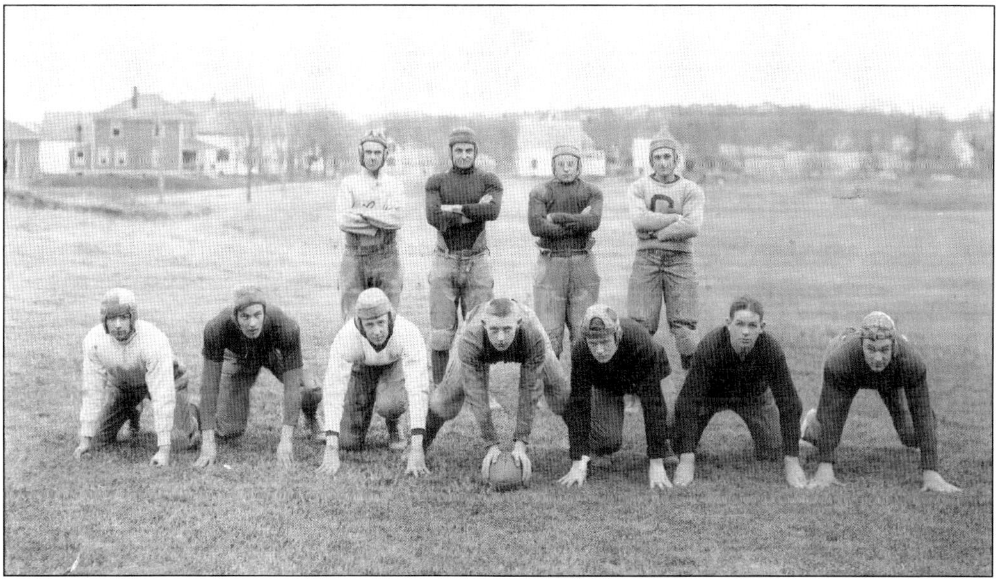

This photograph of a Camden High School football team dates from about 1920, as this was the first time that helmets were starting to be widely used in the sport. Hardened leather helmets were raised above the head, yet they were insufficiently padded, lacked face protection, and the ear flaps, which had little ventilation, made it difficult for players to hear.

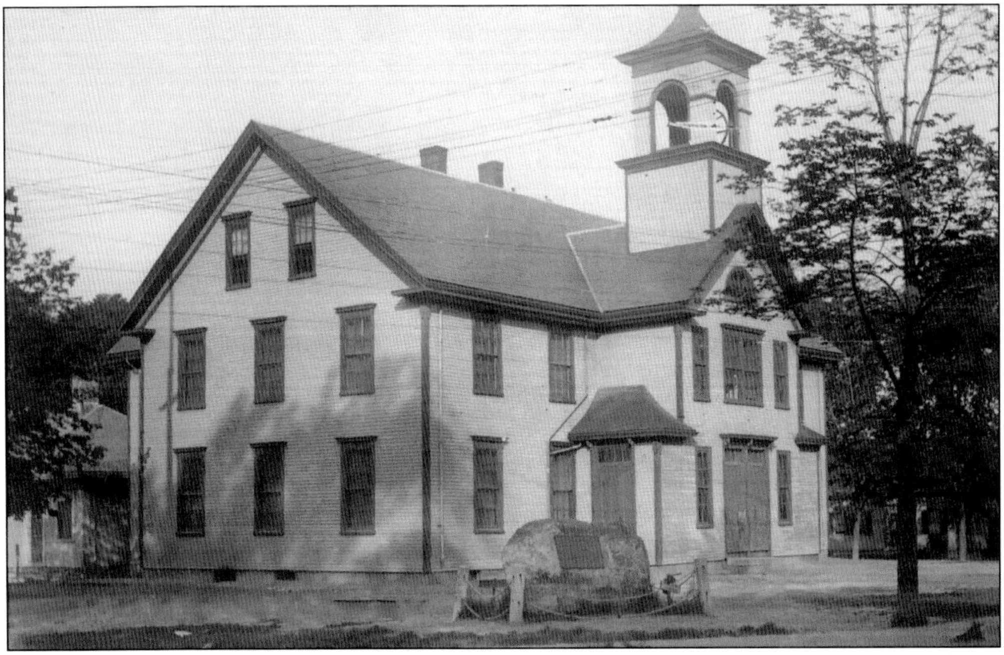

This image of the Elm Street School was taken sometime after the Conway Boulder was placed in front in 1906. The school is an iconic part of Camden, having educated many generations of children since 1869. When the combined elementary school for Camden and Rockport moved to a new site, the Elm Street School became the home of the Children's House Montessori School.

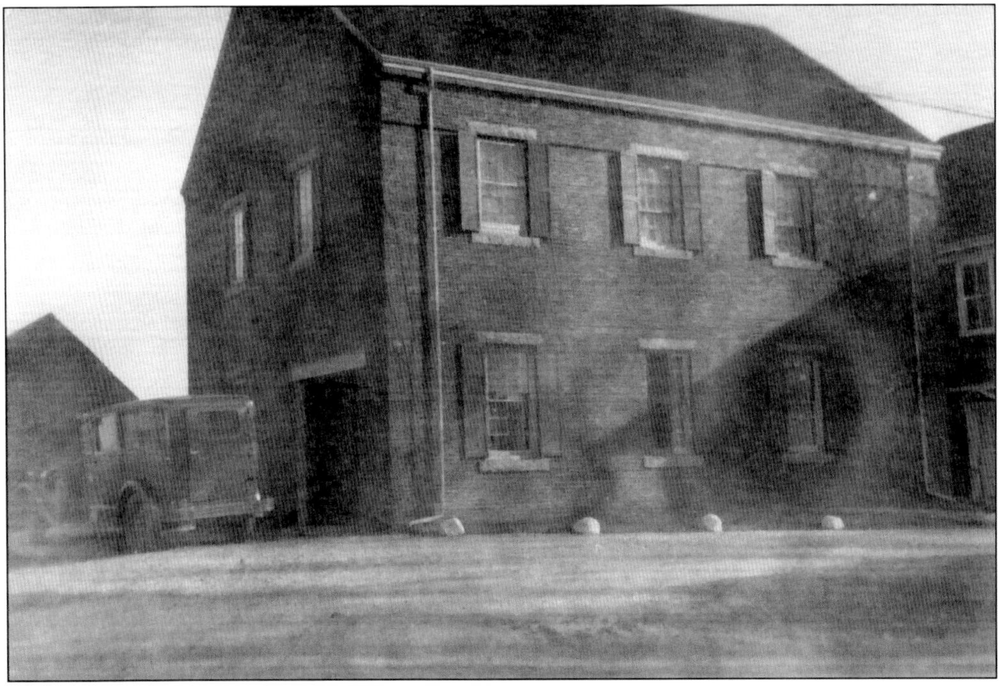

The brick building near the intersection of Mountain and High Streets was known as the Brick School from 1852 to 1905. It later became a Grange hall, after which it operated as the Laite Funeral Home for many decades. The business here in 2015 is the Long Funeral Home.

Four

Working Waterfronts

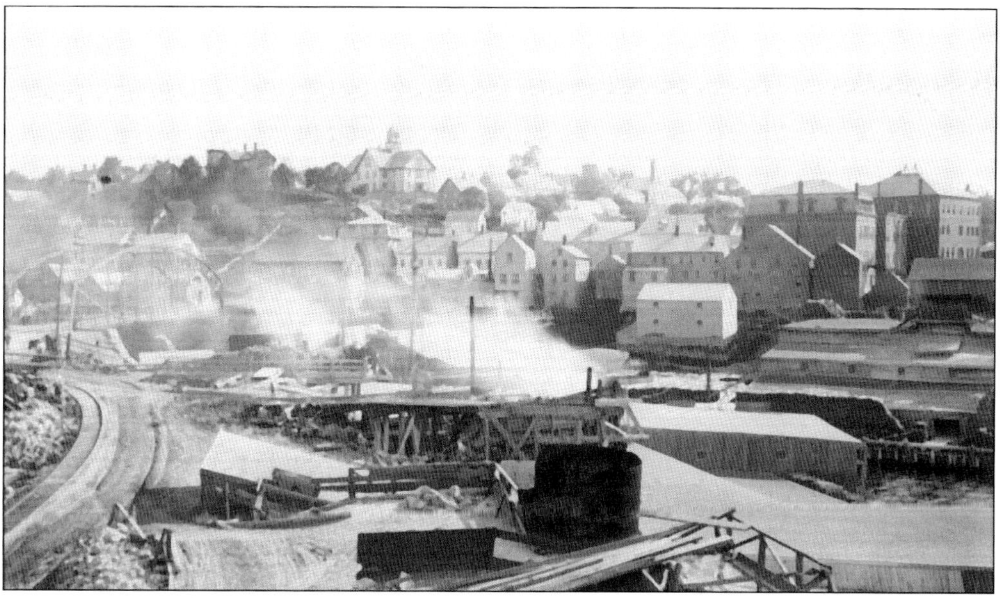

Prior to 1907, Rockport Harbor was a smoky, noisy place, not the serene harbor of today. In fact, Amesbury Hill behind the kilns was often called Smokestack Hill. The view in this image looks north toward the Rockport schoolhouse on the hill with its large bell tower. The school was built in 1891. In the foreground, Pascal Avenue winds its way toward the old iron bridge, barely visible through the smoke hovering over Goose River. By 1919, this bridge was deemed unsafe and replaced. The kilns burned locally quarried lime rock night and day, and the quarry railroad tracks and trestle to load rock into the top of the kilns are visible in the center of the photograph.

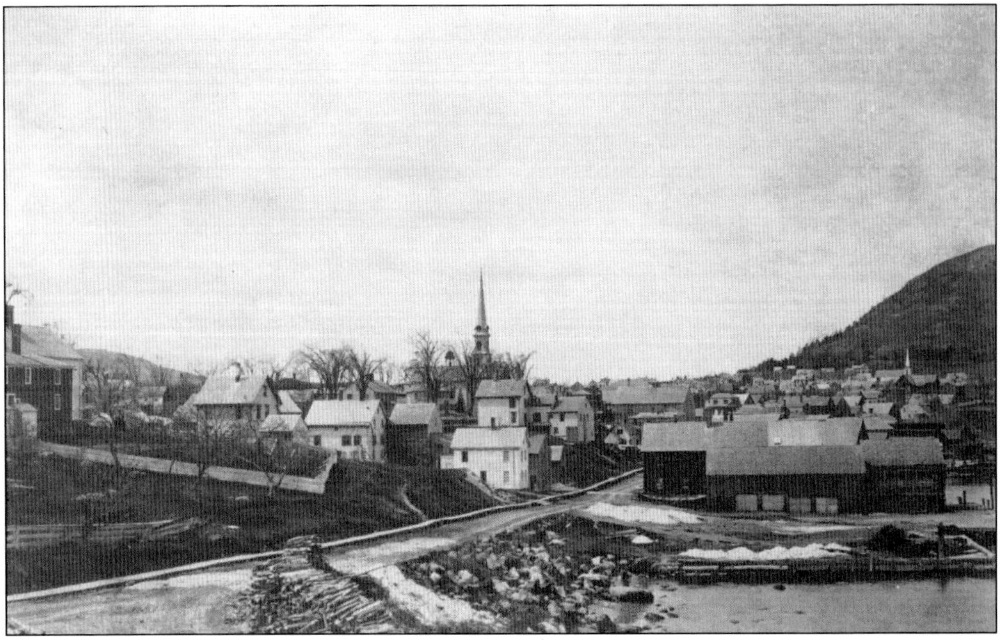

This photograph of Bayview Street in Camden was taken sometime before 1887, when the Chestnut Street Baptist Church spire had to be removed for a second time due to rot. The tower had been a landmark for navigation since the early days of the town, yet the church remained without a spire until 1980, when Eagle Scout Billy Young raised the funds to have it replaced. The clock in the tower has kept time for the town since 1868.

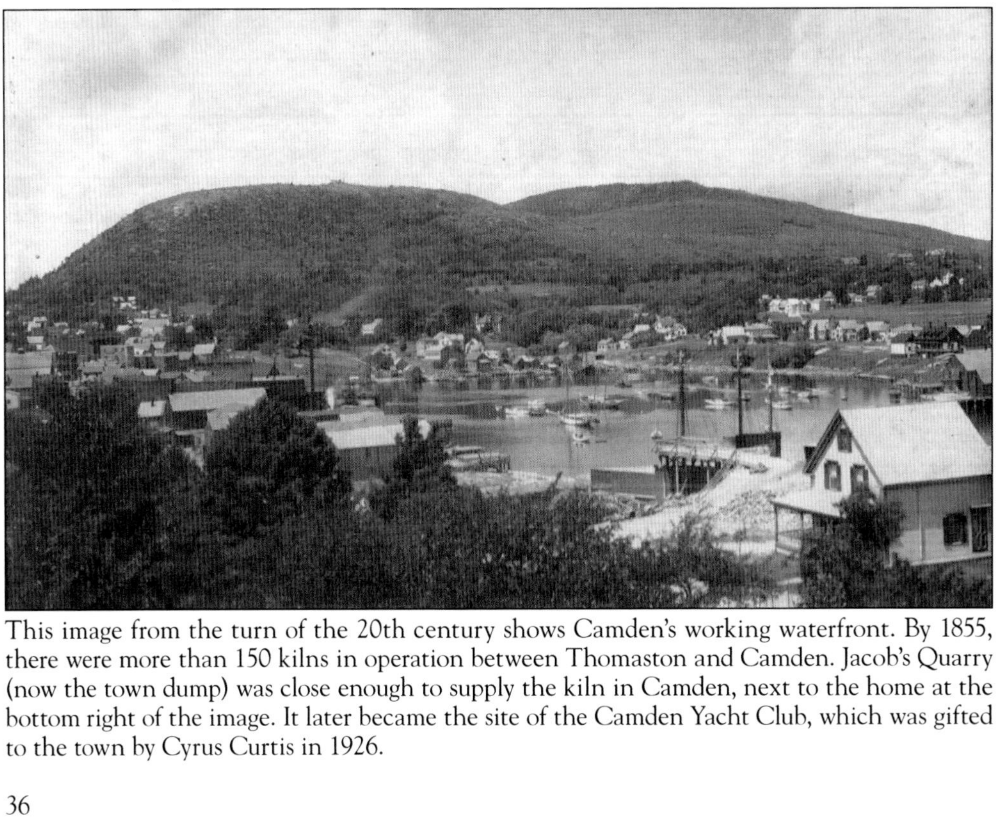

This image from the turn of the 20th century shows Camden's working waterfront. By 1855, there were more than 150 kilns in operation between Thomaston and Camden. Jacob's Quarry (now the town dump) was close enough to supply the kiln in Camden, next to the home at the bottom right of the image. It later became the site of the Camden Yacht Club, which was gifted to the town by Cyrus Curtis in 1926.

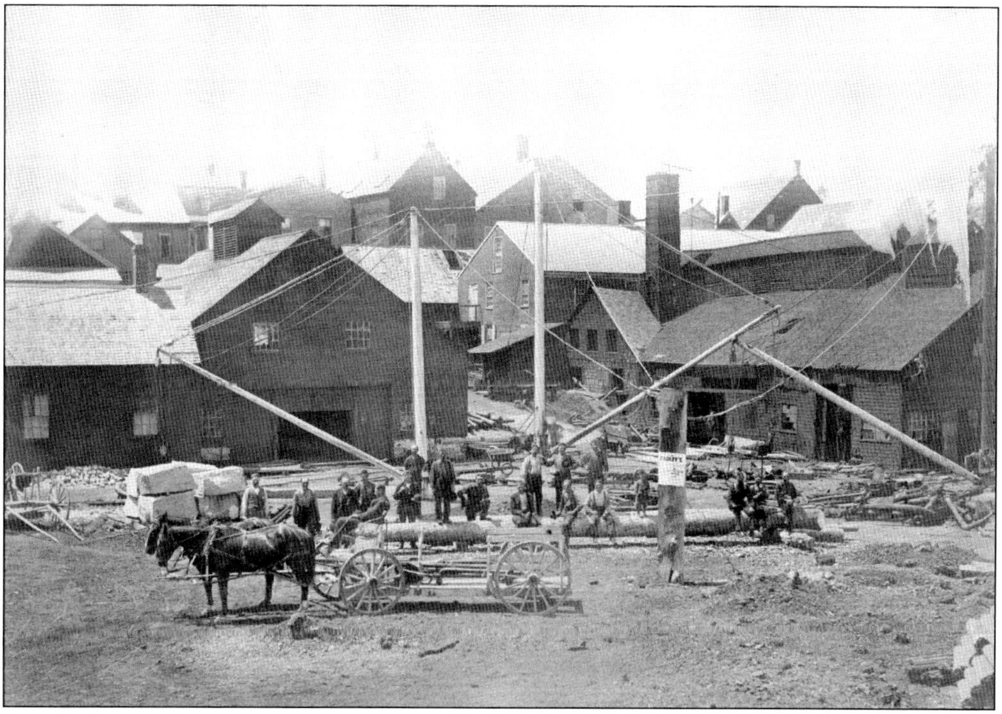

Camden's waterfront area was a very busy place in the 19th and early 20th centuries. Here, the Alden Anchor Factory on Bayview Street is a beehive of activity. Teams of horses and rugged wagons are being used to carry timber, and anchors are visible on the ground. In the background, the white manual cranes are ready to hoist heavy loads.

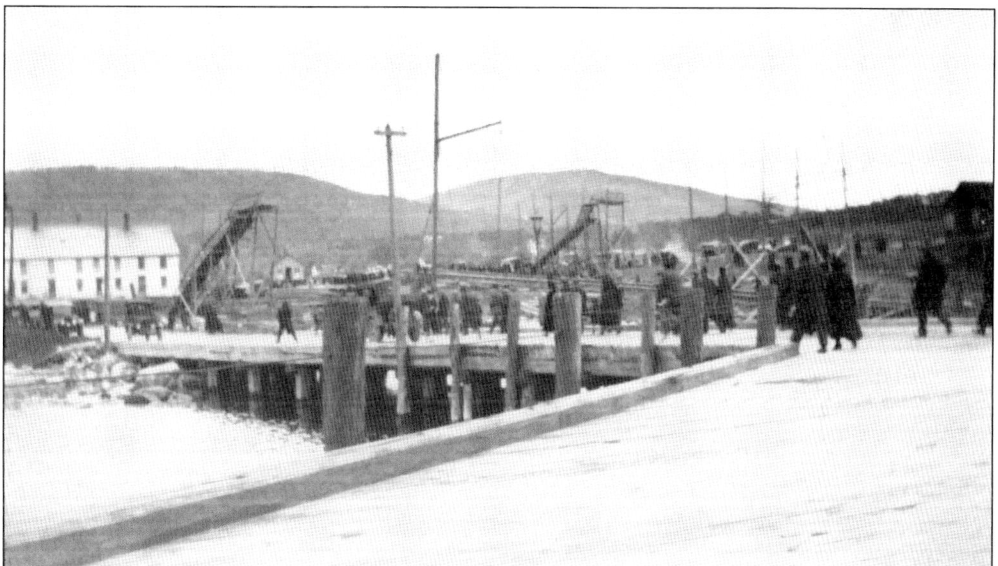

Camden shipyard, a fixture on the waterfront since 1856, was one of the area's largest employers by the turn of the 20th century. In this photograph from around 1920, people are making their way along the Eastern Steamship Company wharf; the white building in the background was part of the shipyard complex.

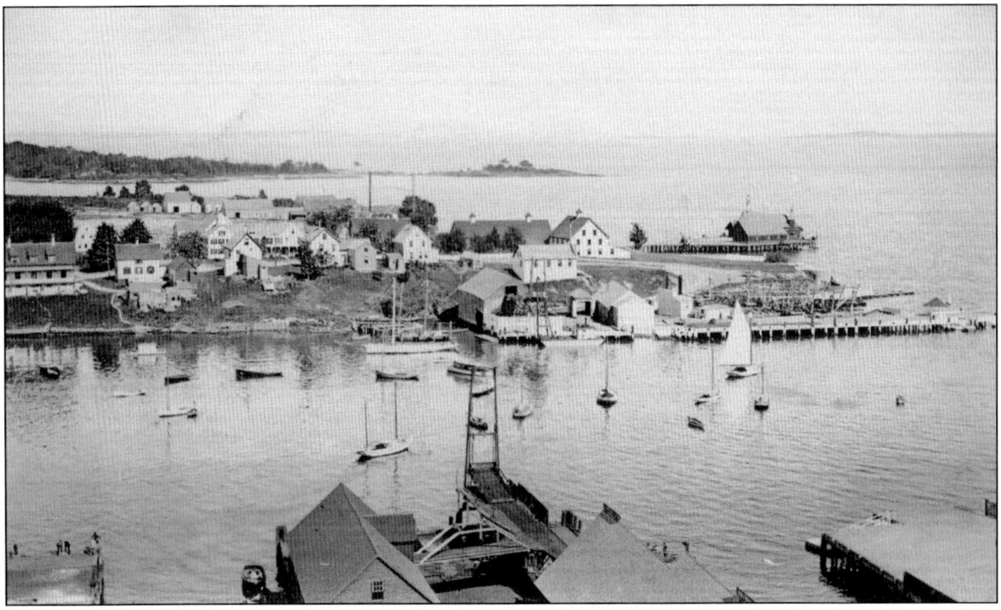

Camden has one of the more sheltered harbors on the Maine coast. The depth of the harbor was ideal for building massive sailing vessels, and master builder Holly M. Bean did just that, exceptionally well. He bought the shipyard in 1875, and it operated until 1920. The largest of these ships was the *George W. Wells*, a six-masted schooner built in 1900.

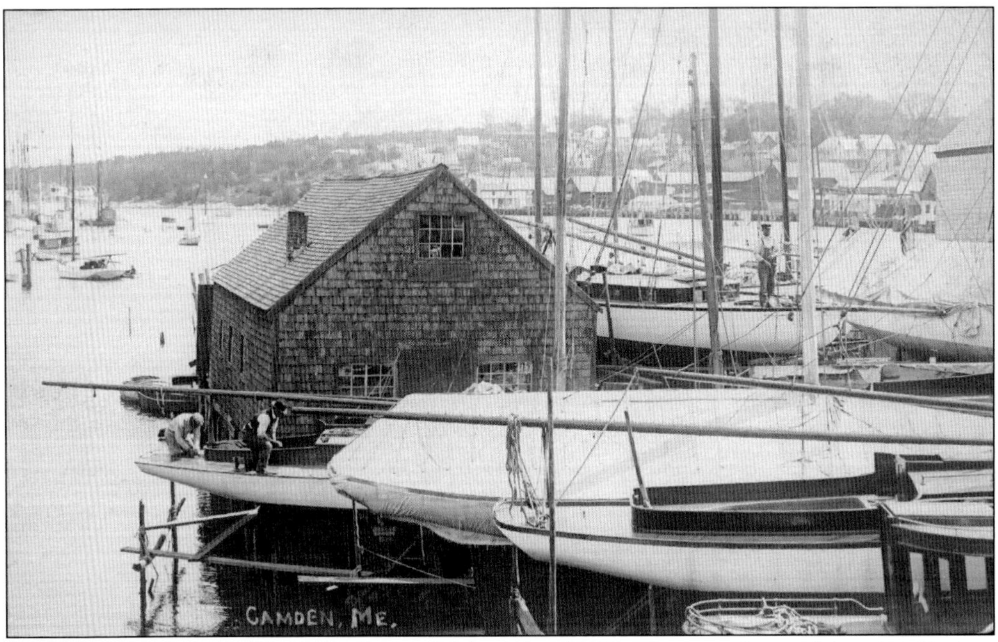

This undated postcard shows a boat repair and storage shed on the waterfront of Camden Harbor. Shipbuilders have been in business on the harbor since Capt. William McGlathery built the sloop *Industry* here in 1792.

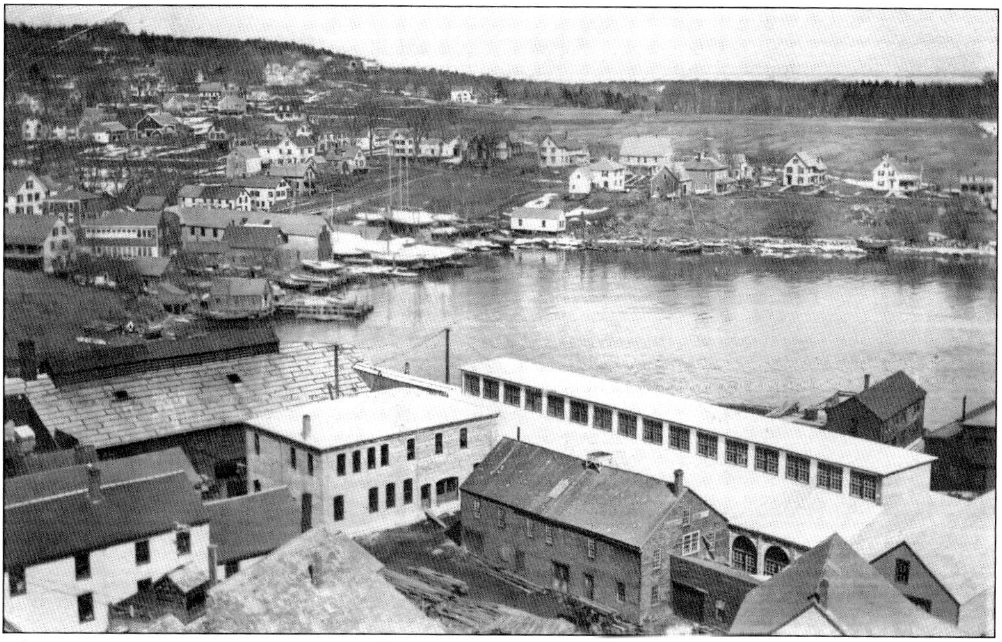

This is an interesting perspective of the inner harbor in Camden, taken from the Chestnut Street Baptist Church steeple. The long, light-colored building in the foreground is the Alden Anchor Factory, begun in 1866, which was known for manufacturing some of the largest anchors in the world. Many boathouses are visible along the left side, known as the head of the harbor, and Eaton's field is in the background. Today, most of these buildings are gone, and the site of the anchor factory is now a parking lot.

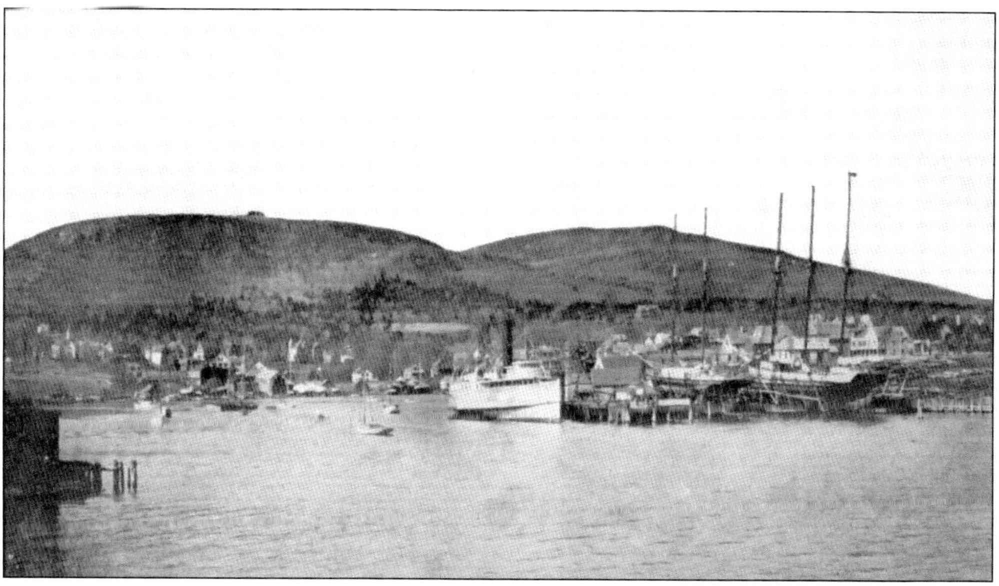

This panoramic postcard view shows Camden Harbor and the surrounding hills. The image is undated, but it appears to have been photographed from the outer harbor around 1902. An Eastern Steamship Company steamboat is docked at the right with two vessels on the ways (slipway) at the Holly M. Bean shipyard.

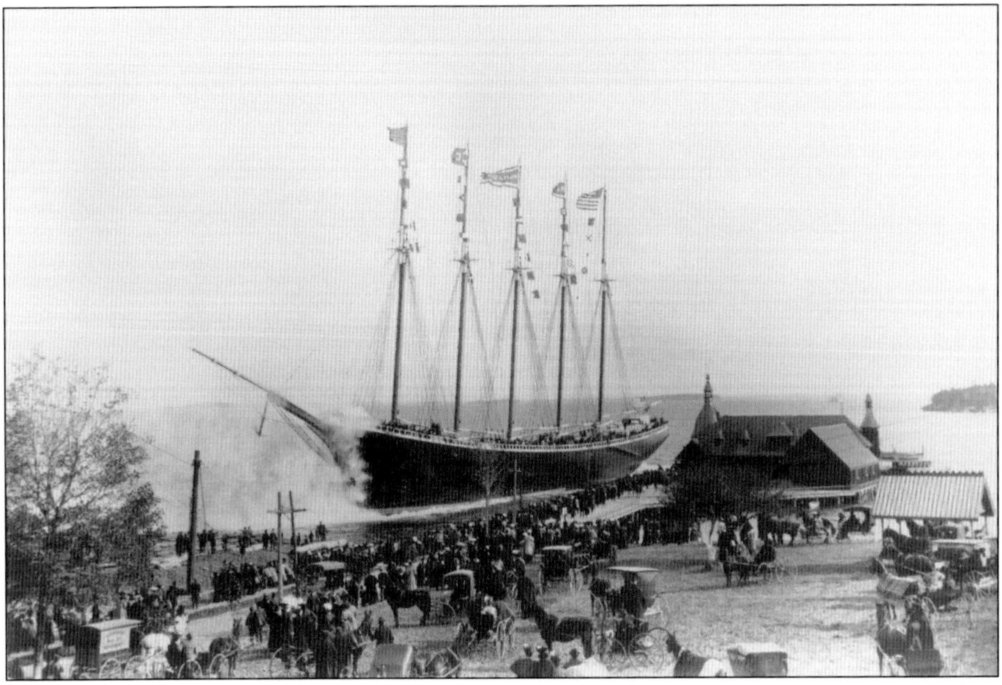

This is a classic image of a ship launching at the Holly M. Bean shipyard in Camden. The five-masted vessel *Helen Seitz* is being sent down the ways amid much fanfare on October 30, 1905. A launch was a great social event, as evidenced by the large number of people and carriages in the image. Sadly, the ship was stranded in New Jersey in a February 1907 storm.

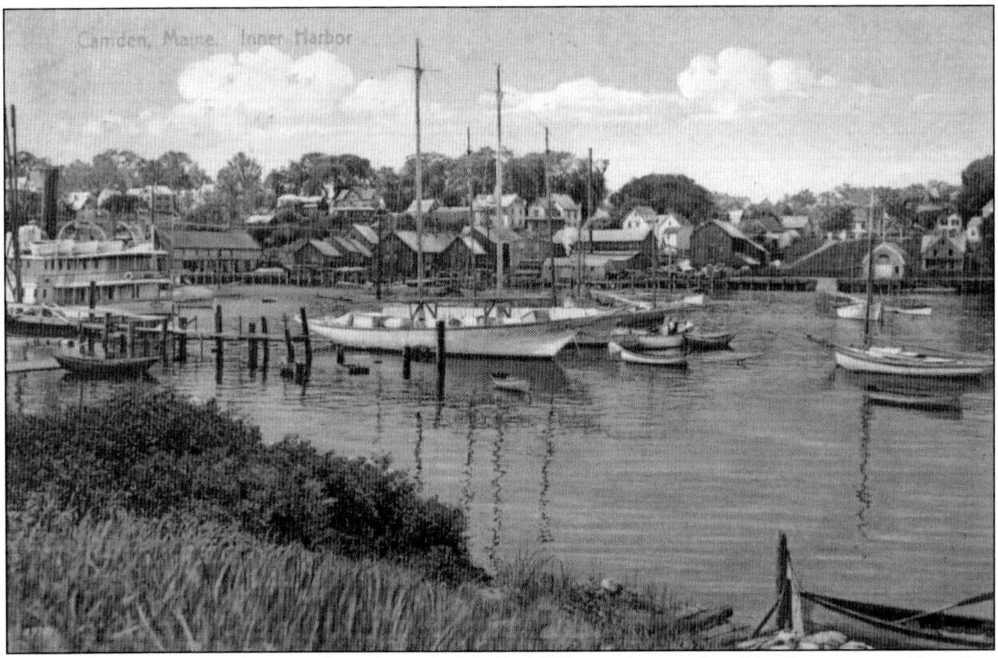

This is a lovely postcard view taken from the Holly M. Bean shipyard and looking across Camden Harbor to the downtown business district. The image dates well before the 1930s, as the anchor manufacturing and gristmill buildings are still there along the distant waterfront.

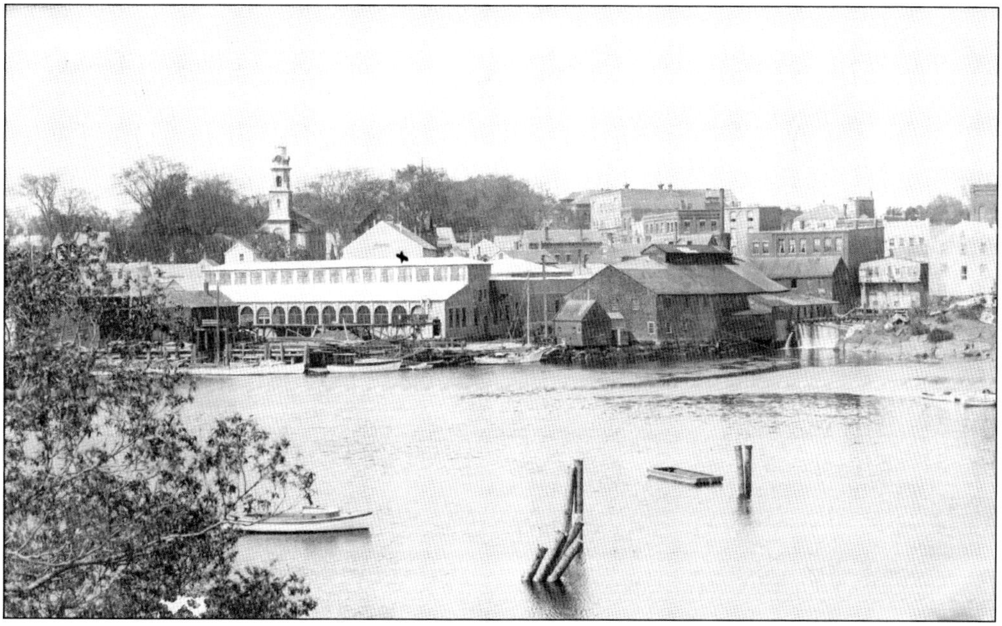

This postcard shows a closer view of the busy Camden waterfront. The light-colored building with the arched windows is the Alden Anchor Factory, manufacturer of some of the largest anchors in the world. The darker building to the right is the gristmill, which was powered by the Megunticook River waterfall at right.

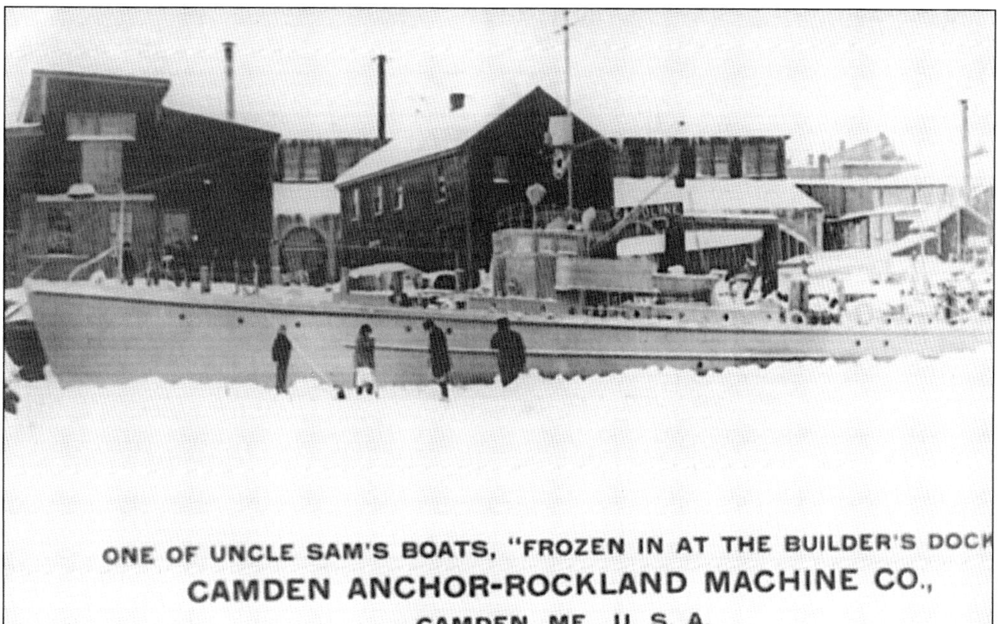

Taken around 1917, this is a fine postcard image of the Camden Anchor-Rockland Machine Company. By 1901, the Alden Anchor Factory had been sold and became known as the Camden Anchor-Rockland Machine Company. Employing more than 100 people, it built submarine chasers like the vessel shown here, as well as the Knox gasoline engine.

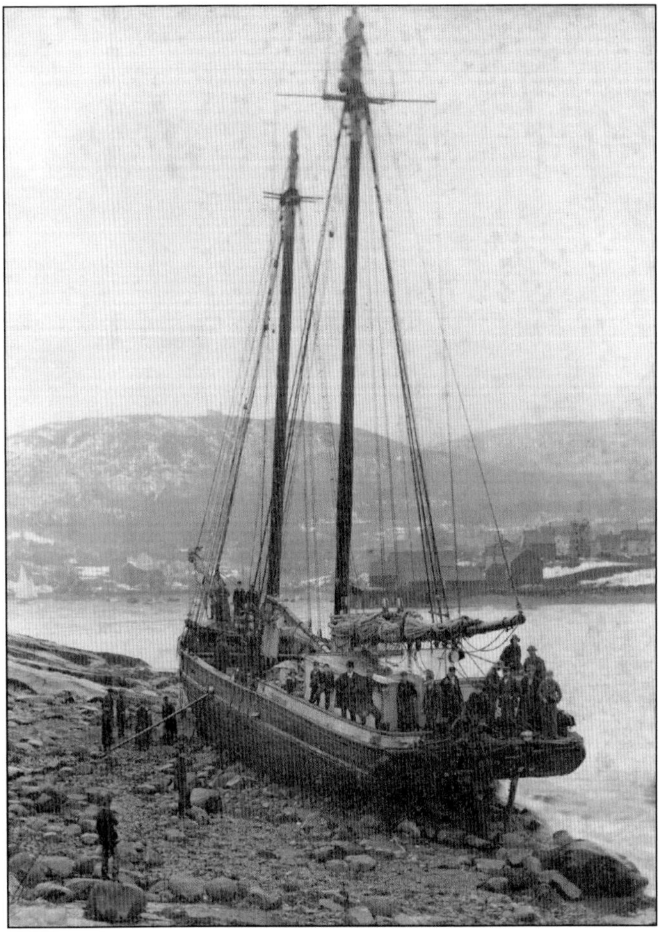

In this remarkable photograph from winter 1898 taken by the Adams & Potter studio, a working coaster or schooner has blown up on the ledges near Dillingham Point in Camden. The shallow-keeled vessel does not seem much the worse for wear and would likely have been floated off in the next high tide. The dark buildings of the Holly M. Bean shipyard are seen behind the rigging.

This serene photograph is of Rockport Harbor around 1900. The massive icehouses that stored blocks cut on nearby Lily Pond await sailing ships called coasters to transport the ice to towns along the coast, and larger vessels would carry ice as far away as the Caribbean. Two of the coasters are anchored in mid-harbor, and just visible behind the large tree at right is a ship under construction at the local shipyard.

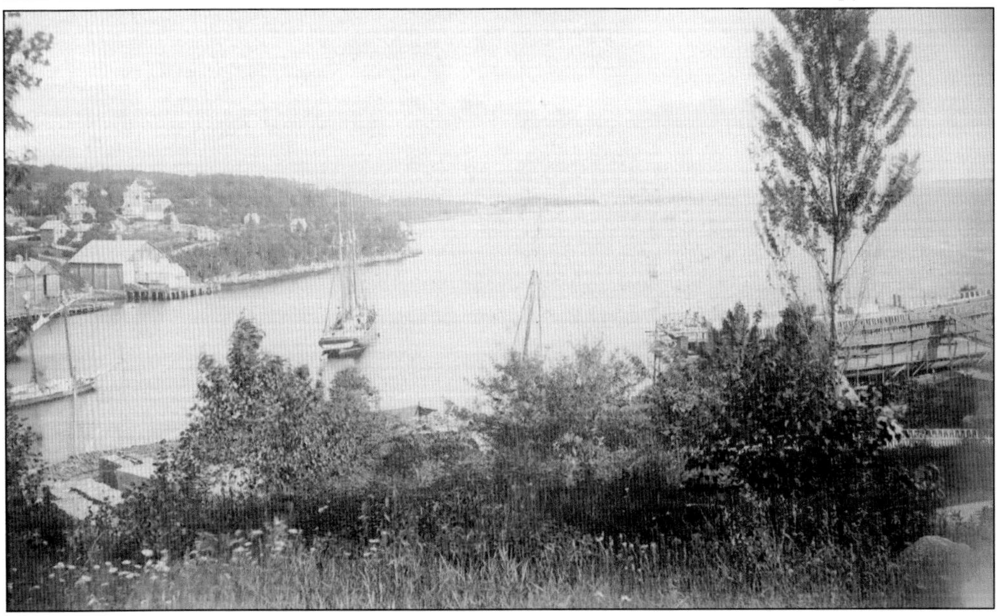

This image was taken in Rockport. Although the subject is unidentified, it appears to be the skeleton of the *Edgar W. Murdock*, which was built in 1902. The roof of one of the massive icehouses is just visible above the top of the ship's hull.

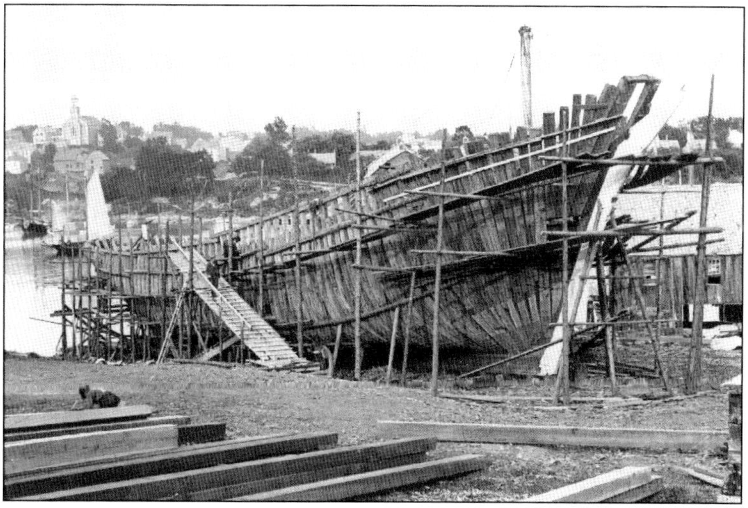

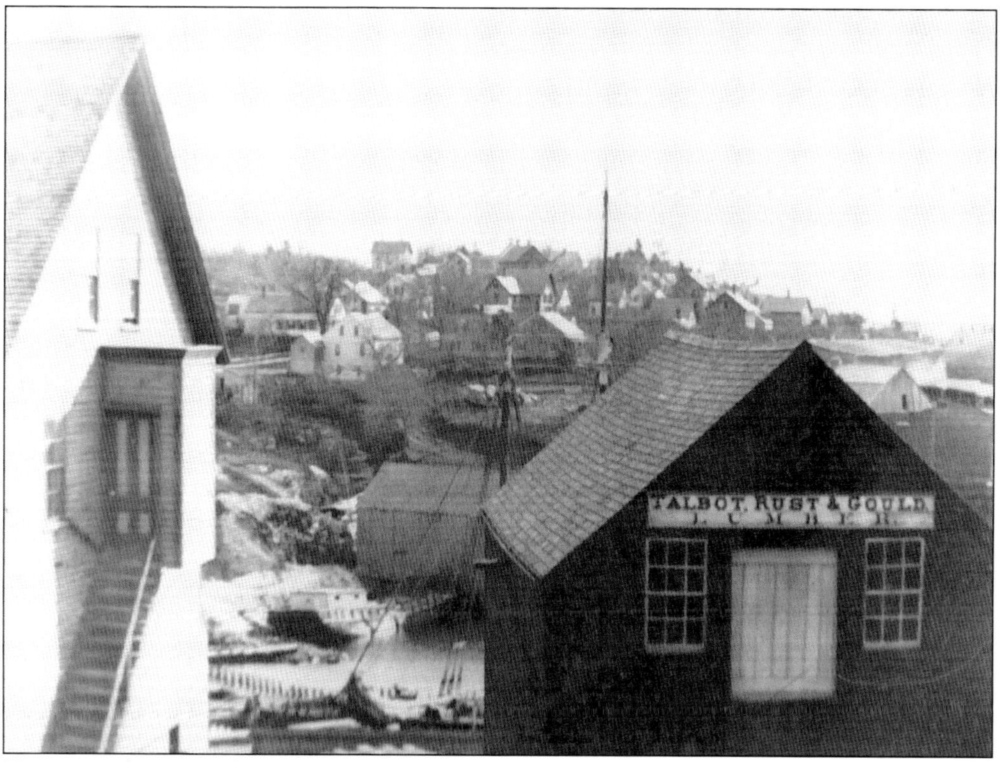

Here is another view of inner Rockport Harbor around 1880, taken from the top floor of a building close by. The Talbot, Rust & Gould lumber shed is prominent in the foreground. Nathaniel Talbot was a lawyer and staunch temperance advocate who joined Gen. John Rust, Joseph Gould, and Hanson Andrews in the ice and lumber business until his death in 1889. Nathaniel's brother David was a prominent lime manufacturer and shipbuilder.

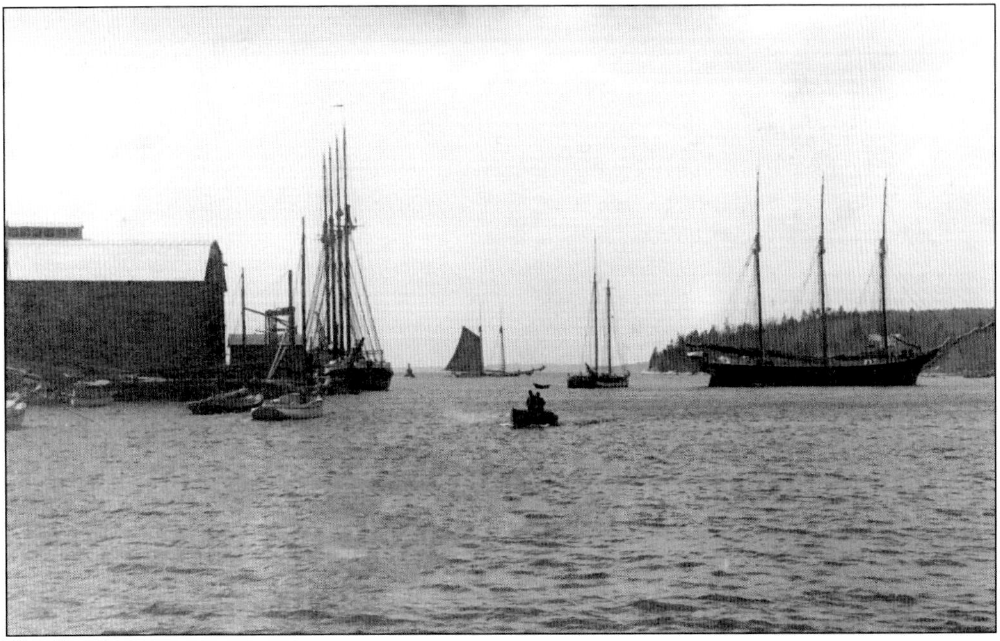

This is an interesting photograph of Rockport Harbor. One of the large icehouses owned by the Rockport Ice Company is at the left of the image, and large three- and four-masted schooners are anchored just offshore. The ice industry was one of the largest in Rockport, as more than 50,000 tons of ice were cut from Lily Pond every year and stored here for transport.

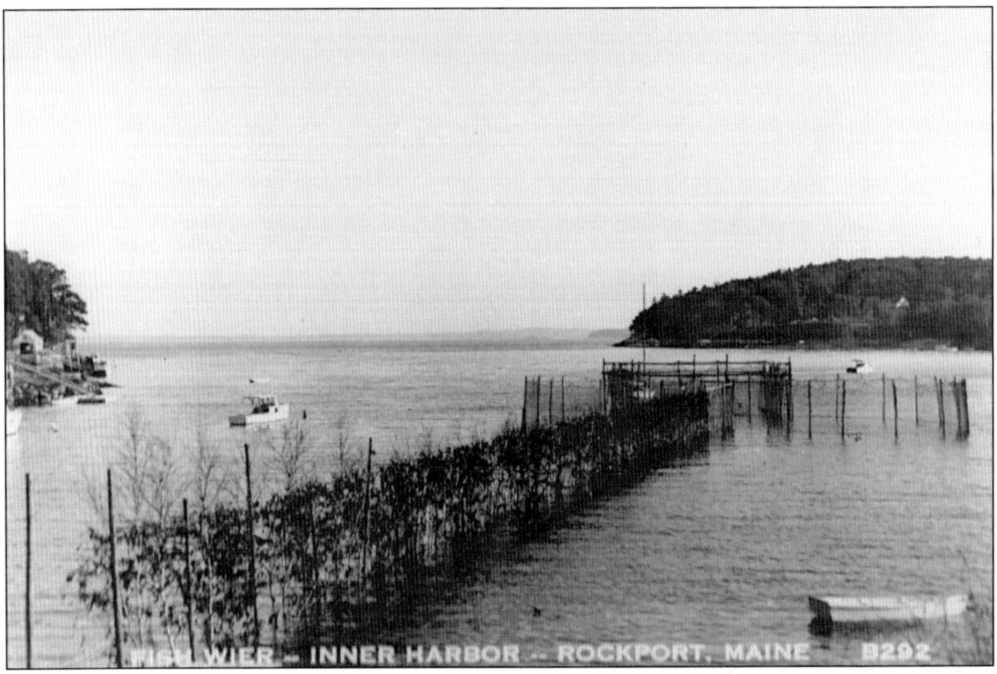

This postcard shows a weir in Rockport Harbor. Smelts, salmon, and other species were abundant at onetime near the rocky shore, along with lobster, which were once considered unsuitable to eat. The ocean was full of cod, hake, and haddock that could be easily harvested until the collapse of the ground fisheries due to overfishing.

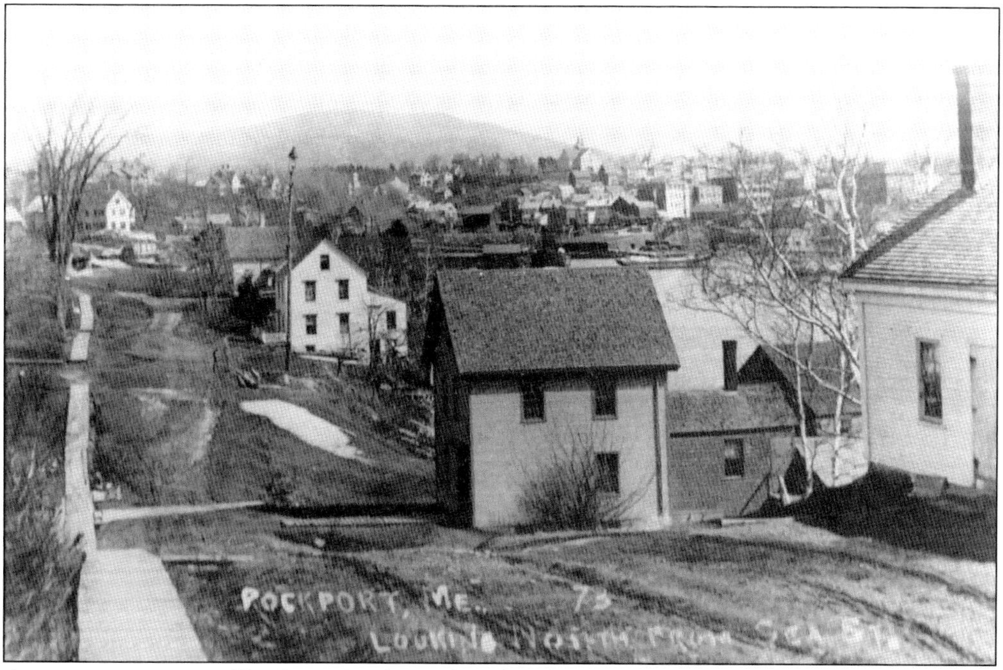

An interesting view of Rockport Harbor is found in this postcard. Many cards from the 19th and 20th centuries depict the harbor from a more central location and are often images of the lime and ice industries. Here, a view of an unpaved Sea Street looks toward the Camden hills. Elevated sidewalks helped keep pedestrians somewhat clean when the dirt road turned to mud.

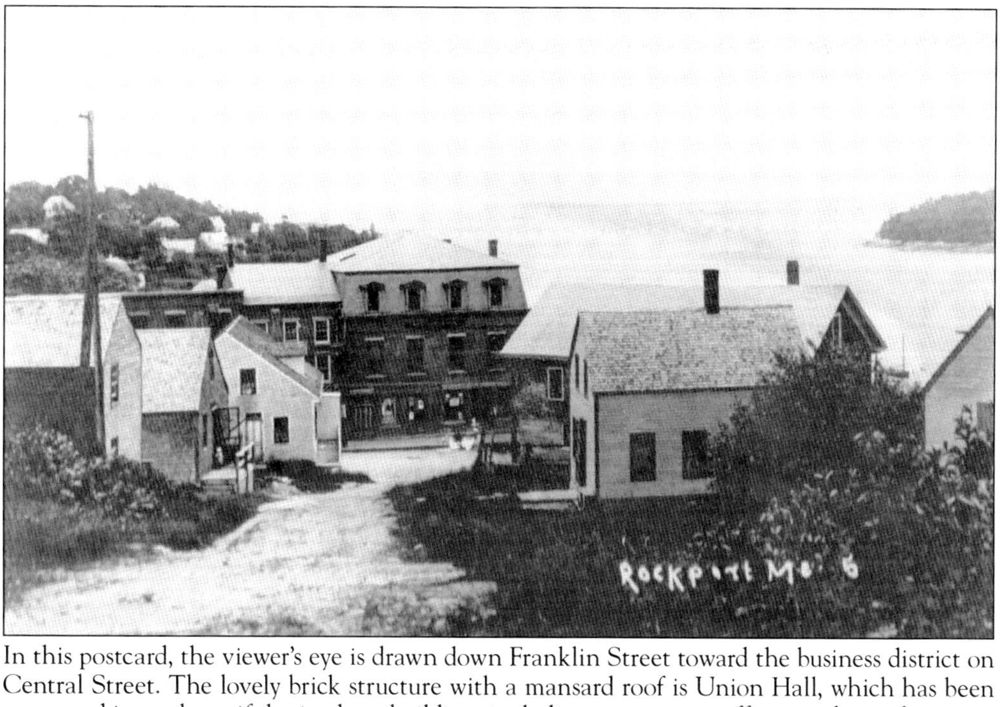

In this postcard, the viewer's eye is drawn down Franklin Street toward the business district on Central Street. The lovely brick structure with a mansard roof is Union Hall, which has been renovated into a beautiful mixed-use building, including restaurants, offices, and a performance space for Bay Chamber Concerts.

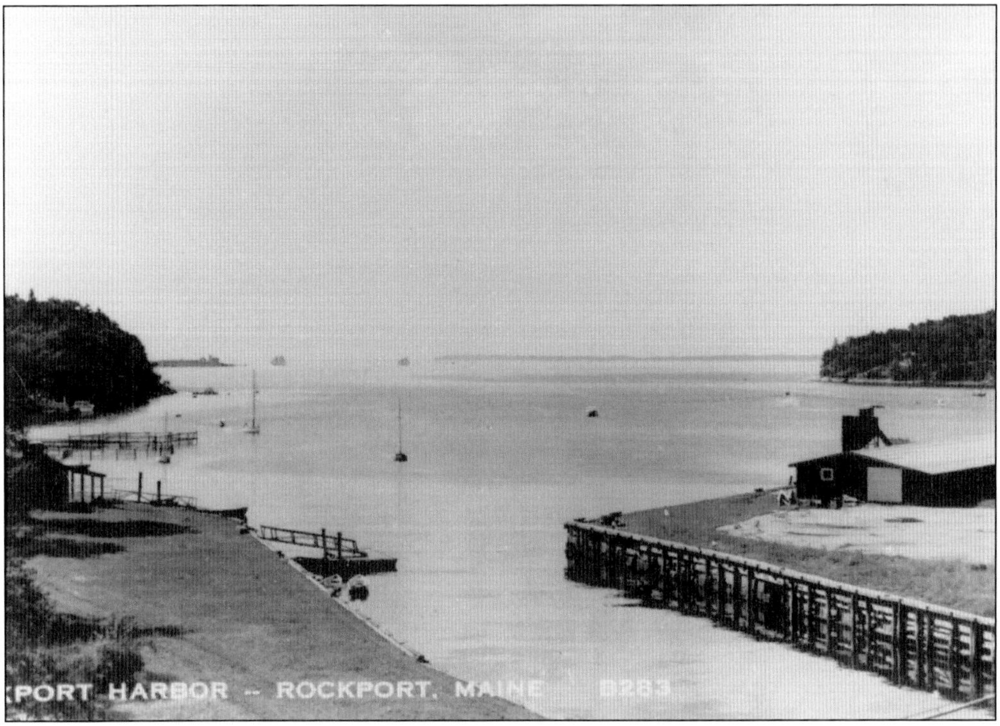

In these two postcards from the mid-20th century, Rockport Harbor has started to recover after the devastating fire at the lime kilns in 1907. The above image shows the Homeport Fish Packing Company in Marine Park. The site of the destroyed kilns was turned into a park and is today the location of the harbormaster's office and offers dockage for daysailers. Beauchamp Point curves around out of sight, and Indian Island is nearly hidden from view just beyond the point. The image below shows a sleek craft sailing past the Rockport Boat Club.

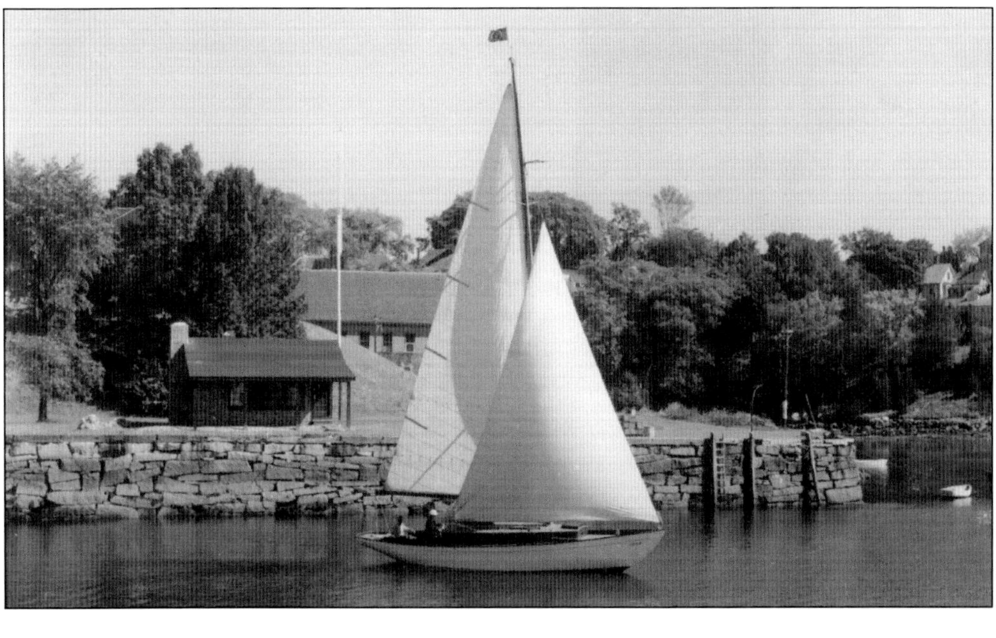

Five

Making a Living

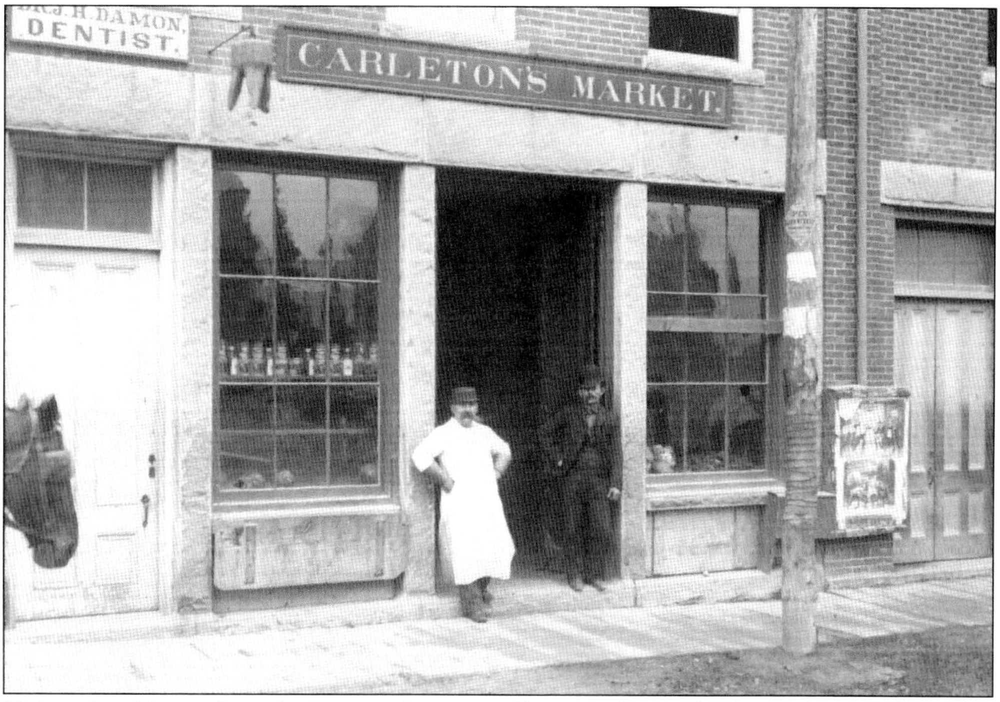

This undated image from the historical society collections shows Charles Carleton (left) outside his grocery shop. According to Williams's two-volume *History of Camden*, "the old Armstrong building at the corner of Washington and Mechanic Streets was remodeled [in 1925]; and Carleton's Market, which occupied the building, found temporary quarters at the American Express building on Washington Street."

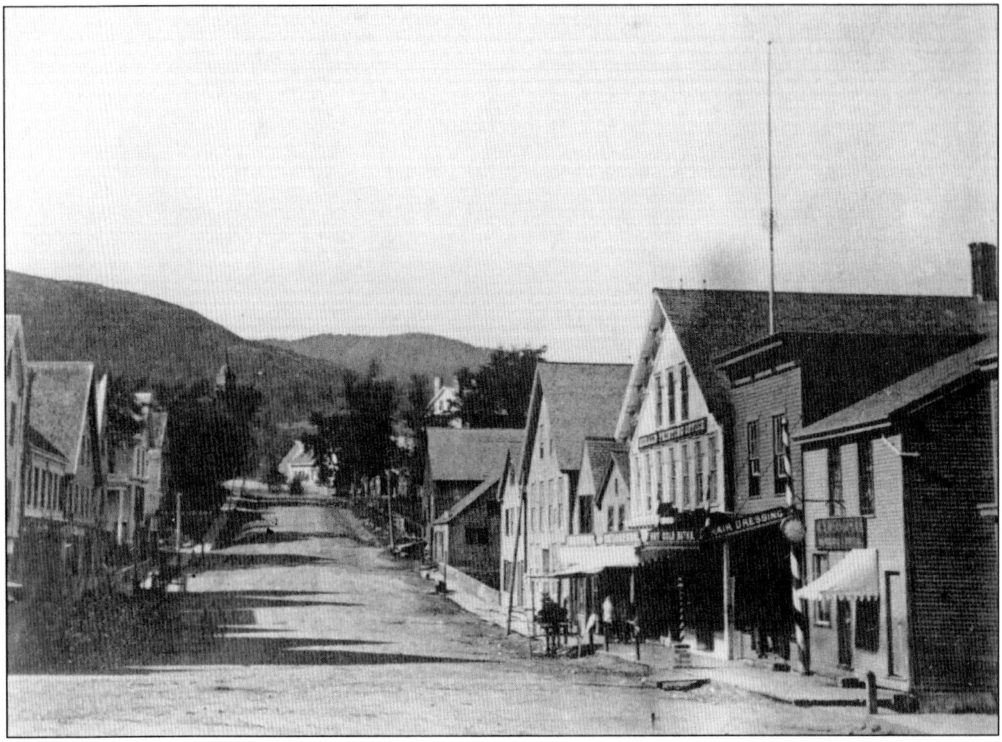

These photographs show how Main Street in Camden evolved over the years spanning the Great Fire of 1892. In the image above, likely taken before 1885, the white, peaked building at the right next to the flagpole appears to be the printing office of the *Camden Herald* newspaper, which was established in 1869. The paper is still in operation 145 years later. In the image below, all the structures in the above image that were destroyed in the fire have been rebuilt in brick. The trolley is visible in the center of the dirt street, and two gentlemen are taking a rest on the back of the delivery wagon in the right foreground in front of the Arau tonsorial artists barber pole.

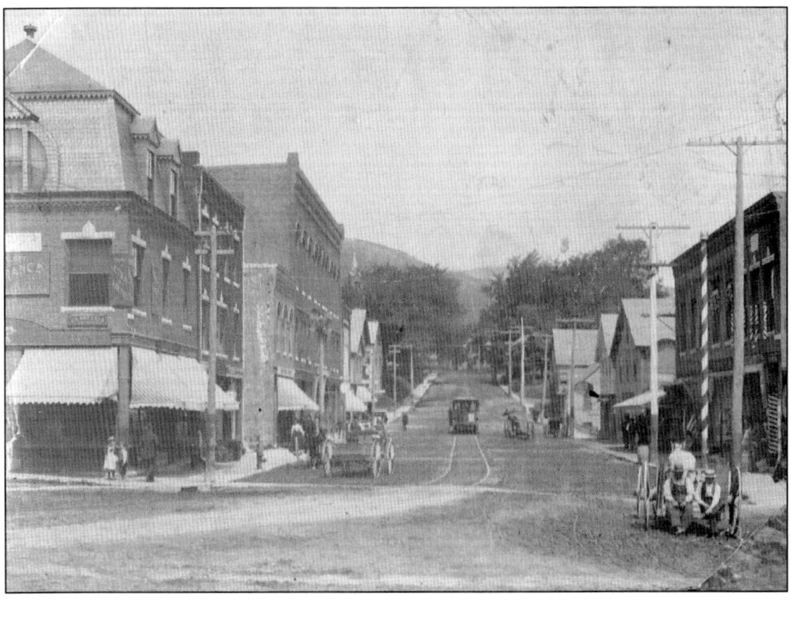

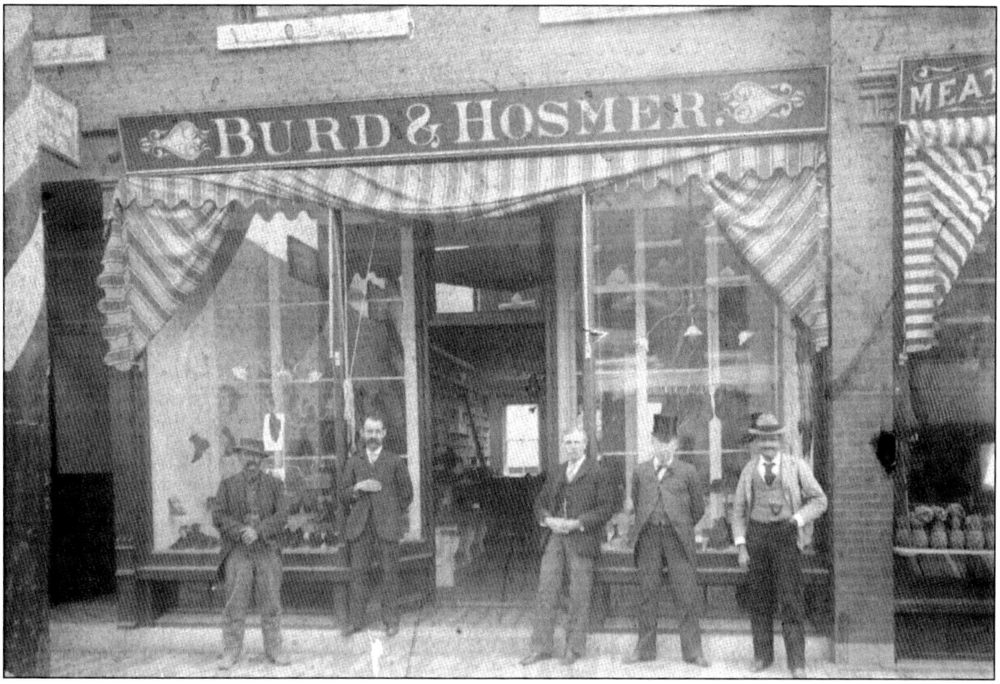

This c. 1900 photograph shows several distinguished-looking gentlemen on the sidewalk outside the Burd & Hosmer shoe shop, located between Hodgman & Co. clothing store and the F.O. Clark grocery on Main Street. At the time of this photograph, George Burd had been in business for more than 45 years and was one of the seminal merchants in Camden. Burd sold boots and shoes and was one of Camden's most prominent and influential businessmen. The advertisement for the shoe shop is found in an early town directory.

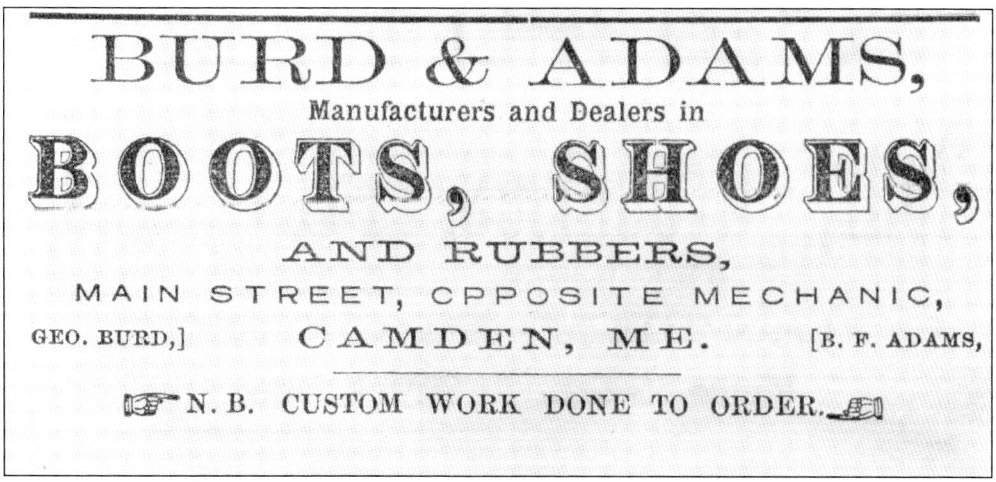

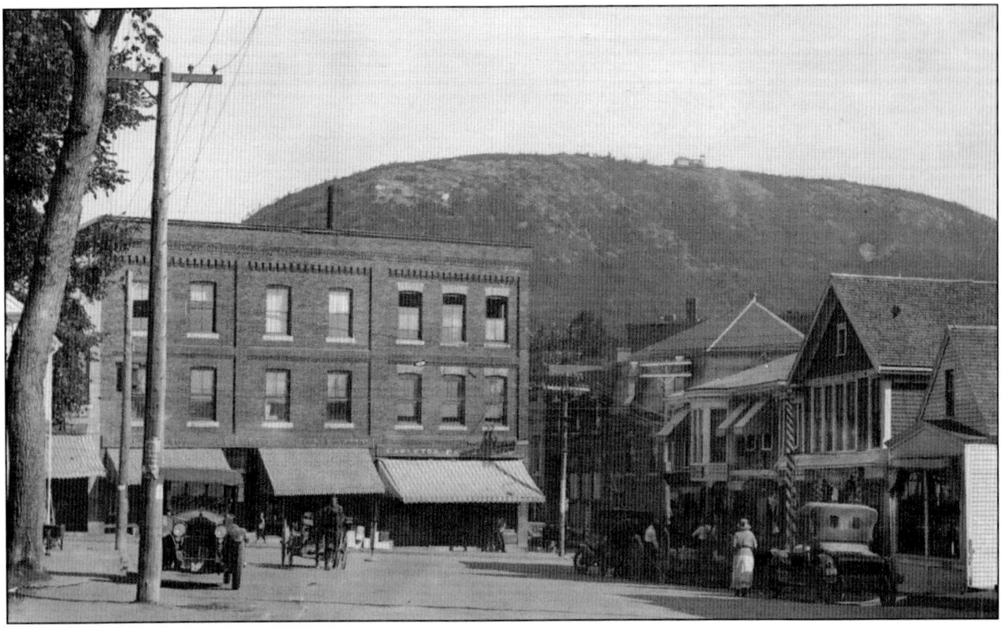

This view of Elm Street looks from Chestnut Street near the Village Green in Camden. The image, though undated, was taken prior to 1920, as the Summit House, which was torn down at the end of World War I and replaced by a stone memorial tower, is visible at the top of Mount Battie. The Carleton-French grocery has the striped awning on the corner, and it remains a popular grocery shop to this day.

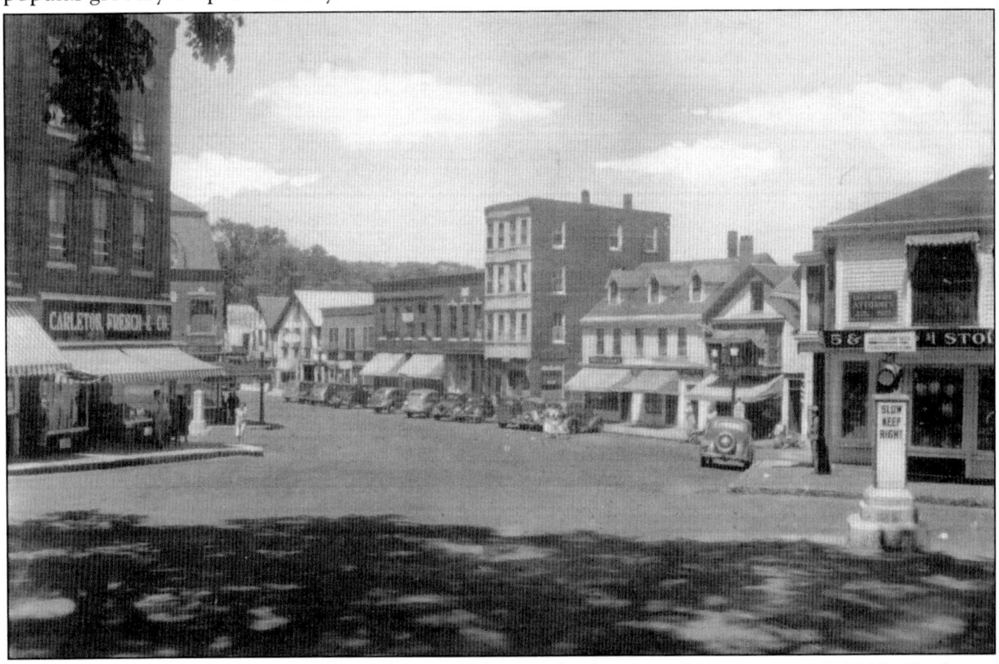

This image shows the intersection of Main, Elm, and Chestnut Streets around 1940. Carleton French & Co. later became known as French & Brawn and is now a popular spot for tourists and locals to stock up on sandwiches and fresh seafood. The building at far right is now the Camden National Bank, but, in the mid-20th century, it was Crockett's five-and-dime store.

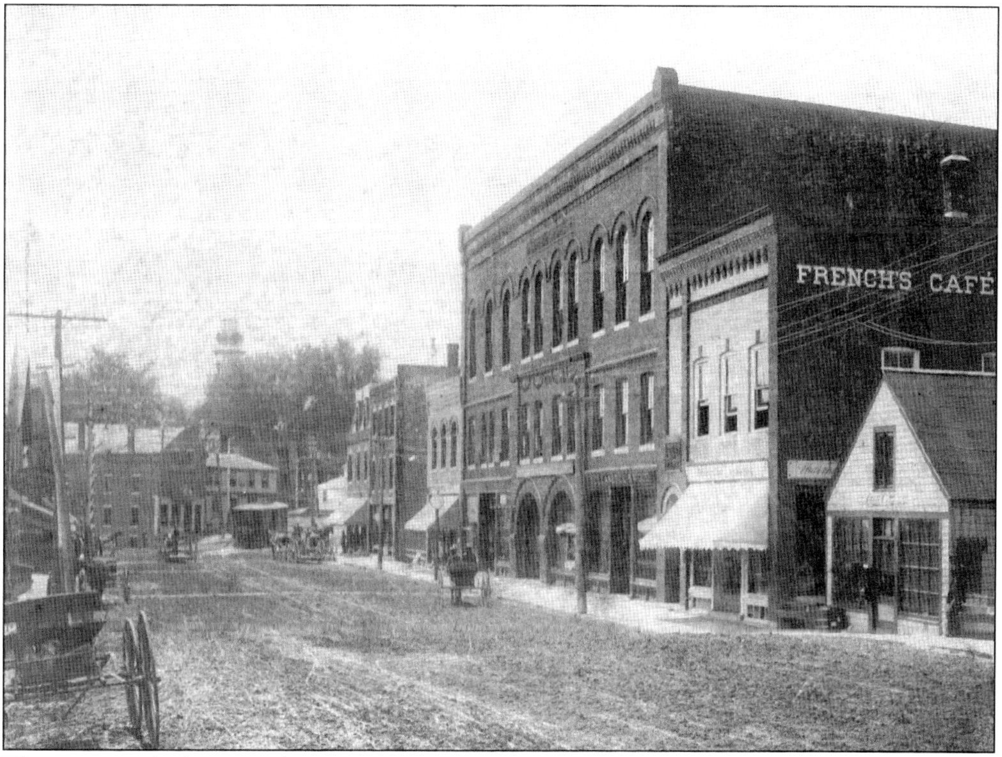

This is a view looking south on Camden's Main Street. It was taken just after the fire of 1892, as all the new buildings shown here were constructed in 1893 of more fire-resistant brick. The imposing brick structure with the distinctive arched entries is now the Lord Camden Inn. The adjacent building, once French's Café, became a drugstore and soda fountain called Boynton-McKay. It is now a popular local restaurant.

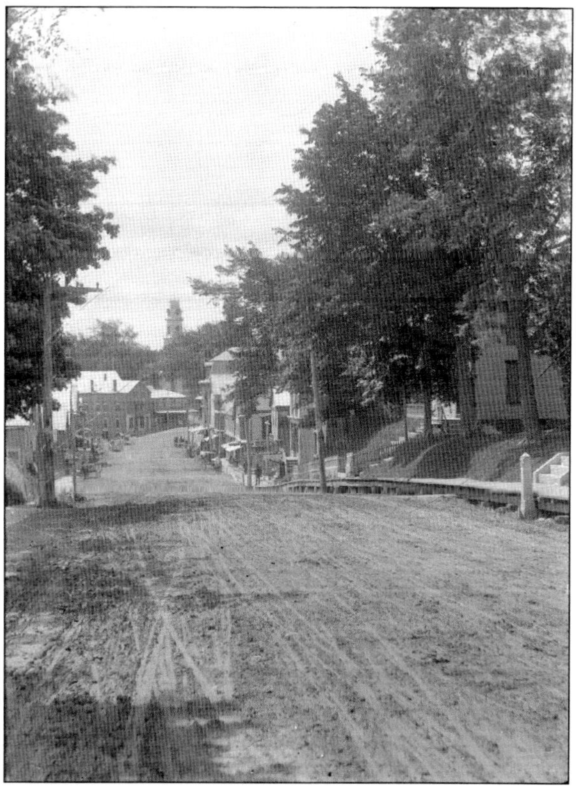

This is an image of a view down Main Street in Camden from Harbor Hill heading south toward the center of town. The main road has not yet been paved at the time this photograph was taken, and the sidewalks are made of wood and elevated above the road. Also notable in the background is the steeple of Chestnut Street Baptist Church, which lost its spire twice after 1837 until a local Eagle Scout raised funds to replace it in the 1980s.

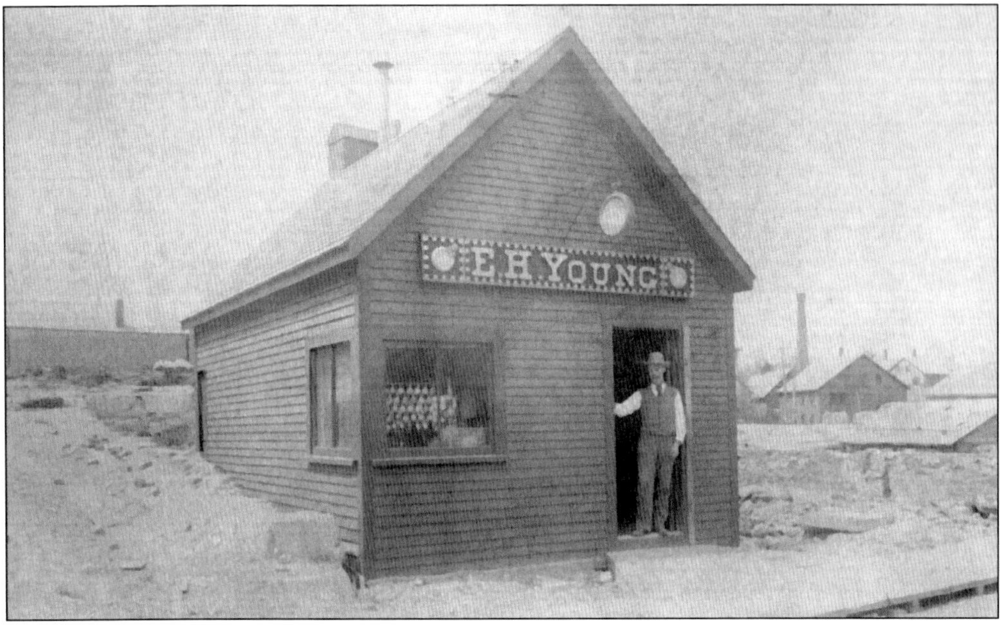

This photograph taken around 1883 shows the shop of Elnathan H. Young, an enterprising young man who owned a jewelry and watch repair shop on Mechanic Street in Camden. The small shop has an outsized watch sign hanging above the entrance, and the smokestack near the Knox Mill complex is in the background.

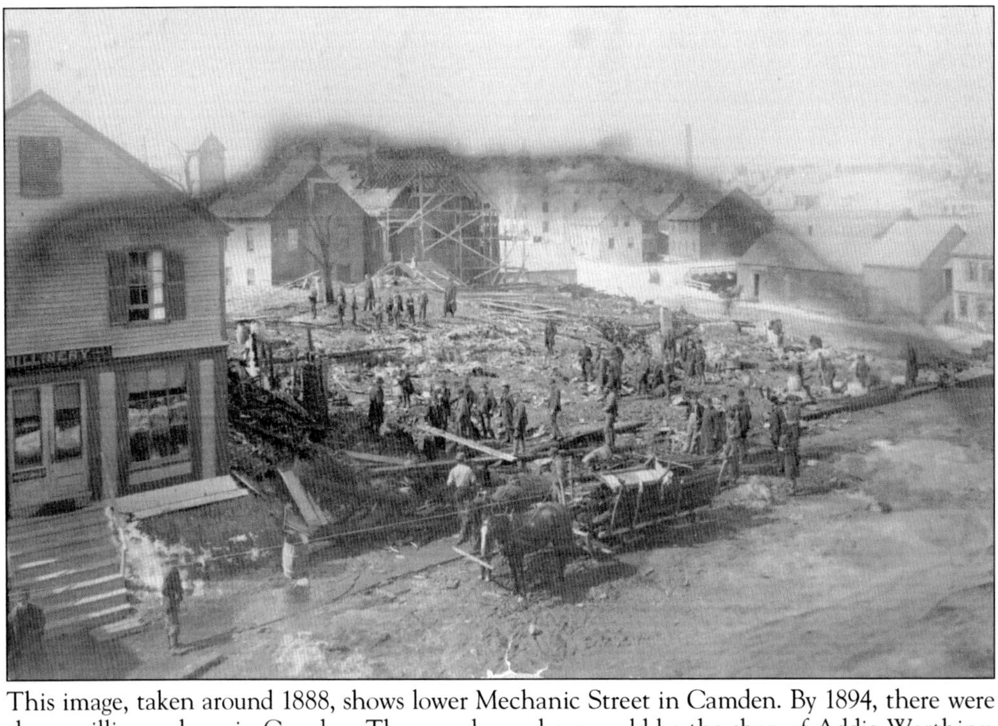

This image, taken around 1888, shows lower Mechanic Street in Camden. By 1894, there were three millinery shops in Camden. The one shown here could be the shop of Addie Worthing, purveyor of "millinery and fancy goods," or perhaps the shop of F.S. & C.E. Ordway. Jameson's Garage occupied the site by 1933.

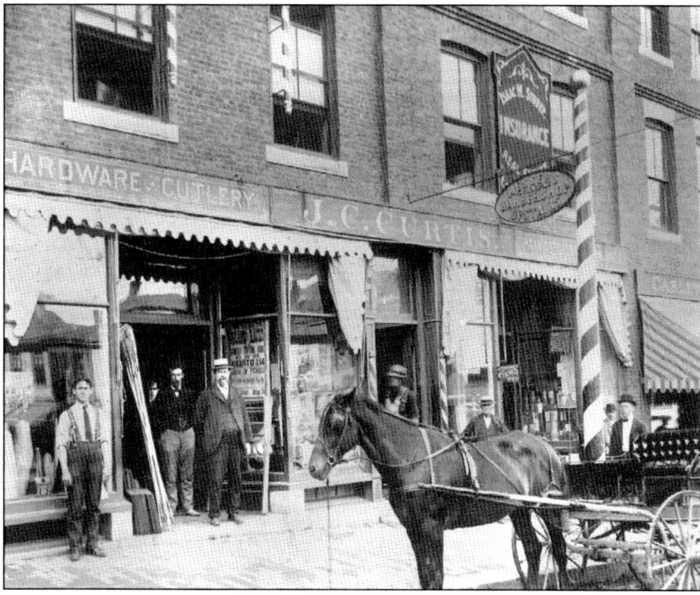

The J.C. Curtis Hardware Store was located for many years on Main Street next to the Carleton-Pascal store with the striped awning. In this image from about 1903, Curtis (in the white hat) stands outside his shop. The other people are, from left to right, Win Bassick, Jane Bickford, A.H Parsons, John Ferrih, Charles Burd, and Herbert Young.

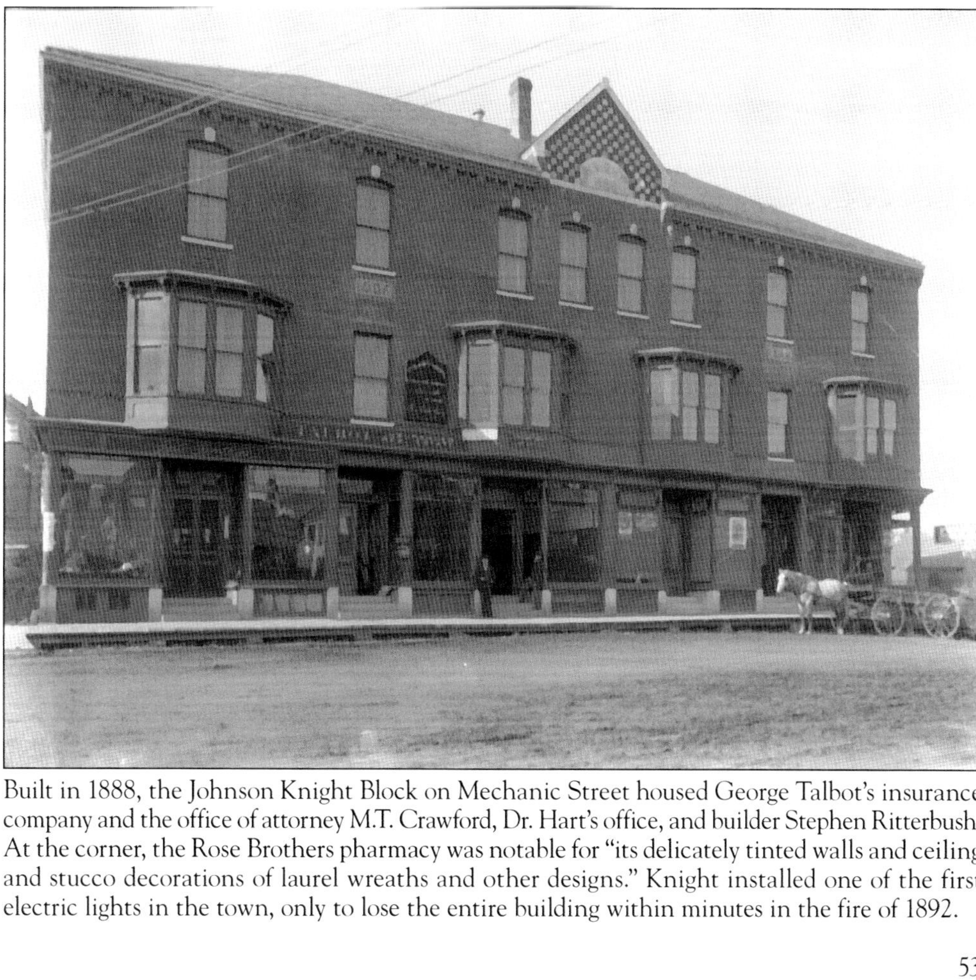

Built in 1888, the Johnson Knight Block on Mechanic Street housed George Talbot's insurance company and the office of attorney M.T. Crawford, Dr. Hart's office, and builder Stephen Ritterbush. At the corner, the Rose Brothers pharmacy was notable for "its delicately tinted walls and ceiling and stucco decorations of laurel wreaths and other designs." Knight installed one of the first electric lights in the town, only to lose the entire building within minutes in the fire of 1892.

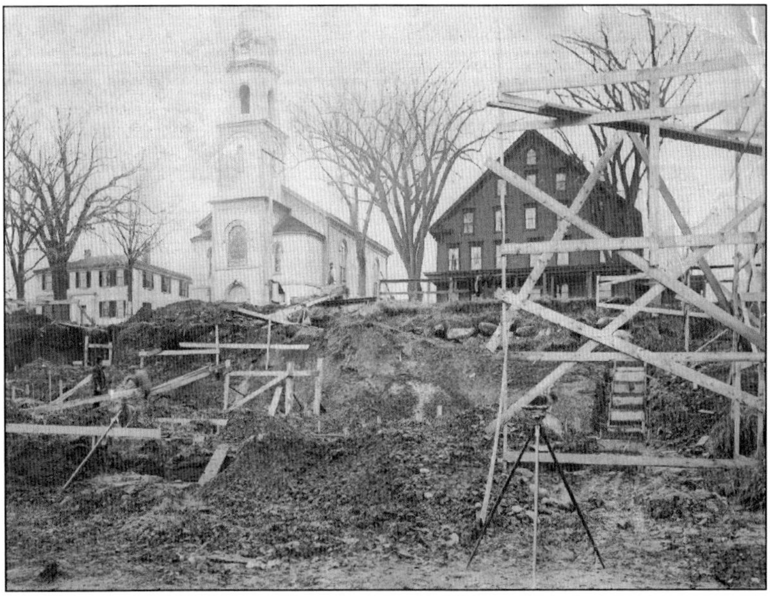

This is a rare photograph of the early stages of the construction of Camden's post office. The image is taken from Bayview Street looking up the rise. Across the street from the construction site are the Cushing house (left), the Chestnut Street Baptist Church, and the Bay View House on what is now the Village Green.

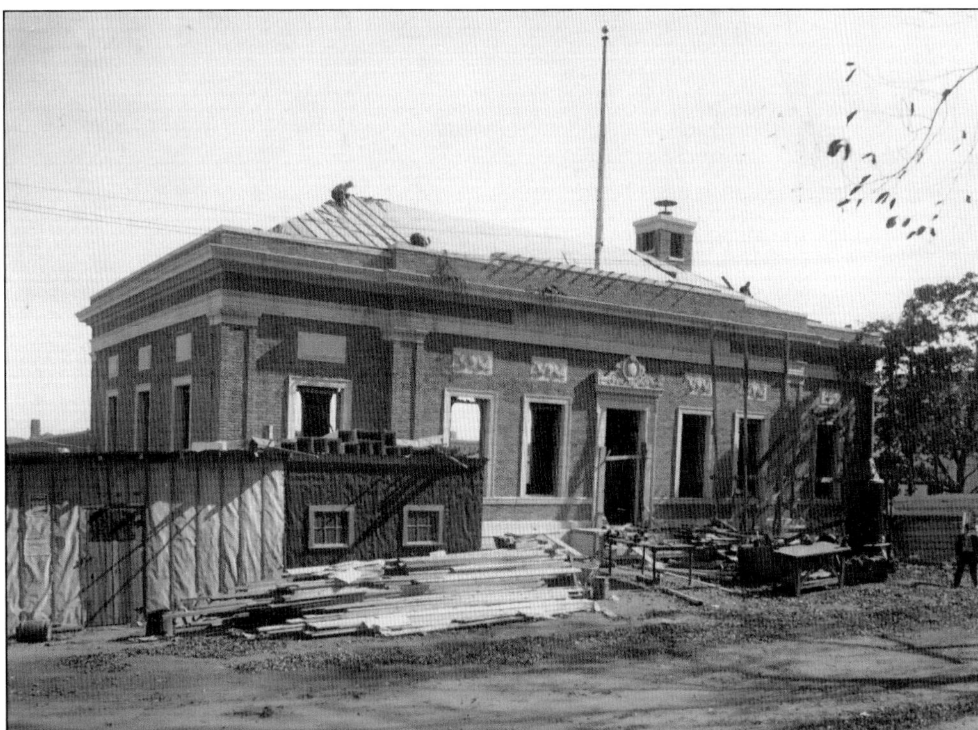

The post office on Chestnut Street in Camden was completed in 1915. Costing nearly $85,000, the first-class facility was necessary in part to handle the massive amount of mail generated by the D.P. Ordway Plaster Company. Established in 1881, the company sold medicinal plasters at 25¢ each and was located on the site of the current Camden Riverhouse Hotel.

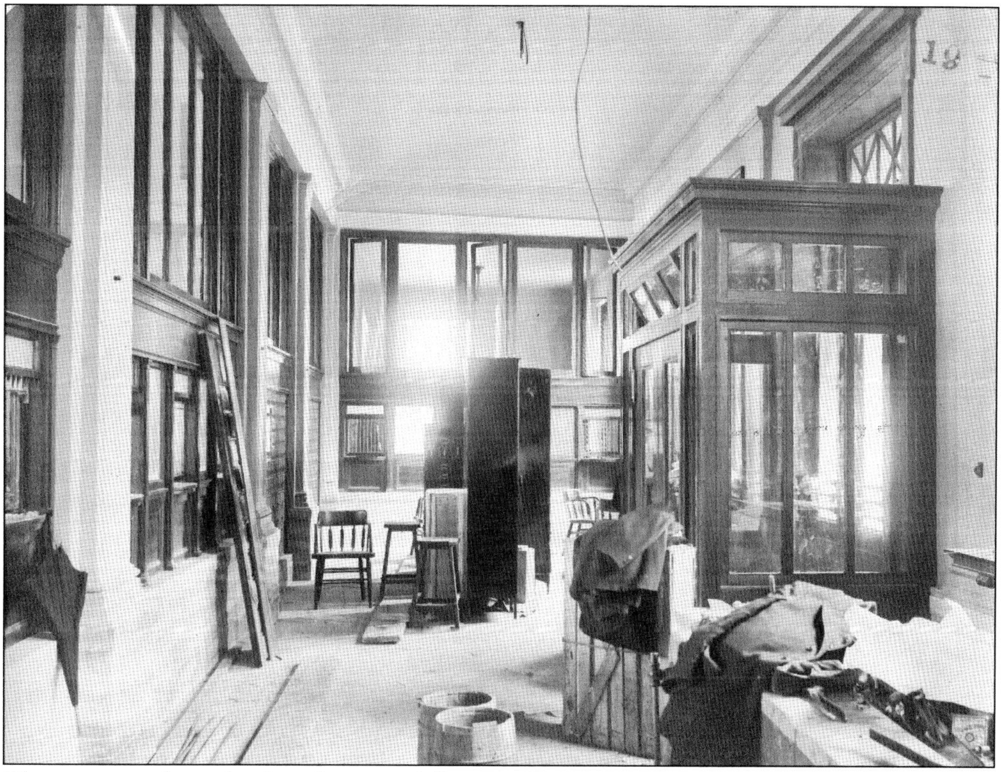

These images show the Camden Post Office nearly complete in 1914. The above photograph shows the interior's beautiful marble floors and dark wood framing. The wood-framed entryway helps shield people from cold blasts of air when the door is opened in the winter. Builder Stephen Ritterbush had the honor of sending the first parcel post from the Camden Post Office, which contained samples of dirt from the post office lot on Chestnut Street. The samples were sent to the architect supervising the plans for the new postal facility, built at a cost of about $85,000 in 1914. The image below is a photograph of the Camden Post Office on Chestnut Street taken about 1920. A cornerstone of the building contains a *Camden Herald* newspaper dated July 31, 1914, a town report, a roster of postal employees with photographs, and a 600-page history of Camden and Rockport written by Judge Reuel Robinson in 1907. Robinson was also editor of the *Camden Herald* from 1898 to 1900 and again from 1923 to 1925. He is remembered as an outspoken critic of Ku Klux Klan activity in town at a time when no other officials stepped forward in protest.

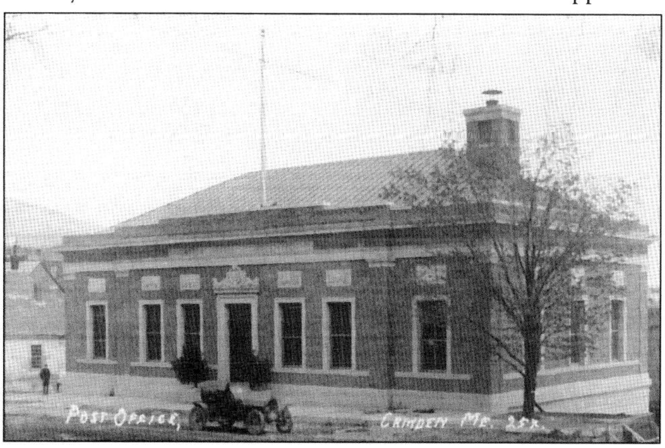

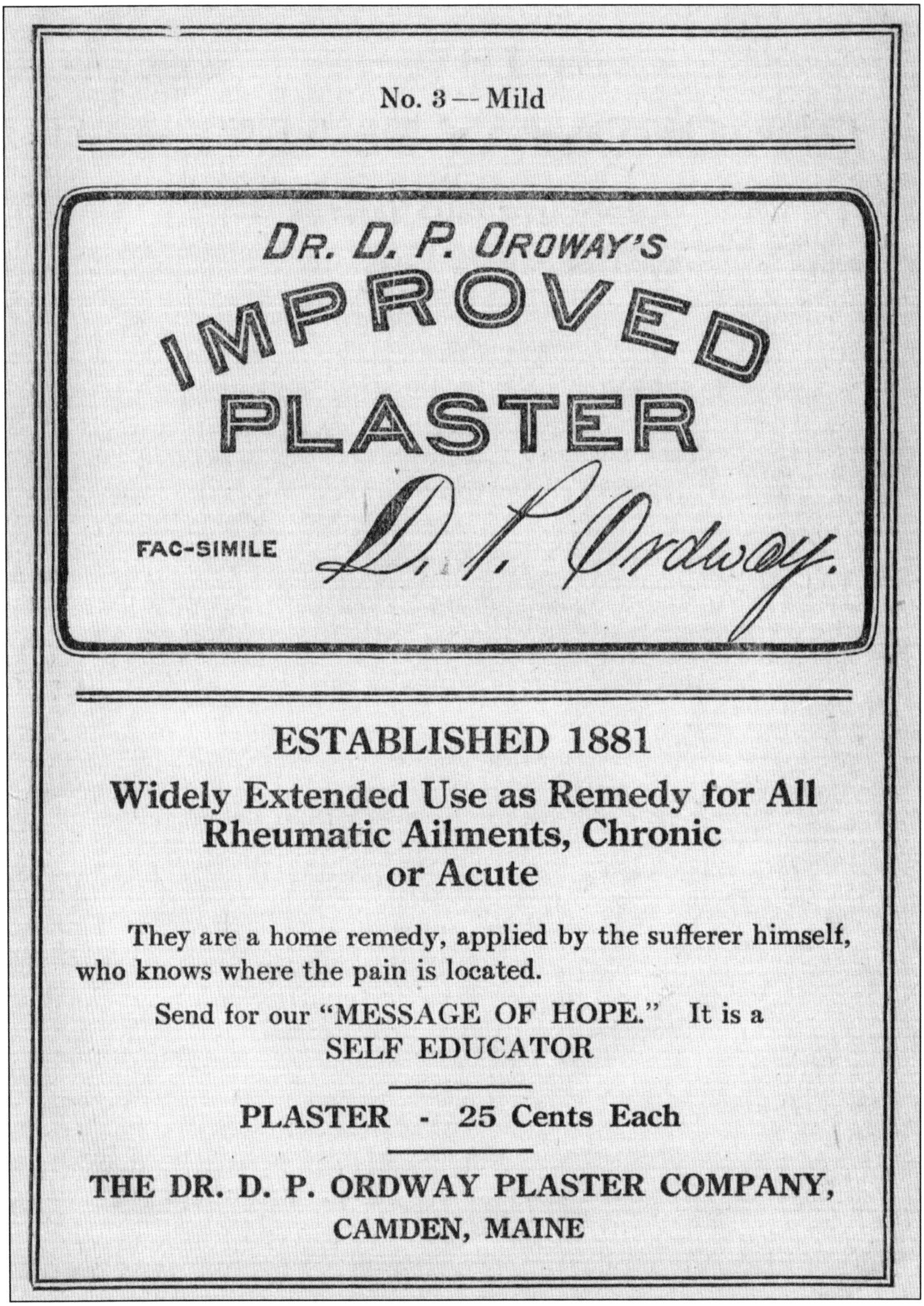

The D.P. Ordway Plaster Company made medicinal plasters at its site on Tannery Lane, which is now the location of the Camden Riverhouse Hotel. The plasters were marketed as a home remedy for many ailments, and the success of the company led to the Camden Post Office's designation as a first-class facility. The plasters were formulated in various strengths from rosin, tar, mutton tallow, beeswax, turpentine, laudanum, oil of hemlock, and camphor gum.

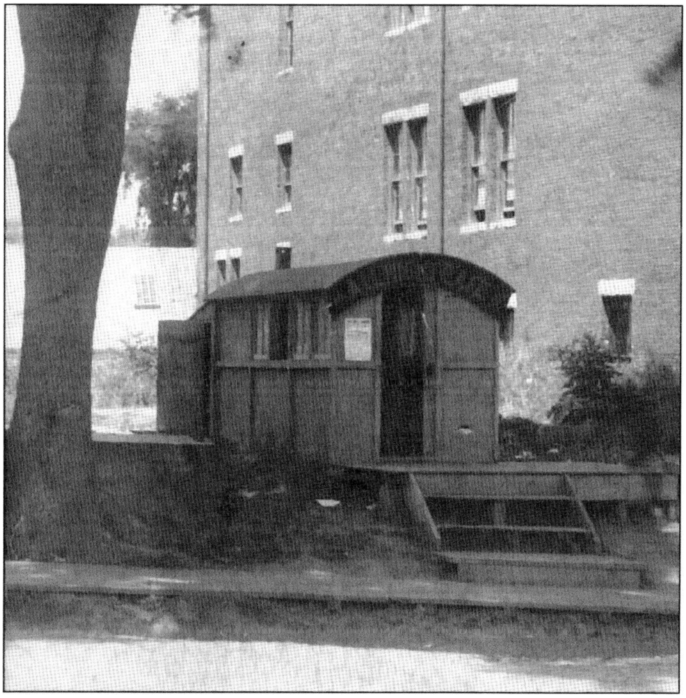

The All-Right Café was a lunchroom located on Elm Street next to the new Camden Opera House. The first café building, shown in the photograph below, was a temporary structure constructed around 1897. The image at right shows the new wooden building that replaced the wagon-like temporary one in 1903. There are still restaurants on this site today.

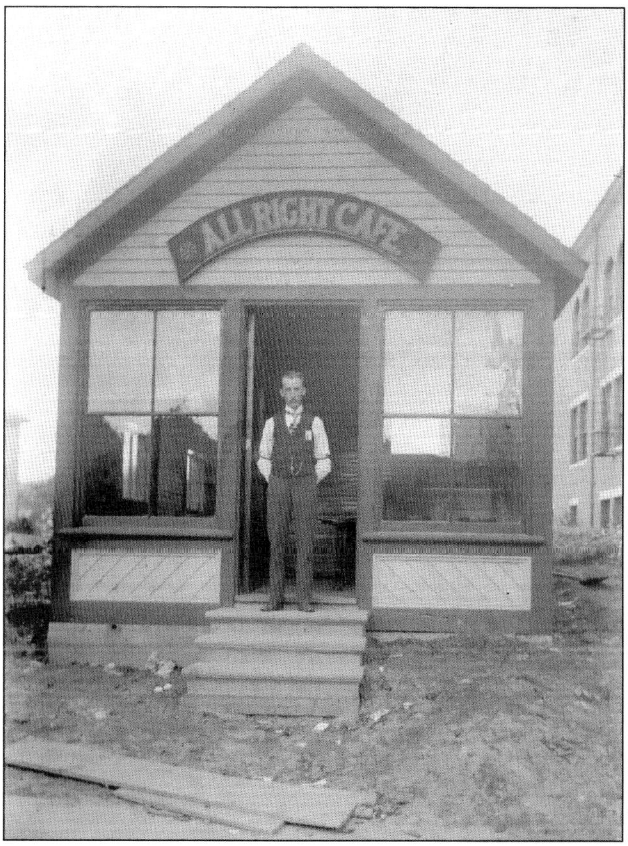

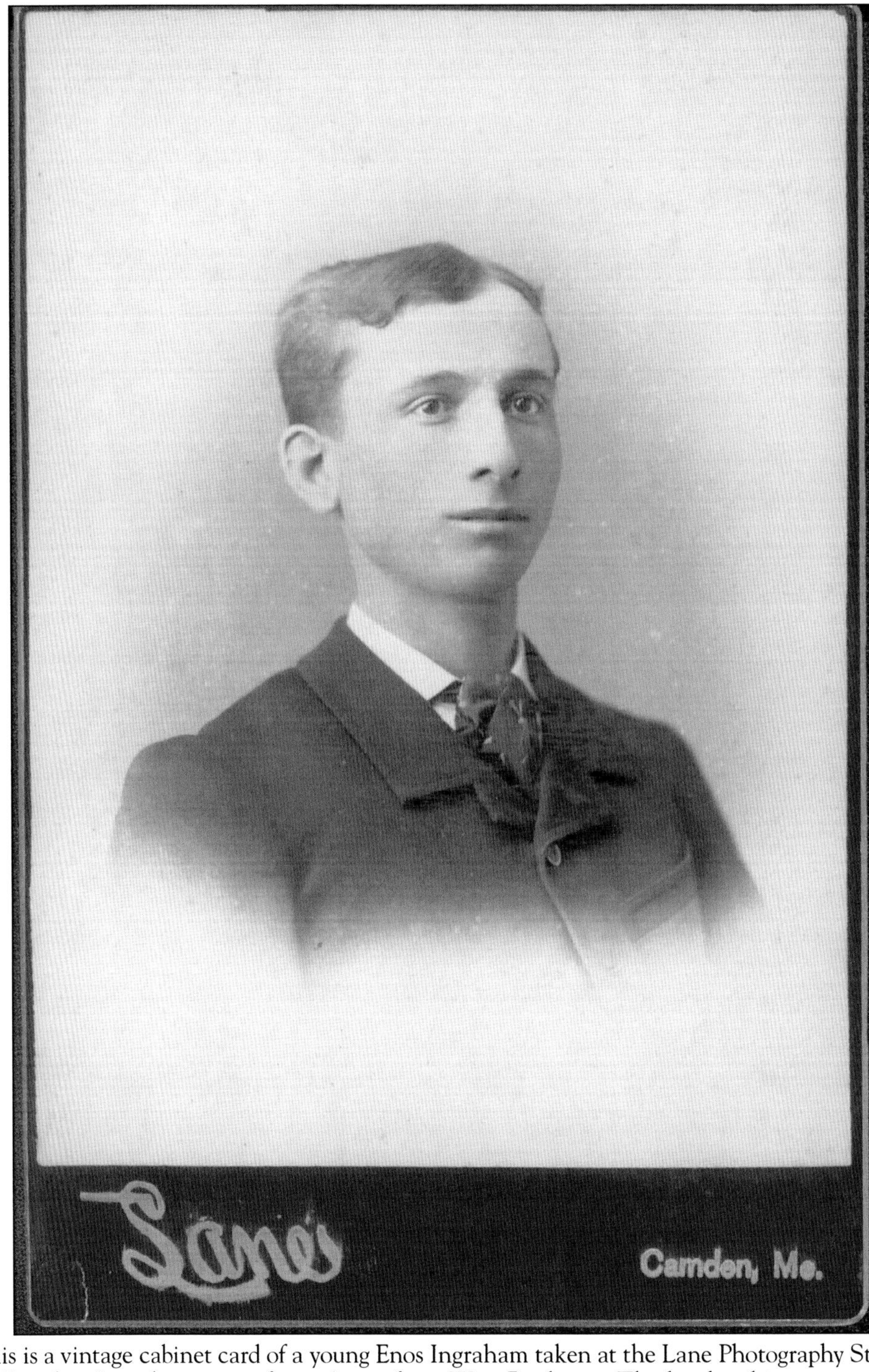

This is a vintage cabinet card of a young Enos Ingraham taken at the Lane Photography Studio in Camden. Ingraham was a farmer's son from West Rockport. The hardworking young man owned a prosperous grocery store on Ship Street in Rockport.

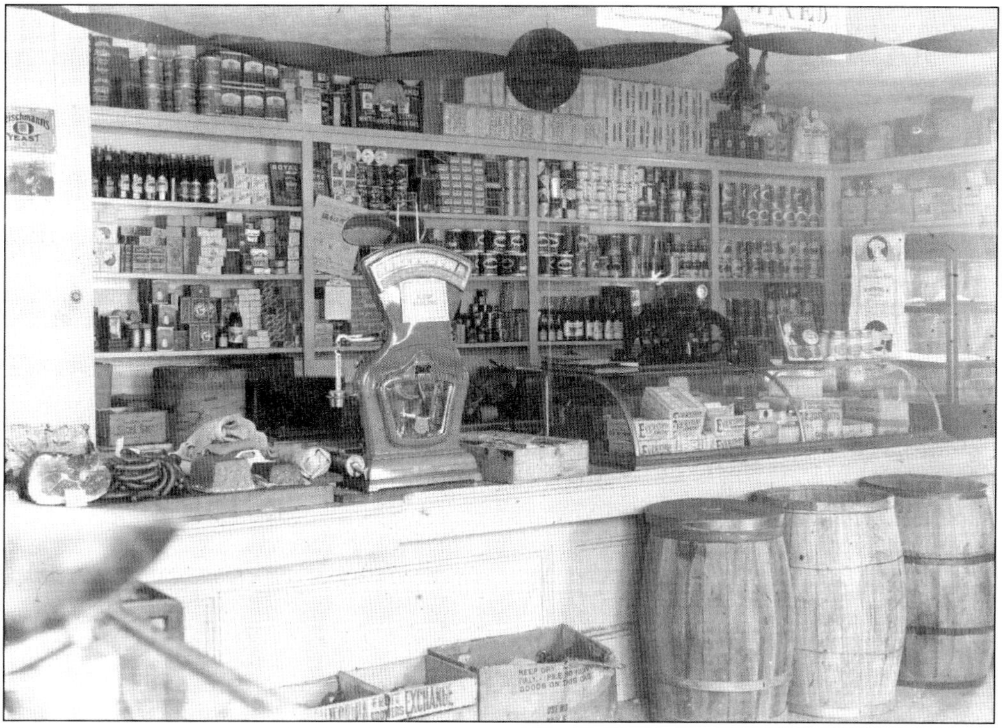

Here are interior views of the Enos E. Ingraham Company store as it looked around 1920. In its early days, the store was located on Rockport's Ship Street, near the head of the harbor. By 1930, Ingraham was prosperous enough to have purchased a three-story building at the intersection of West Street and Commercial Street. Commercial Street was renamed Pascal Avenue in honor of prominent shipbuilder John Pascal.

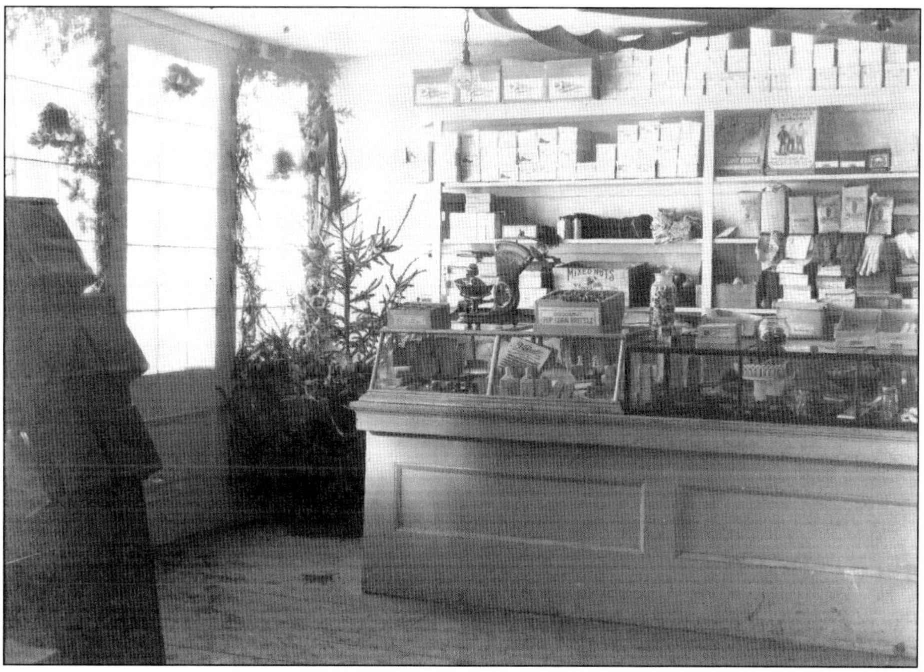

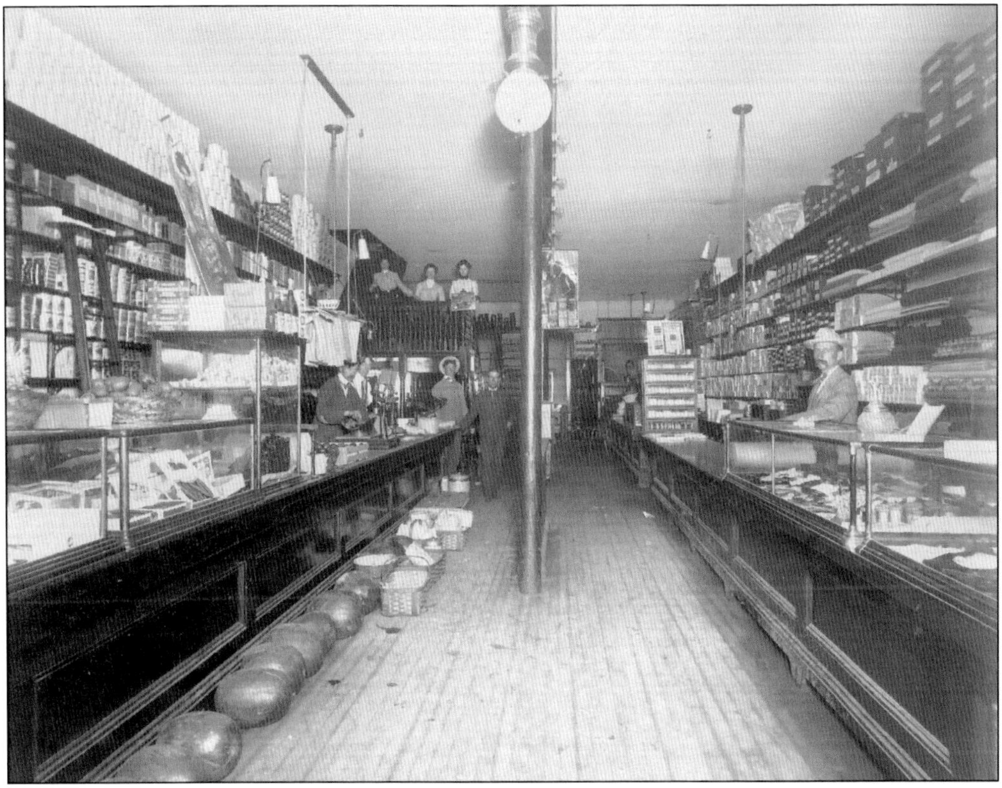

The above image is a nice view of the S.E. & H.L. Shepherd store interior. The S.E. & H.L. Shepherd Company was established in 1845 and incorporated in 1892. It was a vast wholesale and retail business shipping and selling groceries, dry goods, coal, wood, lime, and ice, and it was located in the large brick building in the heart of Rockport's downtown that is still known as the Shepherd Building. It now houses a restaurant called Shepherd's Pie. In the image below, a dapper-looking Enos Ingraham (center, derby hat) stands on the back of his delivery wagon outside the S.E. & H.L Shepherd store.

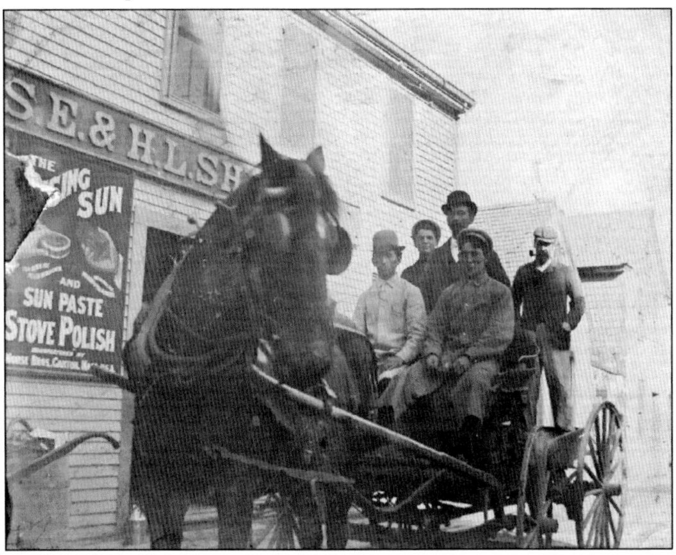

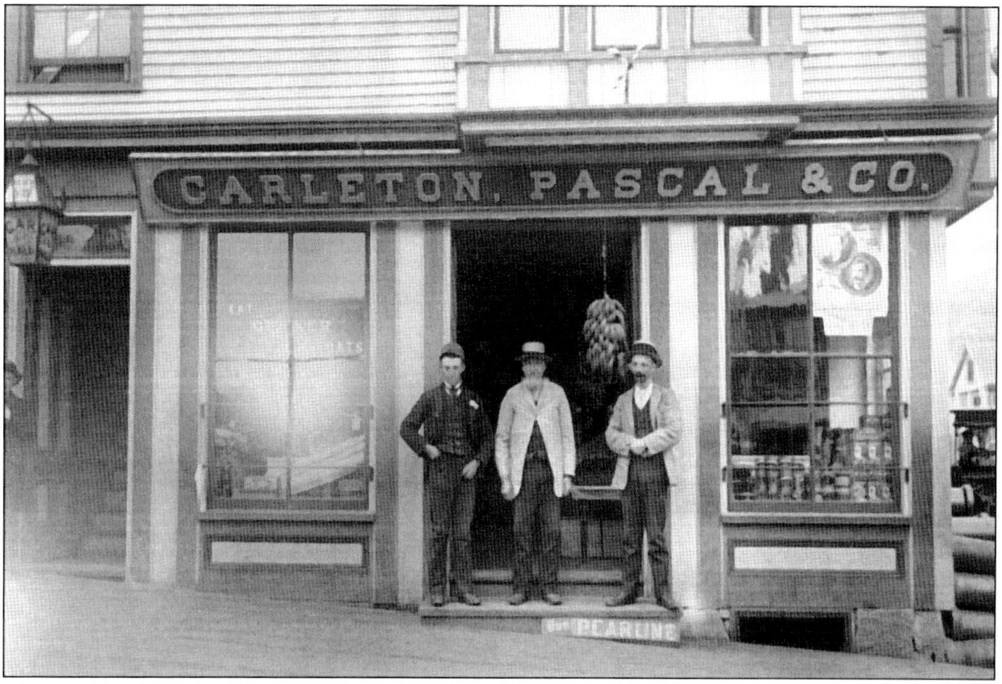

This image of the Carleton-Pascal & Company grocery store dates from about 1888. The building here is clapboard, which dates the image to before the Great Fire of 1892, when the shop and many others on Main and Elm Streets were destroyed in the wind-whipped flames.

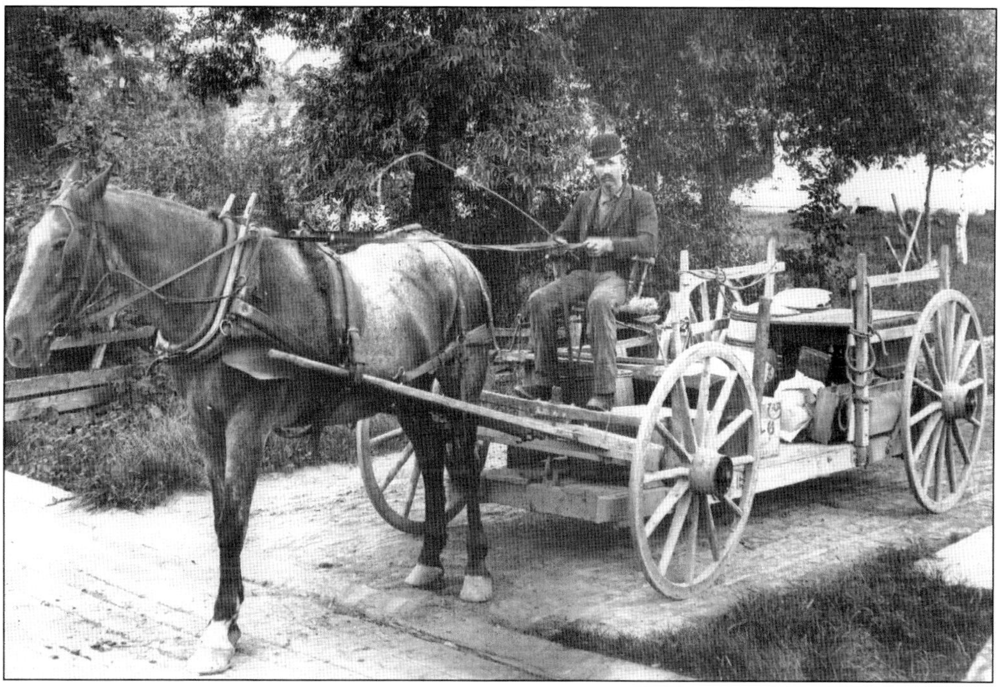

One of the means of delivering goods before the widespread use of the automobile was the use of horse-drawn carts like this one. These low-slung wooden wagons made loading and unloading items easier, but the wooden wheels probably made for an uncomfortably bumpy ride.

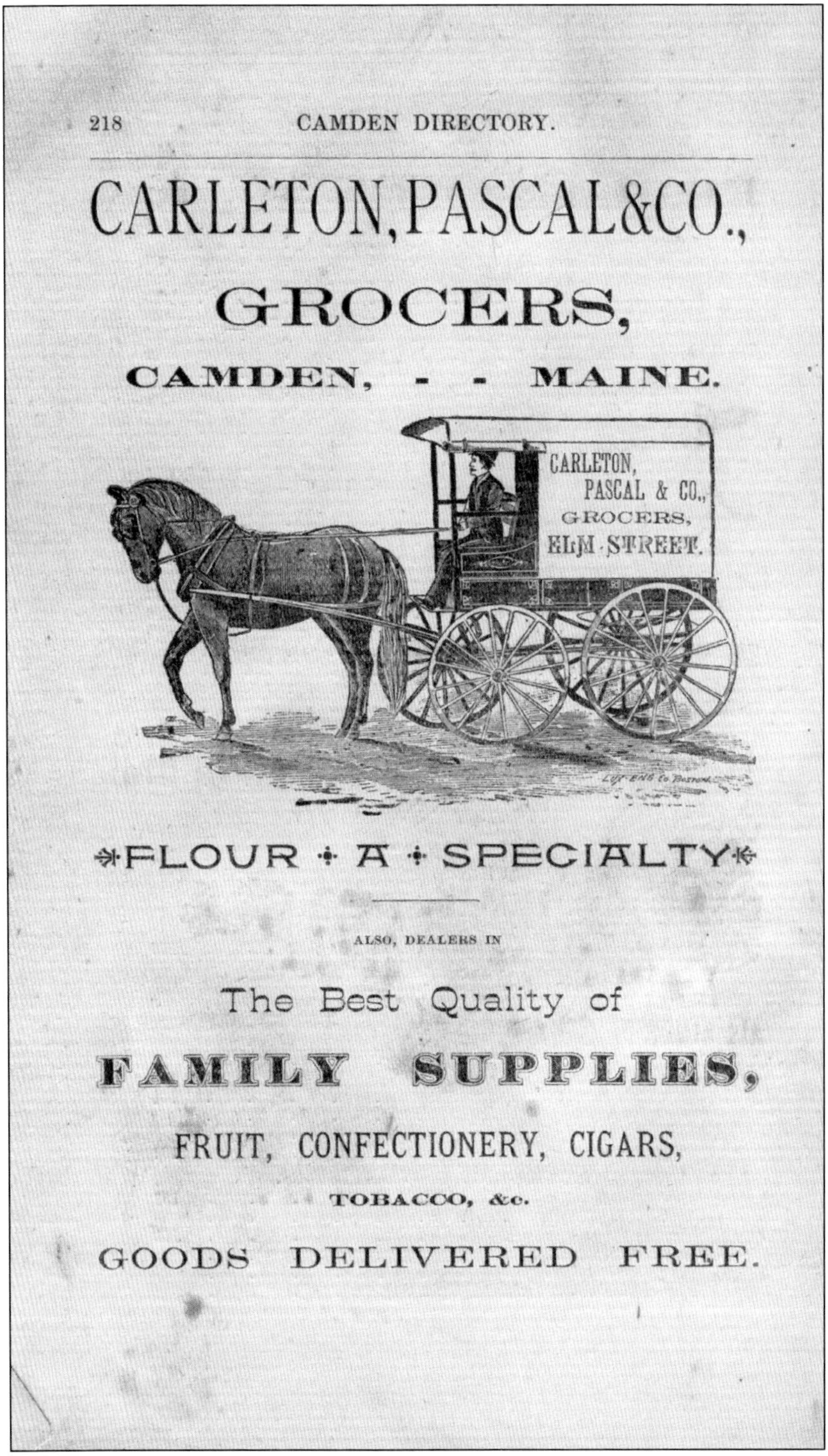

This quaint print from an early Camden town directory shows the Carleton-Pascal grocery advertisement for the store on Elm Street. It remains a small grocery store and is now known as French & Brawn Market. It still offers grocery delivery to area residents.

This photograph shows the interior of the Ralph B. Bucklin tailor shop. It was located at 2 Pearl Street and called the Camden Tailoring Company. In 1916, it was noted in the local paper that Bucklin was stepping down as director of the Bucklin-Marston Orchestra because of the increasing demands of his tailoring business.

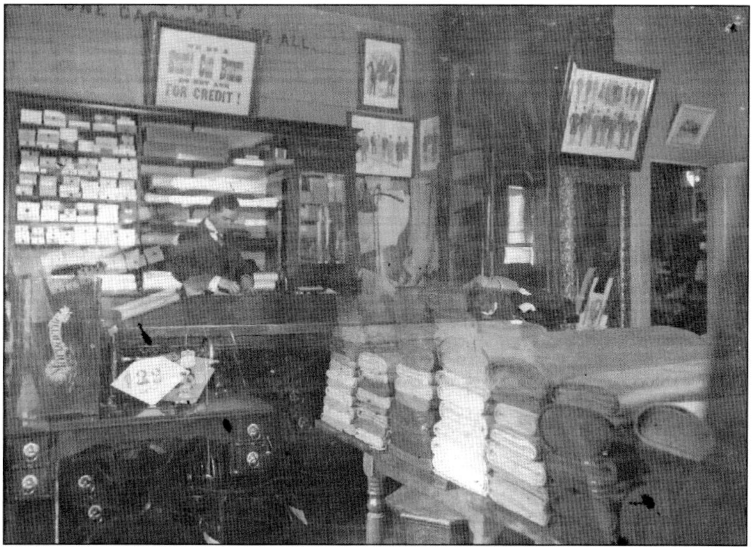

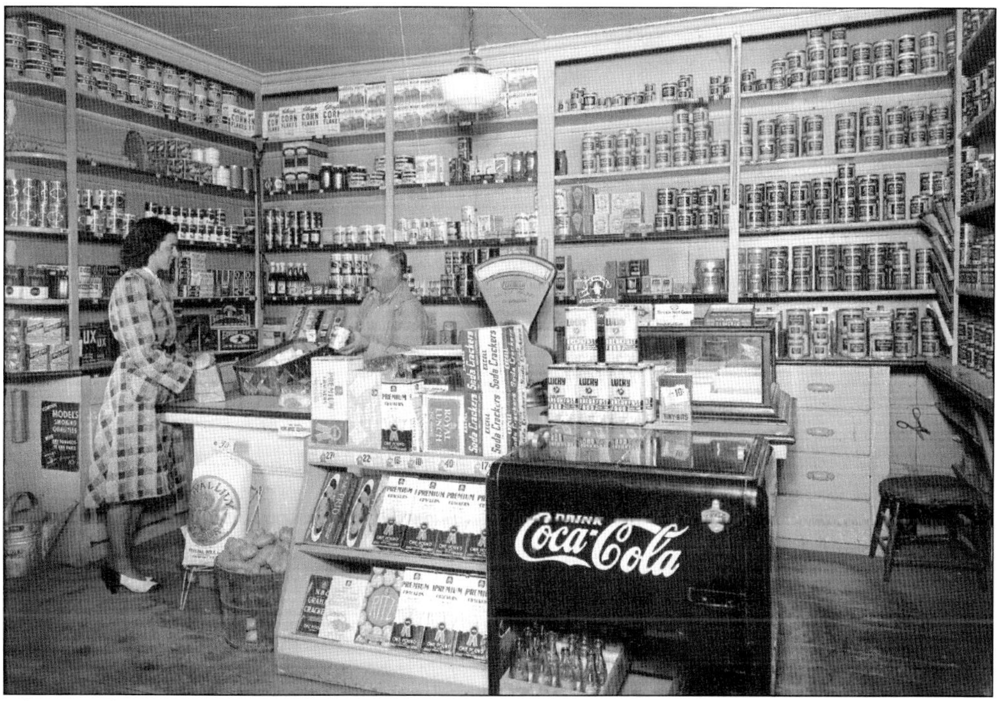

The Camden Farmer's Union in this photograph from the early 1940s was a fixture on Mountain Street for decades. In Camden's early days, it was the location of the Episcopal church until 1924. In later years, the building was turned into a purveyor of farm supplies selling grains, feed, and fuel to area residents. It is now a lovely community space known as High Mountain Hall.

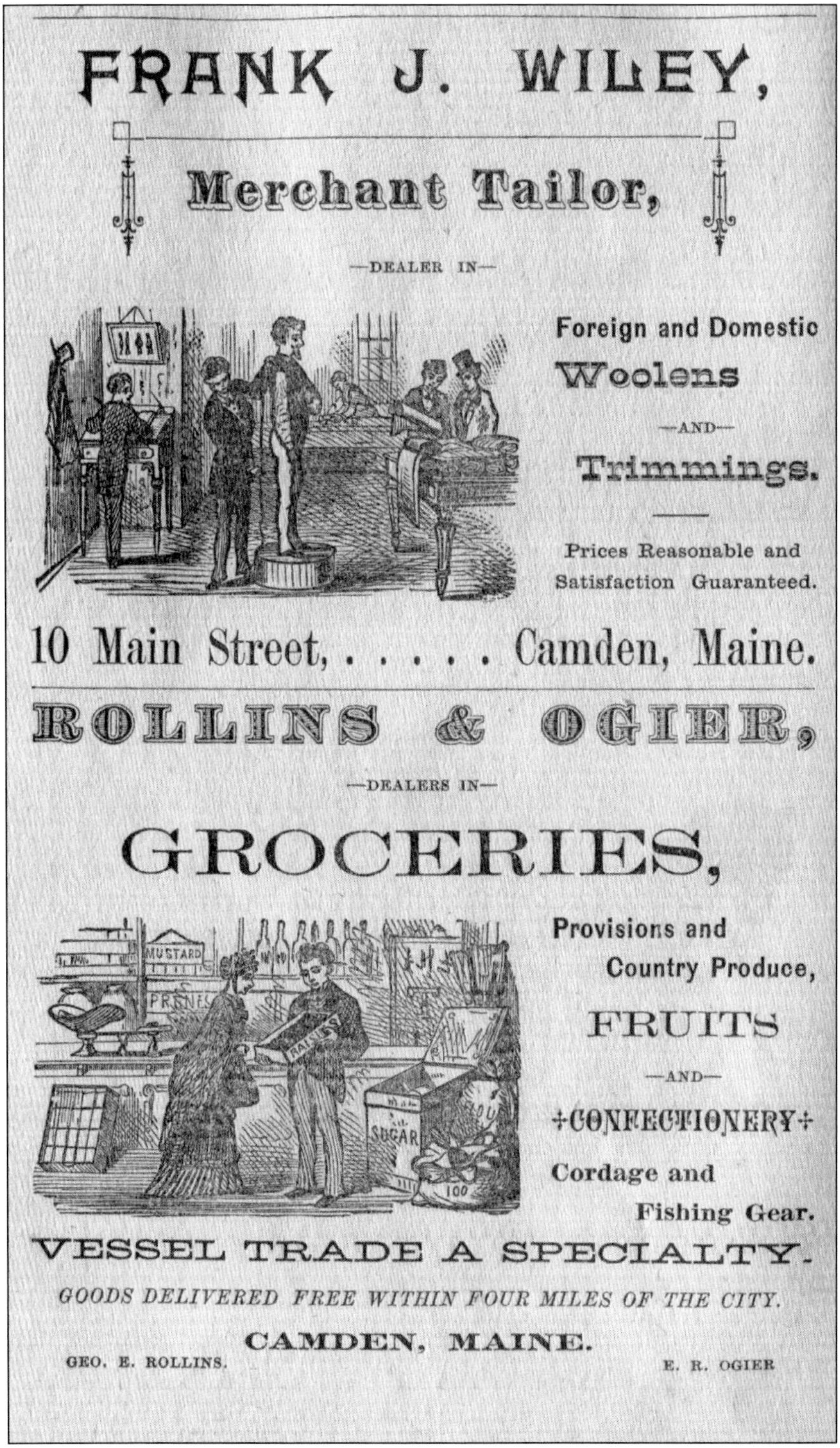

This vintage advertisement from around 1885 was found in an early Camden town directory. The directories were like early telephone books, selling advertising space for area businesses and listing street addresses for residents in the days before the telephone was invented.

An early automobile is parked in front of electrician R.F. Crockett's shop. Roland Crockett lived on Amesbury Hill with his wife, Annie, and together they operated an auto repair garage on Rockport's Union Street in the 1920s.

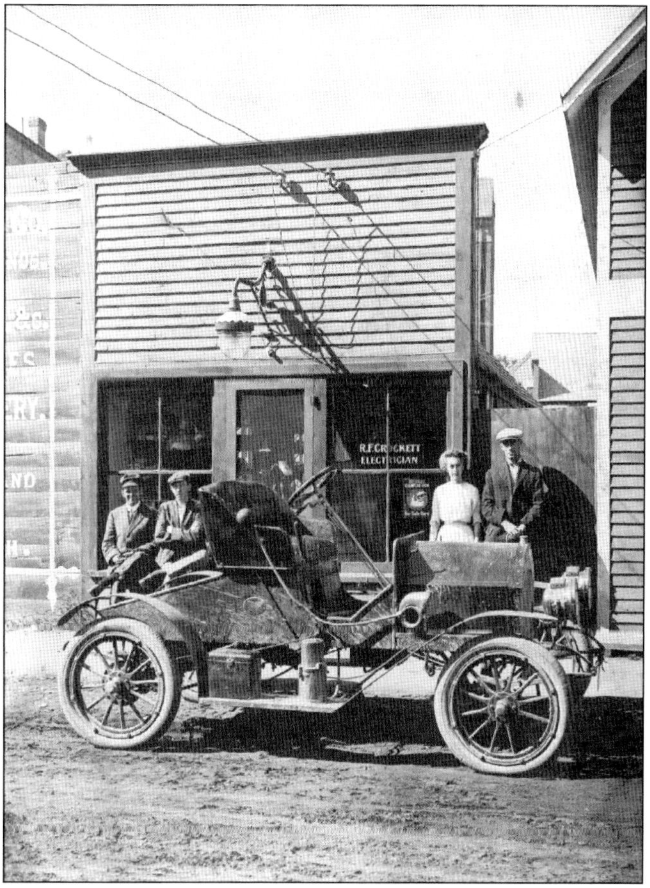

In 1910, Rockport's Masonic lodge moved from the Shepherd block across the street to the granite building on the corner near the bridge over the Goose River. The roof of the building was raised to accommodate a third floor. Laborers were paid $1.25 a day; if the man had a horse, he would receive an extra dollar per day.

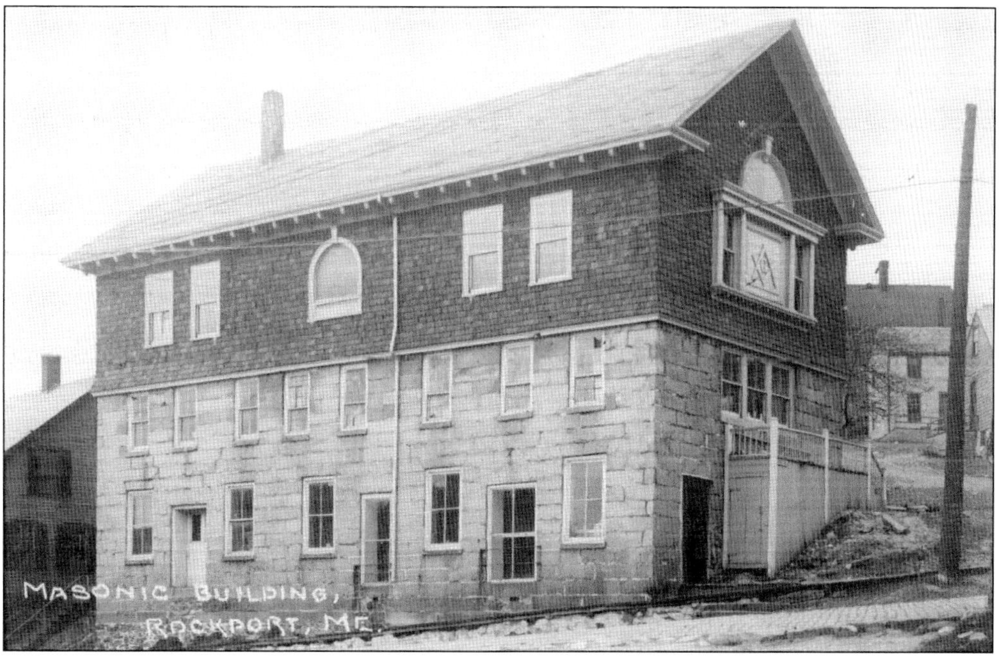

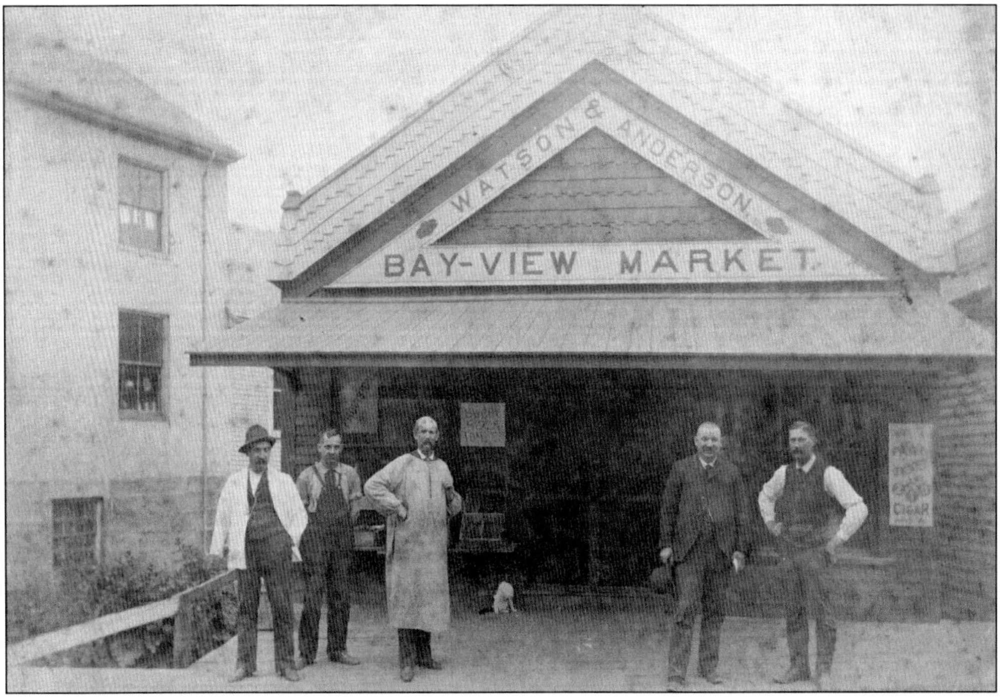

The Watson & Anderson Bay-View Market was located near the corner of Bayview Street next to a whitewashed brick building with a uniquely curved front, which in later years was known as the Unique One knitting shop. The market sold various goods, and it was owned by Orrington and Cora Ella Cross at the time of the Great Fire of 1892. Cross's shop and the rest of Bayview Street were untouched by the conflagration.

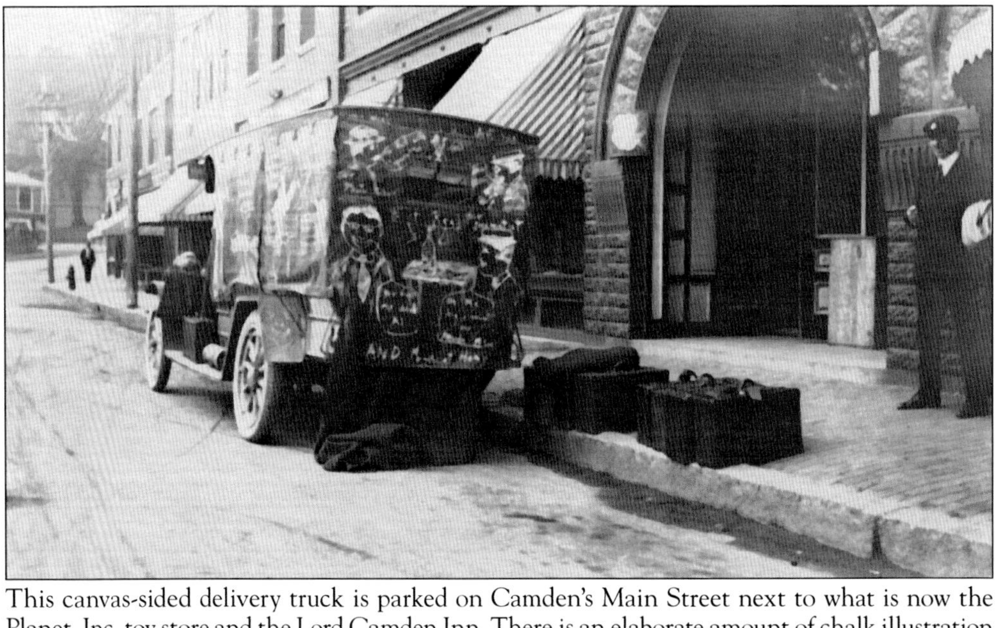

This canvas-sided delivery truck is parked on Camden's Main Street next to what is now the Planet, Inc. toy store and the Lord Camden Inn. There is an elaborate amount of chalk illustration on the sides of the delivery truck, with numerous suitcases on the sidewalk. This photograph was taken around 1920.

Six

ENTERTAINMENT

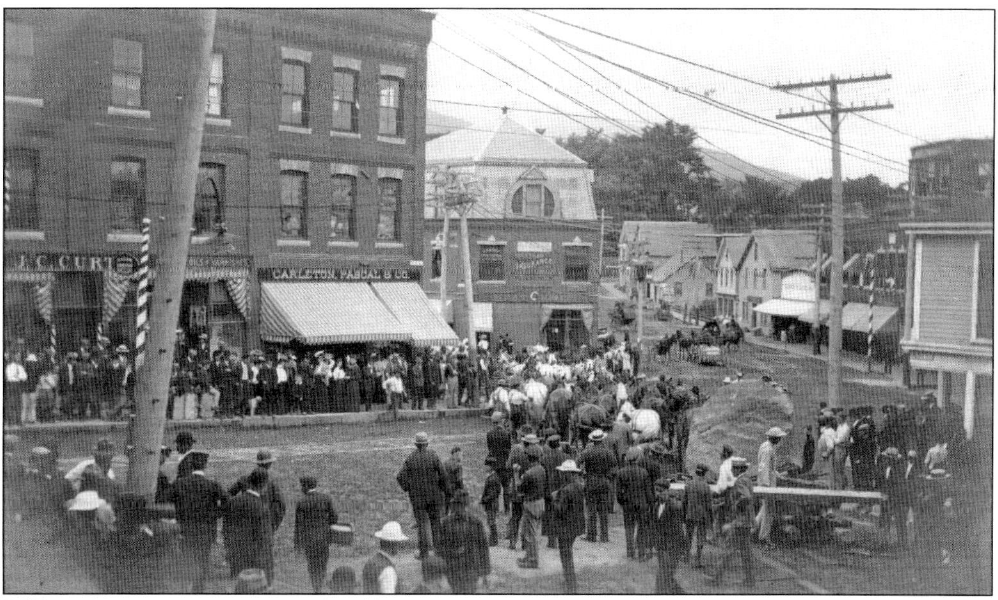

William Conway was one of the local heroes of the Civil War. Refusing an order by the Confederates to pull down the American flag at Pensacola Navy Yard, Conway was thrown in prison for his bravery. On August 30, 1906, the residents of Camden installed a 30-ton boulder in his honor on the grounds of the Elm Street School. It took 30 two-horse teams (60 horses total) to pull the boulder on skids down Chestnut Street from Ogier Hill up Elm Street to its final resting spot. Conway's relatives lived in the 1780s family homestead in Rockport, which is now preserved as part of the Camden-Rockport Historical Society's Conway House complex.

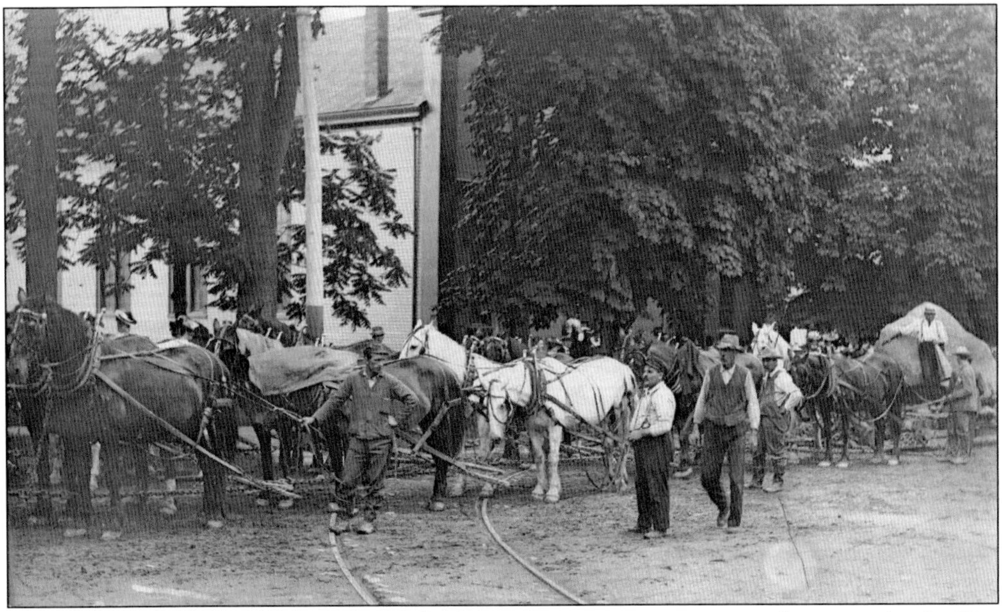

A team of 10 horses with Jim Brown as the boss teamster prepares to turn the corner by the Elm St. School. It took a total of 60 horses to pull the boulder on skids from upper Chestnut Street. The Congregational church is in the background, and trolley tracks are visible in the foreground. The boulder, which weighed 30 tons, was dedicated in 1906 to honor Camden's Civil War hero, William Conway.

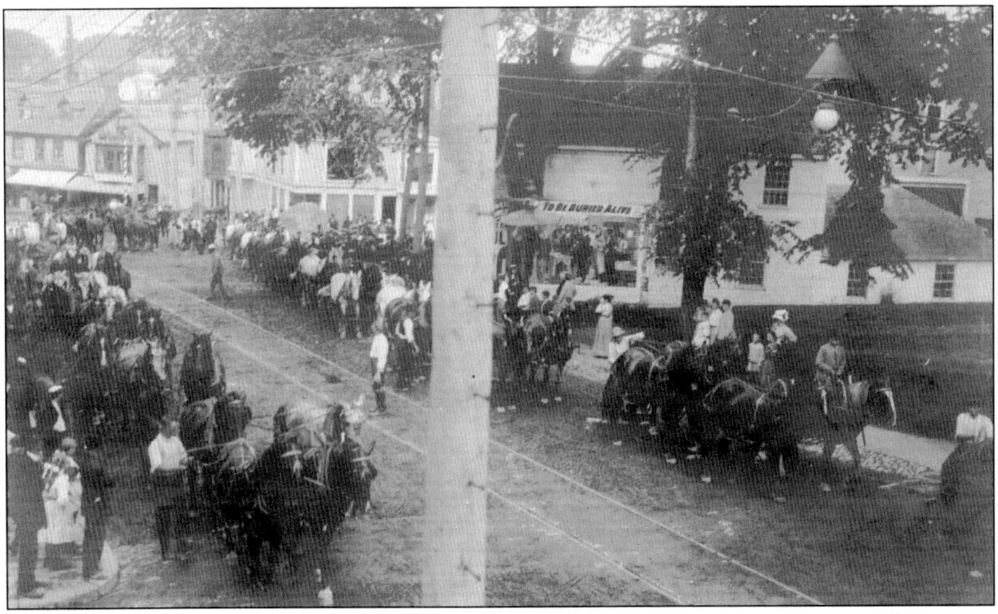

In this image, the massive Conway boulder pulled by the horse teams is just turning the corner onto Elm Street. The trolley tracks are visible in the dirt of Elm Street, and crowds line both sides of the street for this festive occasion. Note the boulder is just visible beyond the light pole.

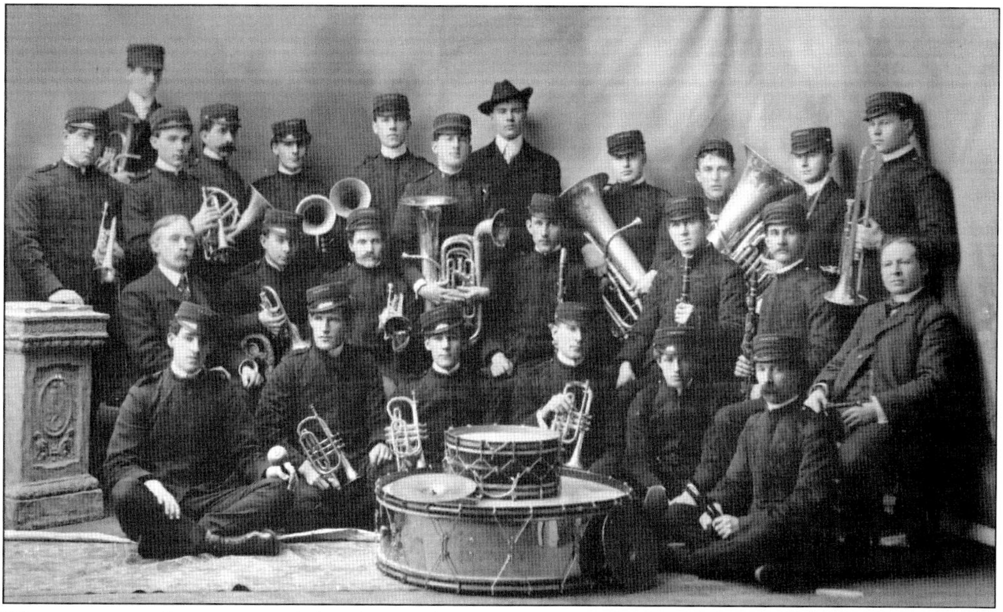

These images show some of the forms of entertainment in the early 20th century. The more formal image of the band seated in a studio shows the elaborately decorated uniforms and caps with the "Camden" above the brim. A young Frank Alexander may be seated in the middle, third from the right. He would become the leader of Alexander's Ragtime Band, a fixture in Camden entertainment circles. The last photograph of the group seated onstage is likely at the Rockport Opera House, though the type of event is unknown. It appears to be some sort of play or musical revue, with placards reading, "That's a Joke" and "Ain't It a Shame."

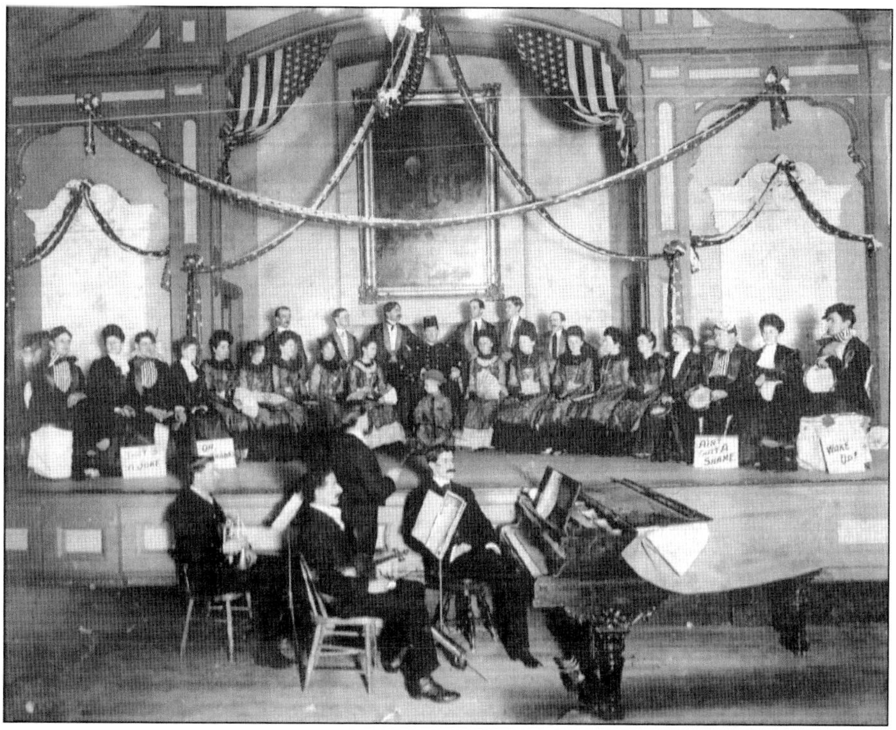

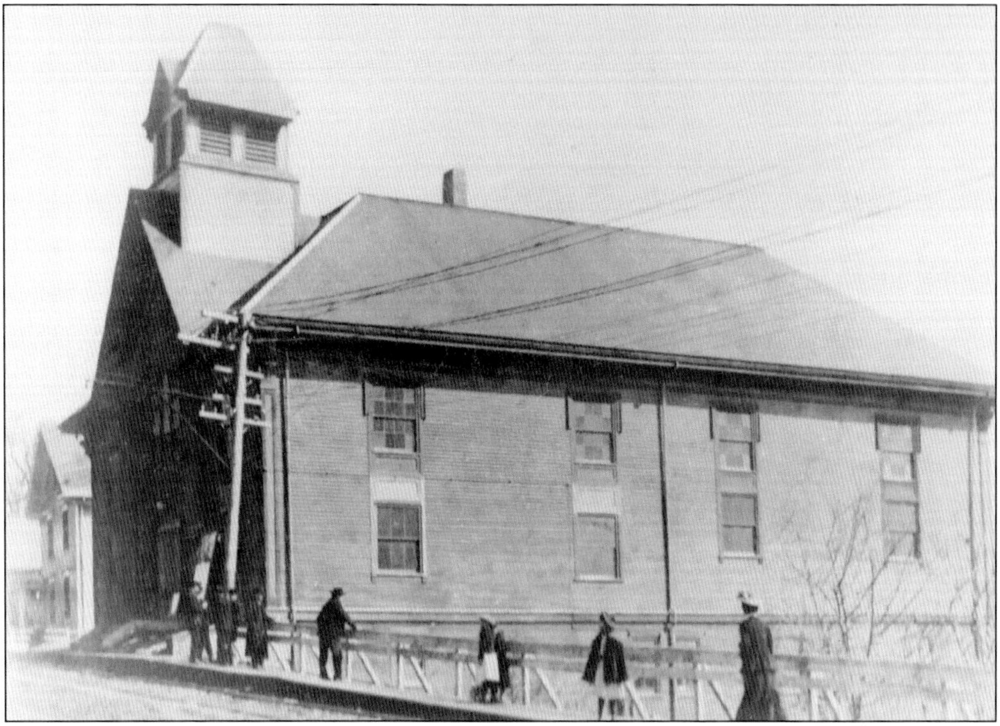

The Rockport Opera House was built in 1892 on the northern hill overlooking the harbor. The clapboard resembles an old-fashioned Grange hall and is quite different from the imposing brick of the Camden Opera House, built in 1893. The Rockport Opera House's huge interior balcony allowed spectators to watch dances and basketball games. By 1907, the YMCA raised $10,000 to buy the building for its exclusive use. By the early 1970s, the lovely old building was showing its age, and the balcony area was unsafe. Lacking adequate heat from an aging coal furnace, the building was renovated in the mid-1970s and underwent major restoration again in 1993. Today, it is a gorgeous performance space and home to the Bay Chamber Concerts.

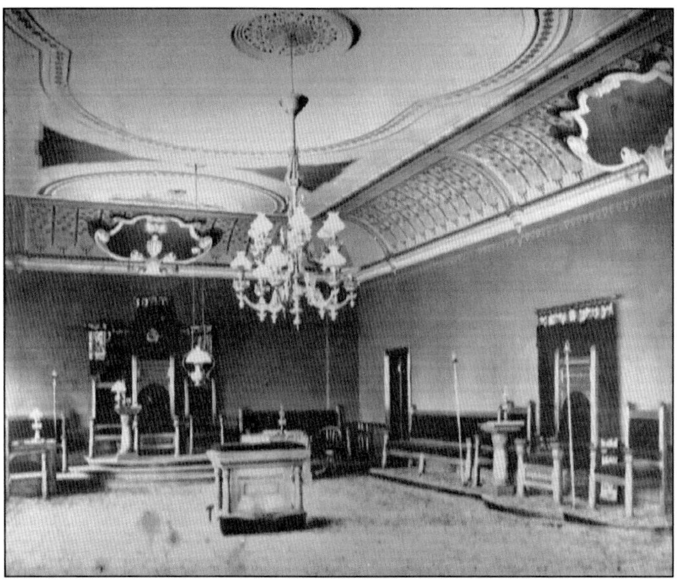

The image shows the St. John's Day parade down Chestnut Street toward the center of Camden in 1906. The Masons adopted St. John the Baptist as their patron saint and celebrated his birth on June 24. The Camden Commandery, part of the fraternal Masonic order, always celebrated St. John's Day on June 24 and invited others to participate along with various town bands in a parade through the downtown area. Festivities also included ceremonies at the Masonic Hall and dinners, sports events, and concerts.

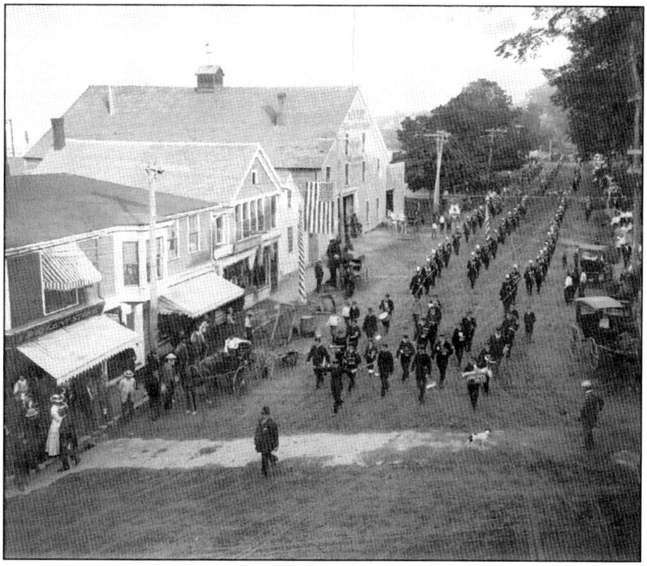

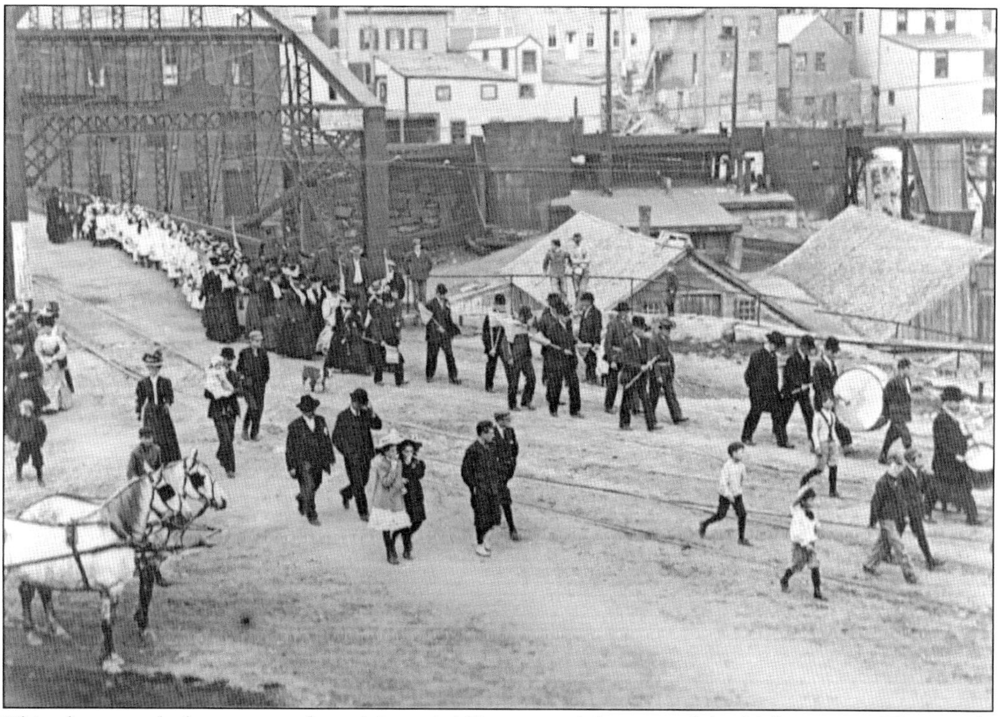

This photograph shows a parade on Memorial Day around the turn of the 20th century. The parade line is just coming across the old, iron Goose River Bridge at the head of Rockport Harbor, and the children running alongside are dressed in their best clothes. The industrial structures at the head of the harbor are visible, including the quarry train trestle and the roof of the lumber sheds.

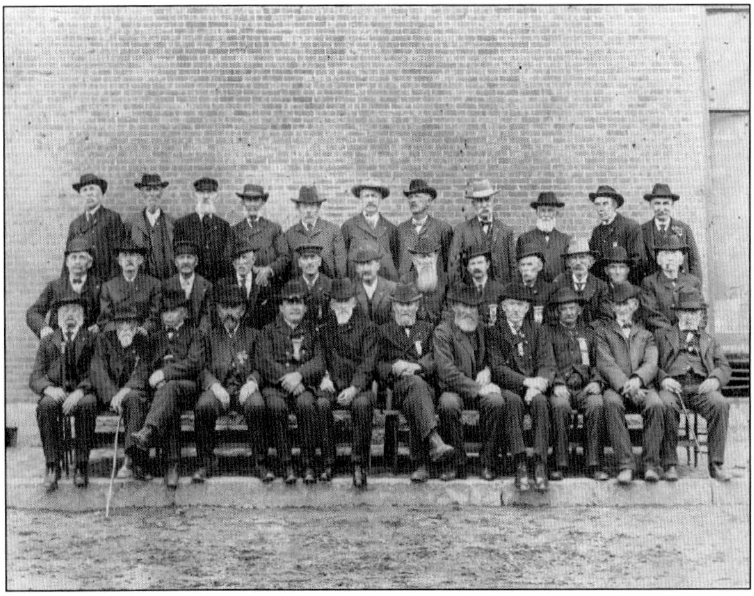

This is a rare photograph of men of Rockport and Camden who served in the Union army during the Civil War. The George S. Cobb Post No. 63, Grand Army of the Republic, was chartered in Camden on October 26, 1882, and had 220 members. In 1886, the Fred A. Norwood Post was formed in Rockport with Gen. John Rust as the first commander.

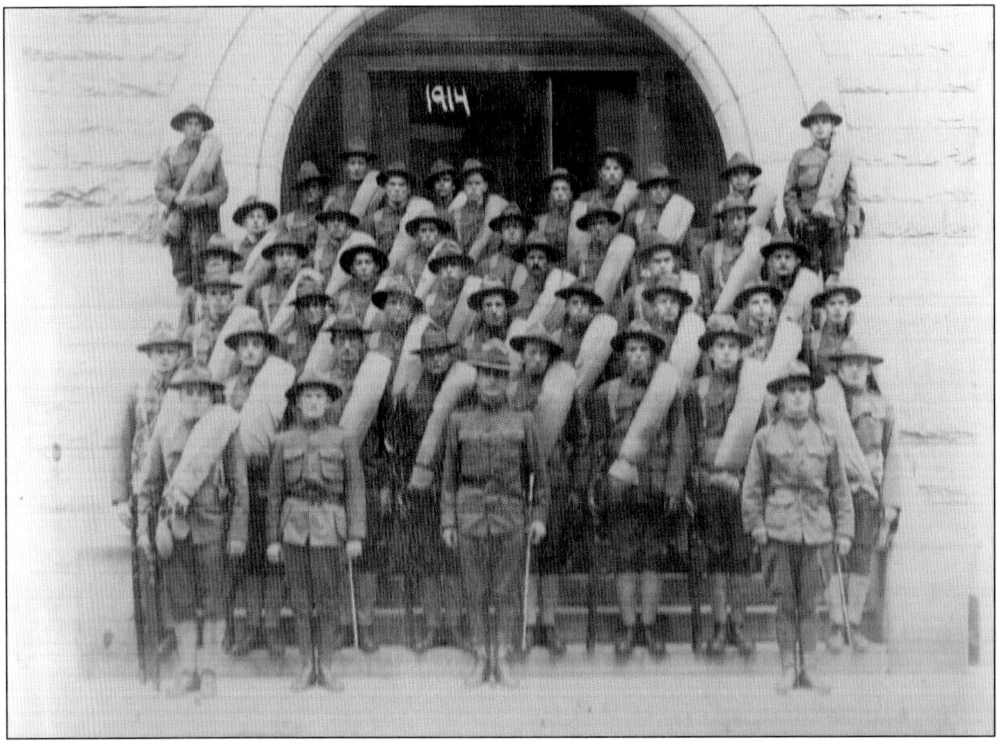

The years during World War I would take a great toll on Camden and Rockport residents. In this image from 1914, Capt. Ralph Stapleton of Rockport is pictured at the right front of the frame with his Army buddies. In June 1917, registration for the draft was enacted as law, and by 1918 Camden had lost the first of its men, Russell Arey and Harold Heal. The killer Spanish influenza also raged in the fall, taking many more lives at an already difficult time.

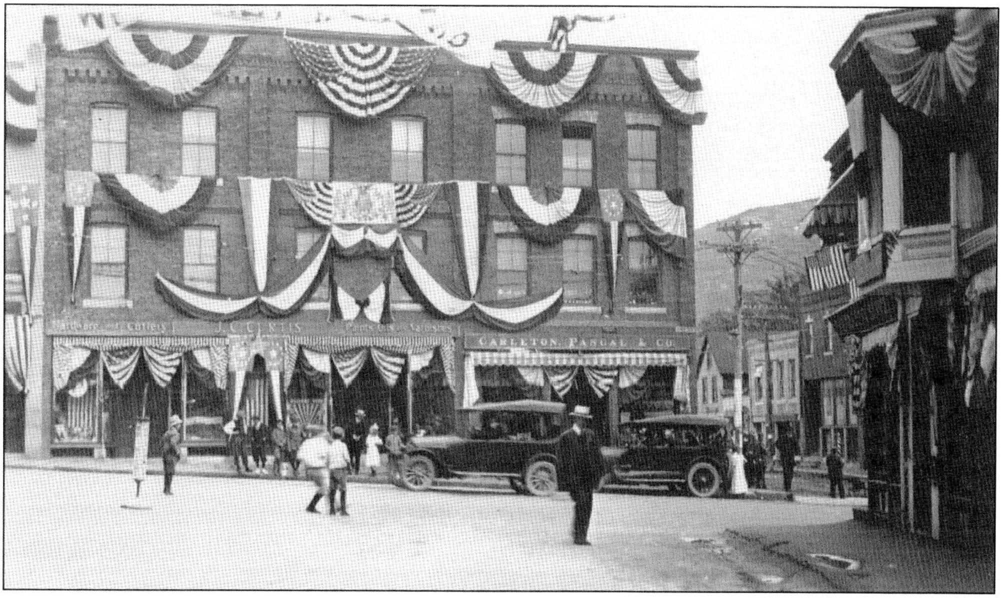

Parades were events at which the entire town turned out. One of the largest was at the end of World War I, when Camden hosted a "Welcome the Boys Home" event to show its appreciation for the efforts of the local soldiers. The parade on August 19, 1919, formed on Bayview Street and was one of the largest the town had ever seen. It was over a mile long, and all the buildings and storefronts were festively draped in patriotic bunting and flags. In the image below, the returning ranks of soldiers are visible just beyond the line of cars heading north up Main Street. At the end of August that same year, Helen Chatfield organized a planting of 44 liberty pine memorial trees at Aldermere Farm. In 1921, the 24-foot Memorial Tower on the top of Mount Battie, built from the foundation stones of the Mt. Battie Clubhouse, was dedicated to the fallen of World War I.

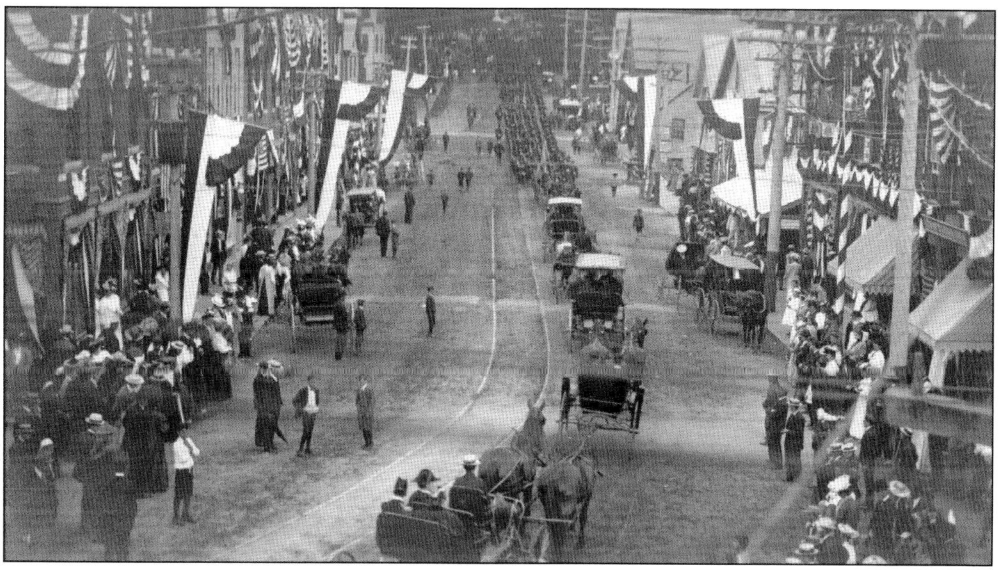

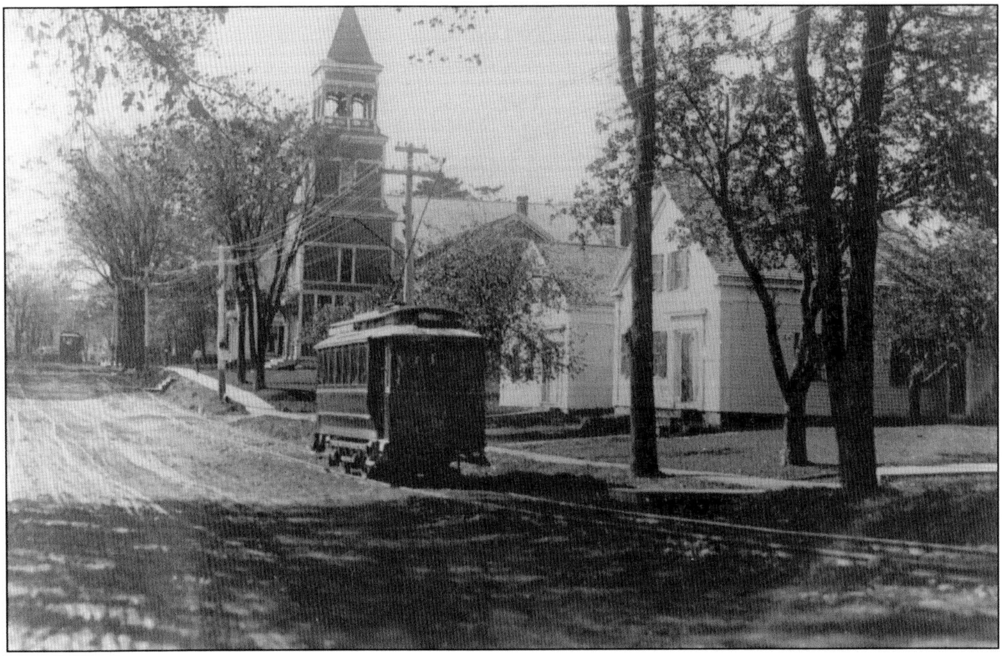

This photograph of the Rockland, Thomaston & Camden Street Railway was taken around 1907 on Rockport's Commercial Street, now called Pascal Avenue in honor of respected shipbuilder John Pascal. This was the main thoroughfare through town until a bypass in 1948 completely relocated Route 1. By the 1950s, Rockport's business district had all but ceased to exist.

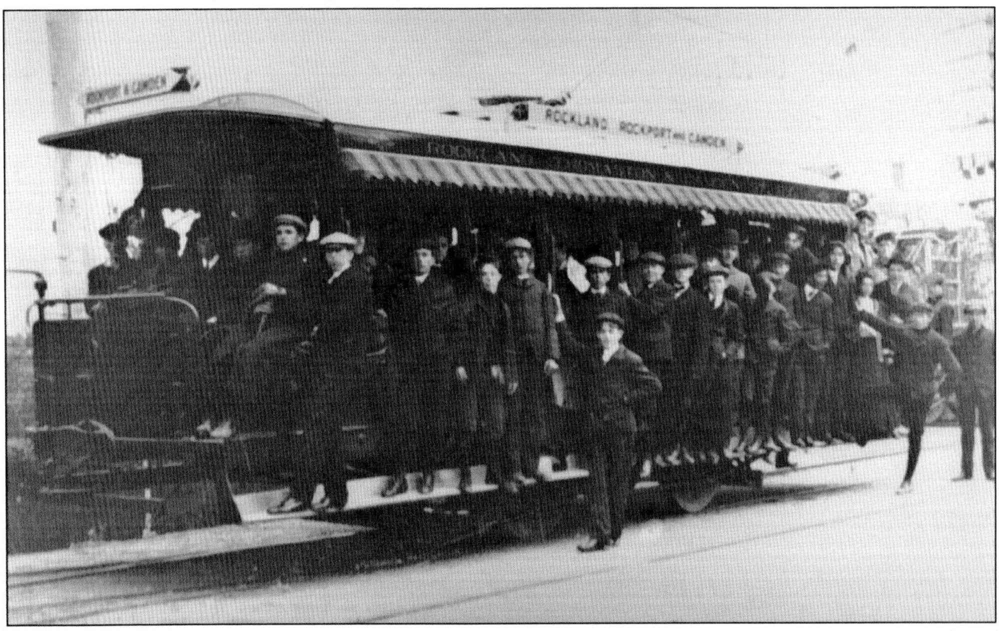

Known as electrics, the trolleys between Camden and Rockland were a primary mode of transportation in the area from about 1892 to 1931. The fare was 5¢ to travel from town to town, which is the equivalent of about $1.40 today. Oakland Park, a 72-acre recreational facility off of Route 1 in Rockport, was operated by the Rockland, Thomaston & Camden trolley company to generate additional revenue for its business.

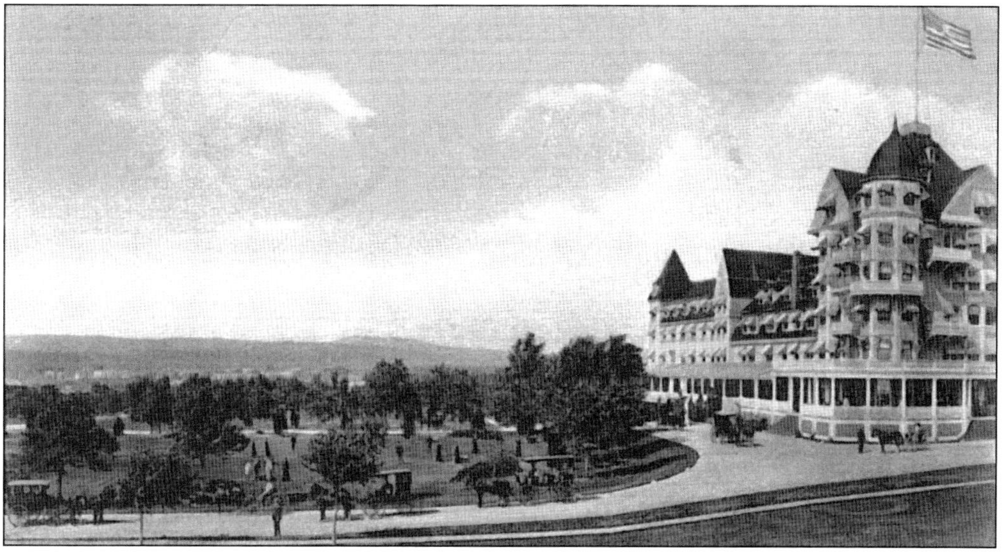

The Samoset Hotel was built overlooking Rockland Harbor in 1889. First known as the Bay Point Hotel, the lodging attracted thousands of visitors annually who came to escape the summer heat in the larger cities. In 1902, it was sold to the Ricker family, who had made their fortune as owners of Poland Spring Water Company. It was renamed the Samoset Hotel, and Ricker set to work embellishing the building with turrets, porches, and wooden latticework popular at that time. Sadly, the Great Depression brought hard times to the country, and the beautiful old hotel passed through many owners. By 1969, it was derelict, and it burned to the ground in 1972. In 1974, the hotel was rebuilt, and though much changed in architecture, it continues to be a popular resort today. The image below is a postcard of a tramp chair on exhibit at the Samoset Hotel. The caption explains that vagrants were confined to the chair for up to 10 hours and perhaps pulled through the streets in the chair as a deterrent to further vagrancy.

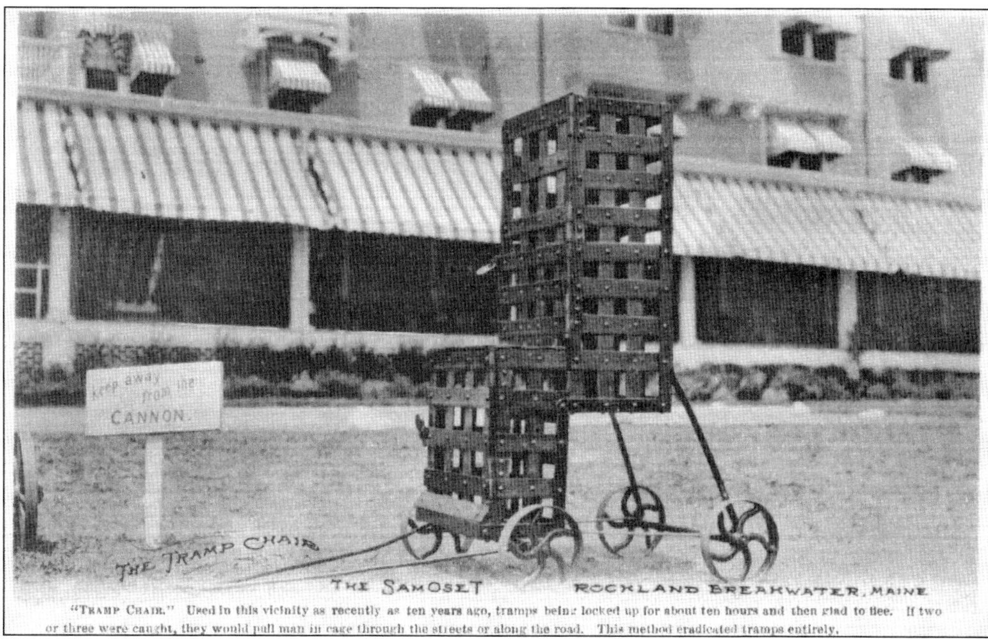

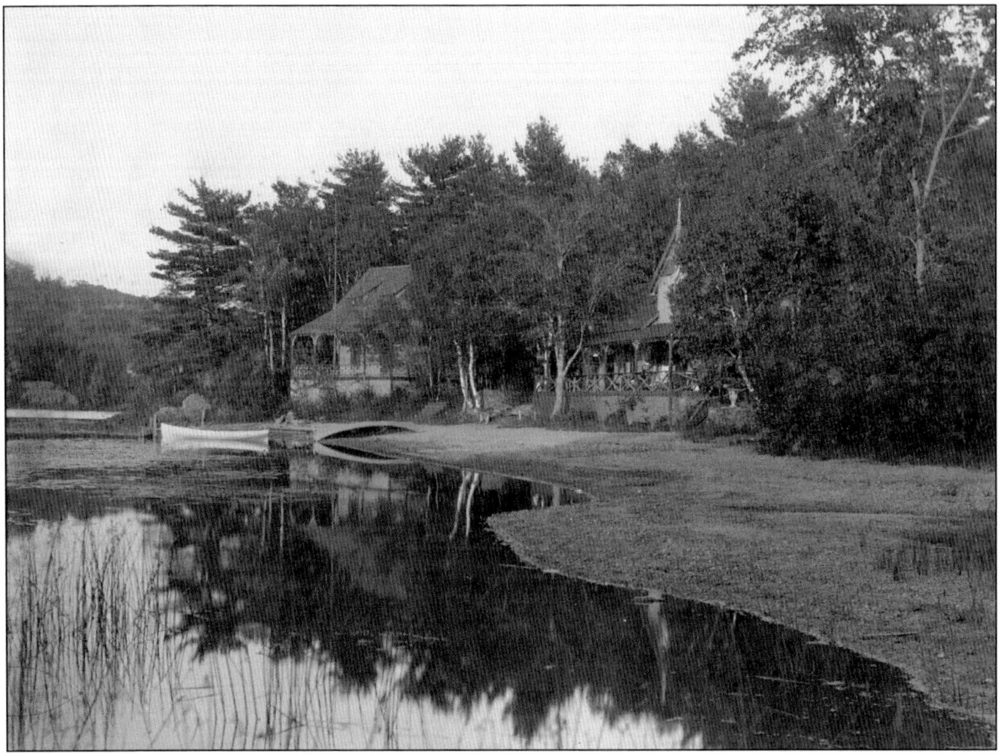

This image depicts the typical summer camps that dotted the shorelines of Megunticook Lake, the Megunticook River, and Hosmer Pond. Because the harbors of Camden and Rockport were industrialized areas by the early 1900s, these inland camps offered a secluded respite from the summertime heat and crowds of the East Coast. Many residents of the industrialized cities farther south spent their summers here in mid-coast Maine. Lots of 50 feet by 100 feet were sold along Megunticook Lake at a cost of $35 per lot. Hosmer Pond lots were selling at an equally fast clip; the newspaper reported the sale of six in one week in 1915.

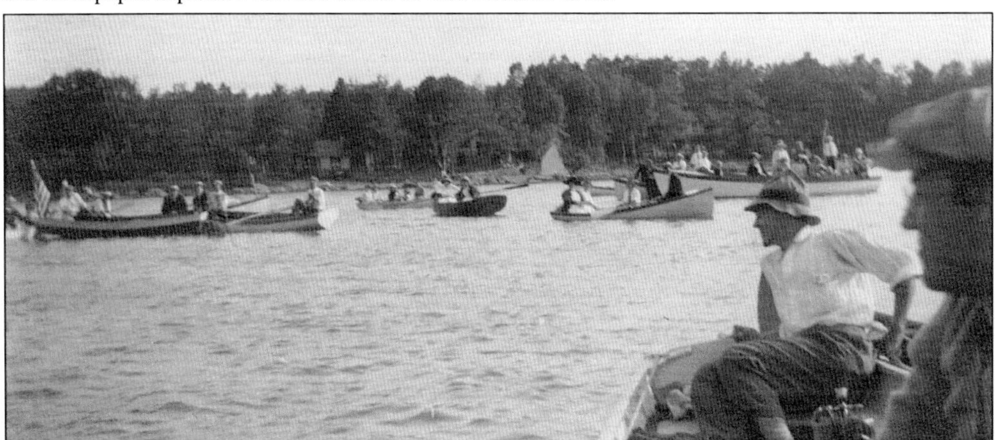

One of the summertime entertainments in the Camden and Rockport area was this regatta held on Megunticook Lake in 1912 or 1913. Barrett's Cove and the Lake City development of cottages were a popular destination for those seeking to get away from the more industrialized harbors in town. The warm lake water of Barrett's Cove is still a popular swimming spot for area residents.

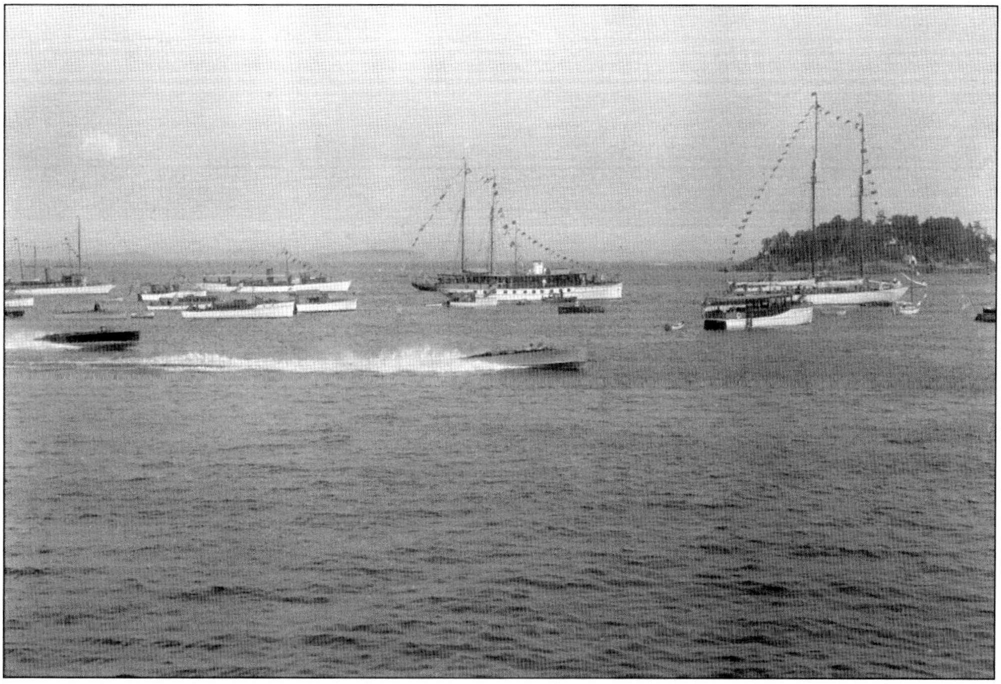

Among the major summer entertainments of the yacht club set were the numerous races and regattas held in Camden Harbor. In the photograph above, taken about 1930, speedboats blast their way past Curtis Island and the spectators aboard their yachts with signal flags flying. There were three motorboat regattas at the end of the Roaring Twenties. On race day, the stores and mills closed around noontime, and there were weeklong parties, dances, and banquets. There was even a 140-foot dirigible to give passengers a bird's-eye view of the races below. By 1932, the yacht club decided to postpone the regatta due to the Great Depression affecting the country at that time, and sailing regattas featuring the new Finn boats became popular. The Finn boats, built in Finland, were $600 each and could be manufactured and shipped in a week.

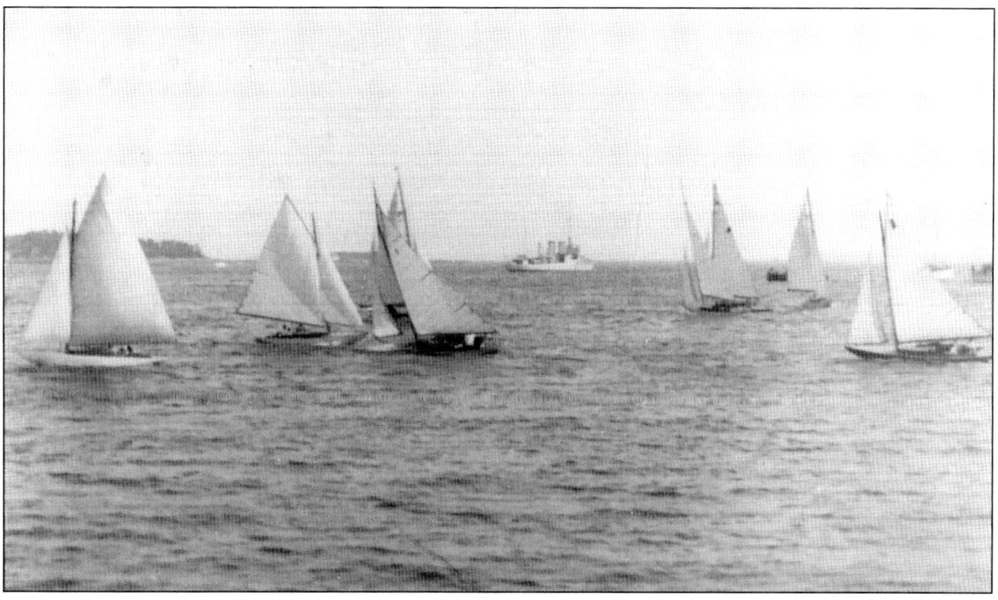

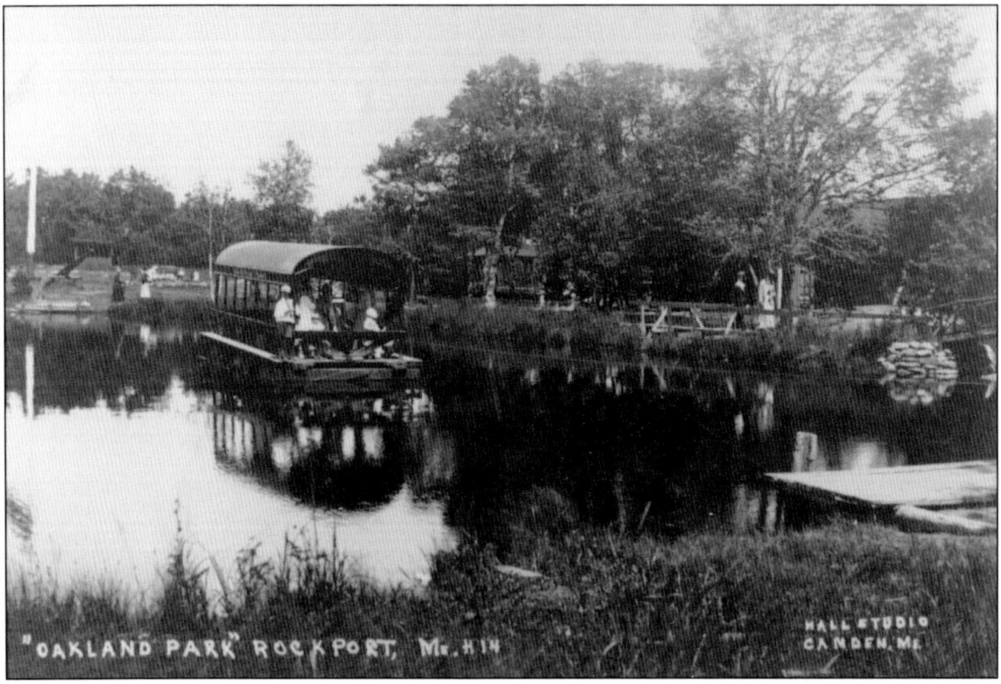

These photographs were taken on Labor Day in the mid-1910s at Oakland Park, a 72-acre facility off of Route 1 in Rockport that was operated by the Rockland, Thomaston & Camden trolley company to generate additional revenue for its business. Advertising enough parking for 1,200 cars, the facility had a casino that showed free motion pictures, a bandstand, a croquet field, and a baseball field. In the above image, a small ferry transports passengers across the pond, on which there was ice-skating in the winter. Labor Day was one of the largest annual events at the park. The day ended with a spectacular fireworks display. An estimated 7,000 people attended these festivities between 1913 and 1918. In the photograph below, two small children and their mother are outside the main building enjoying the sunshine. The rustic bridge in the foreground adds a charming element to the photograph.

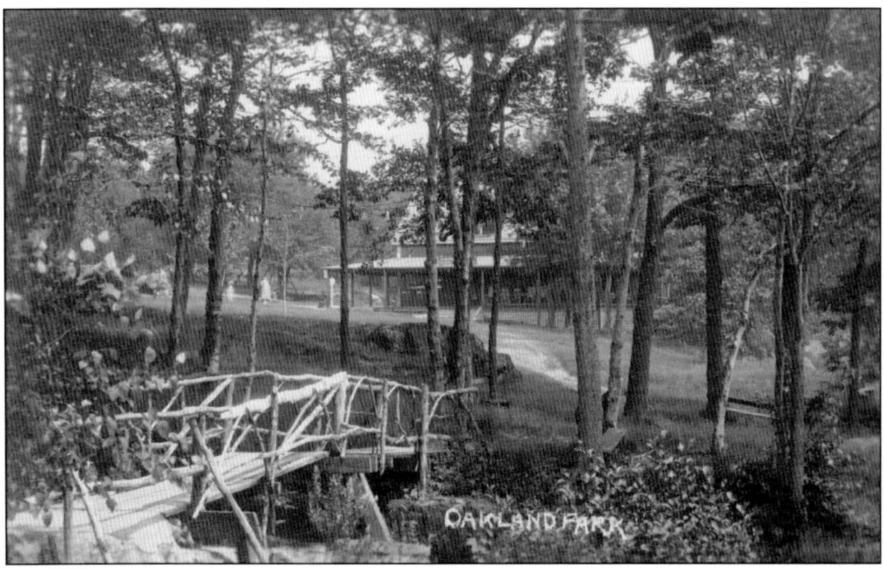

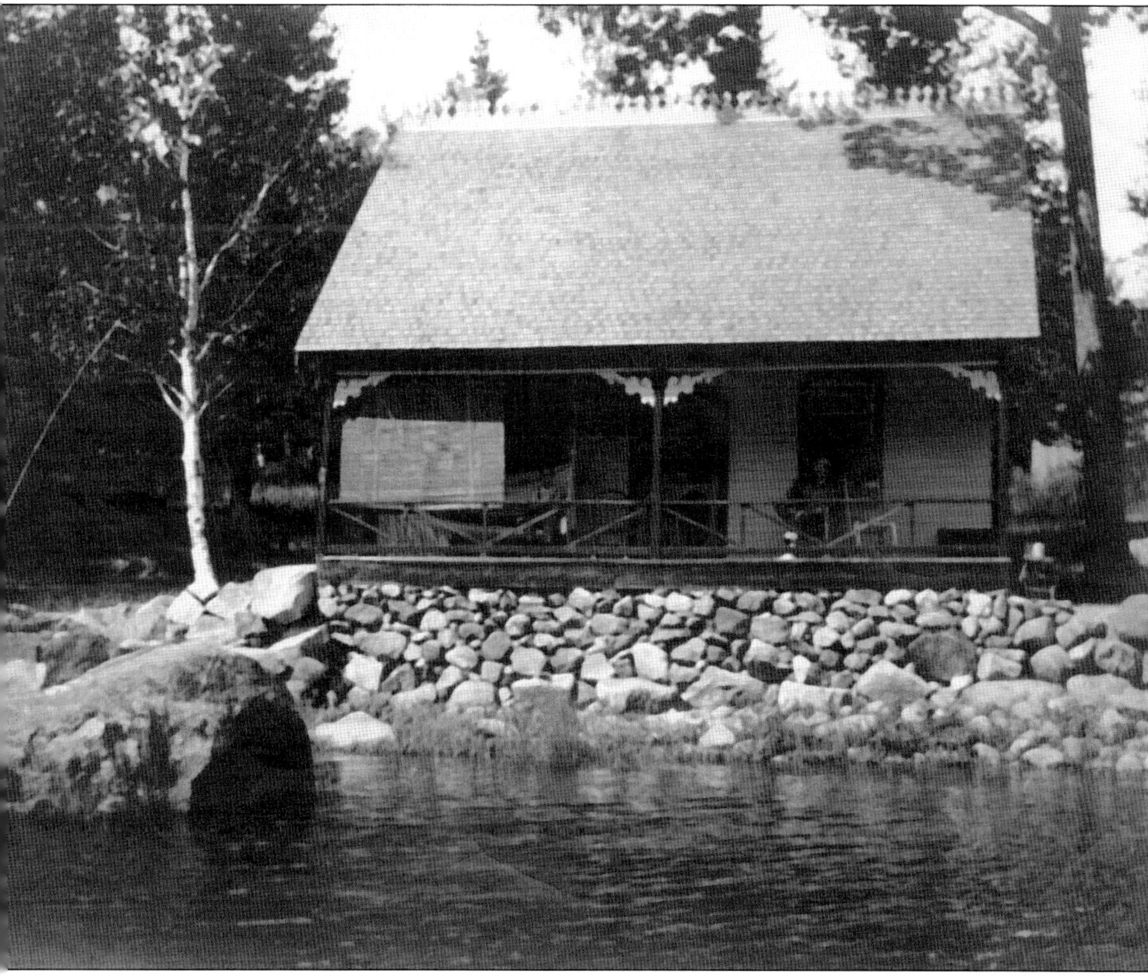

This image is from the Munson family scrapbook and shows the Munson bungalow at Barrett's Cove on Megunticook Lake. The cottage was bought by the Munson family from local builder Mark Whitmore in 1907 and later was enlarged and became known as the Burgess Cottage. The Reverend Dr. H.B. Munson was a prominent Methodist minister in Brooklyn, New York, who often summered at Megunticook Lake with his friends and family. He is shown here on the porch with his friend Dr. F.W. Hannan of Brooklyn.

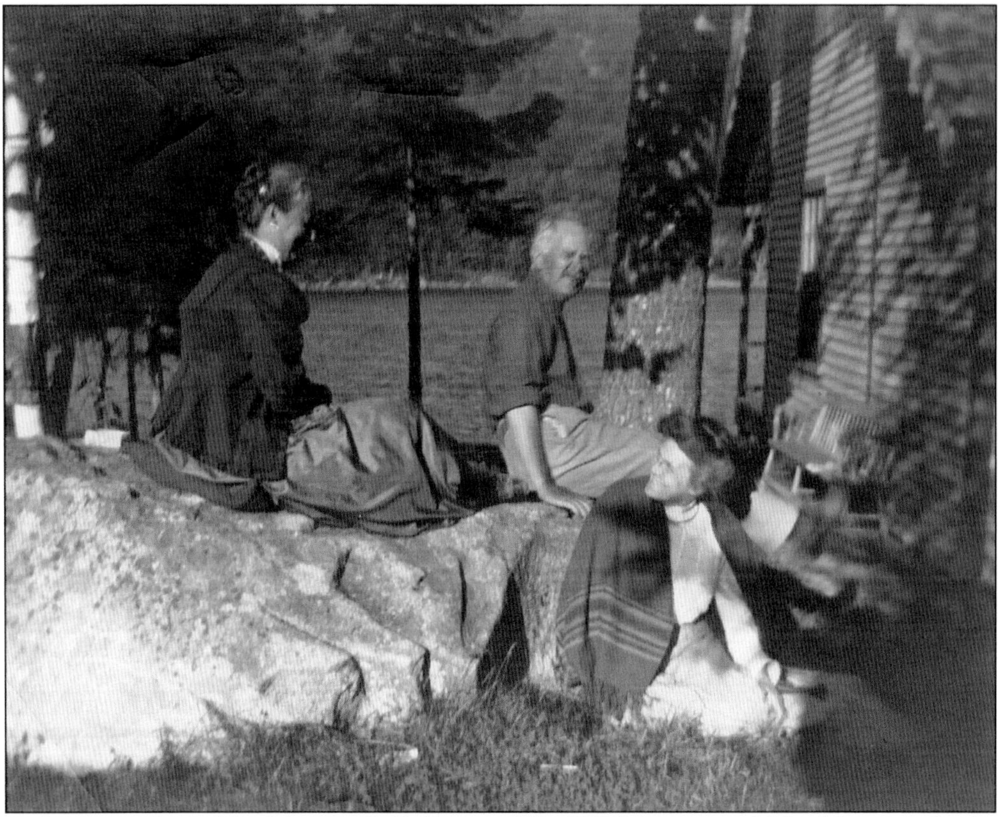

In the image above, Mrs. Munson (left), Reverend Dr. H.B. Munson, and Mrs. Hannan relax by the big oak beside the Munson cottage about 1912. Megunticook Lake was a cool retreat from the hot and humid cities of the East Coast as well as the industrialized harbors of Camden and Rockport. In the image below, Dr. Munson's visitors include, from left to right, Mrs. Hubert B. Munson, Donald Munson, Dr. CM Vandewater (of Madison, New Jersey), Helen Munson, Dr. Isaac Vandewater (of Madison, New Jersey), and Gorham Munson (in shadows).

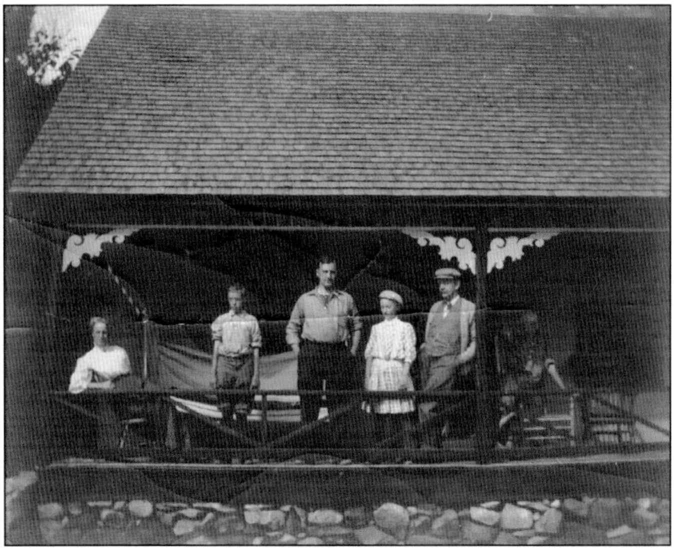

Seven

Evolving Transportation

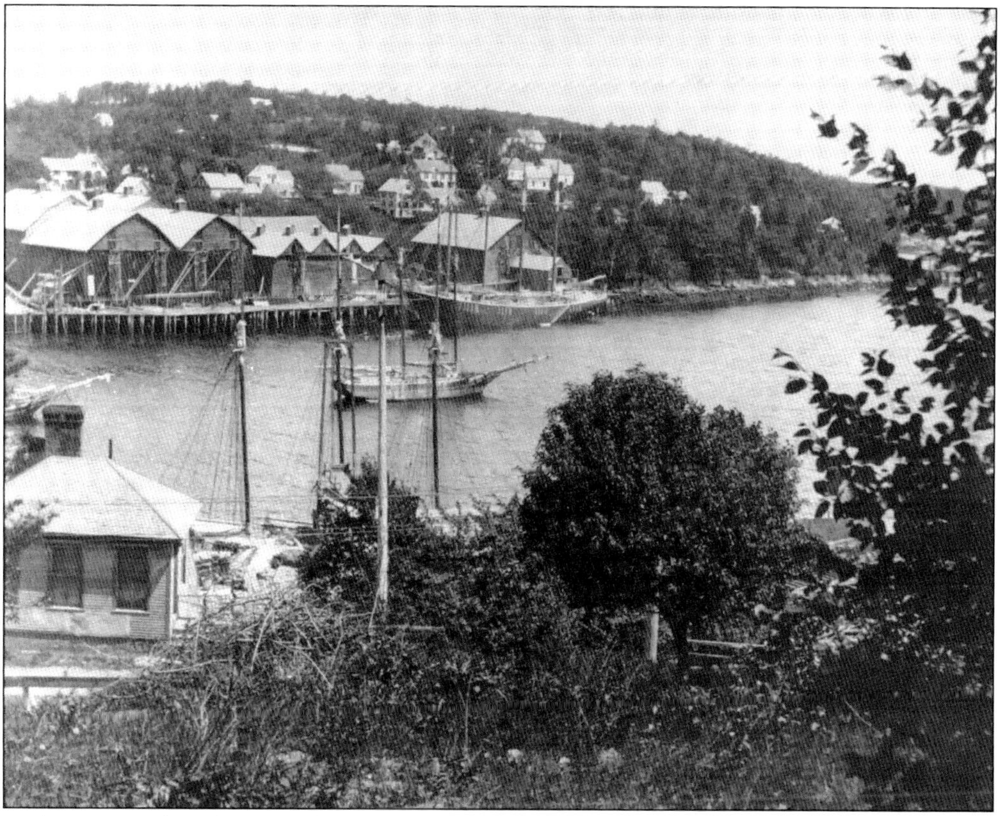

In this image of Rockport Harbor around 1900, a two-masted schooner, or coaster, lies at anchor with sails furled. Wind power was the primary energy for transport of goods and people up and down the coast of Maine, as at that time the rough dirt roads were rudimentary at best. By the 1920s, these majestic working ships had lost their usefulness to the faster steam-powered vessels. In the 1940s, Capt. Frank Swift of Camden renovated several of these windjammers and created a popular cruising fleet for tourists

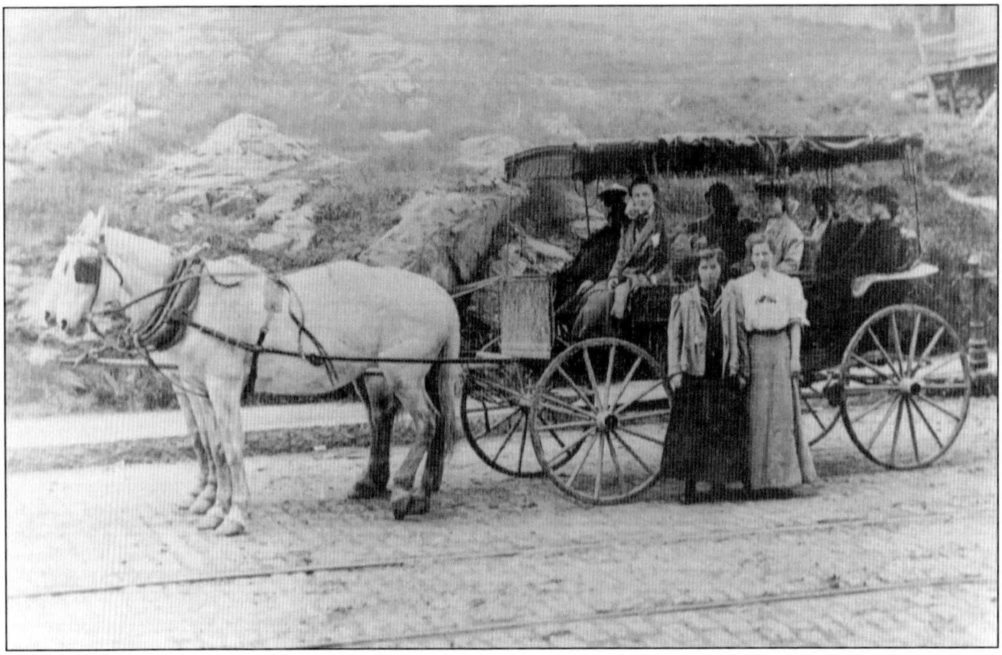

This charming photograph from the late 1800s shows a group of passengers in warm weather finery being conveyed by a horse team pulling a carriage with fringe on top. The image is otherwise unidentified, and there appear to be trolley tracks in the foreground.

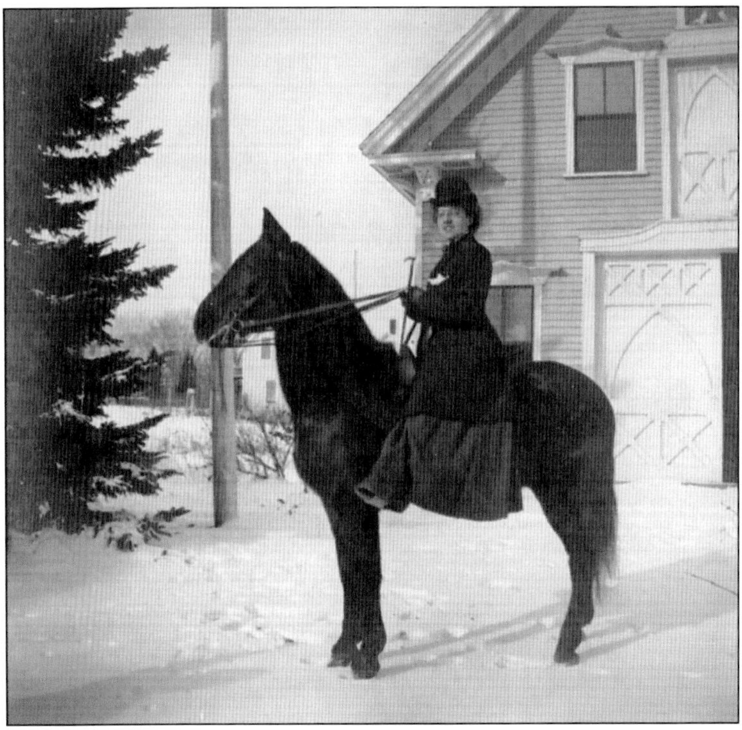

In this photograph, Alice Knowlton French, wife of Jonas French, rides her horse along Pearl Street in Camden around 1905. Horses were still the primary mode of transportation at this time. Her beautiful black woolen clothing, known as a riding habit, is housed at the Camden-Rockport Historical Society.

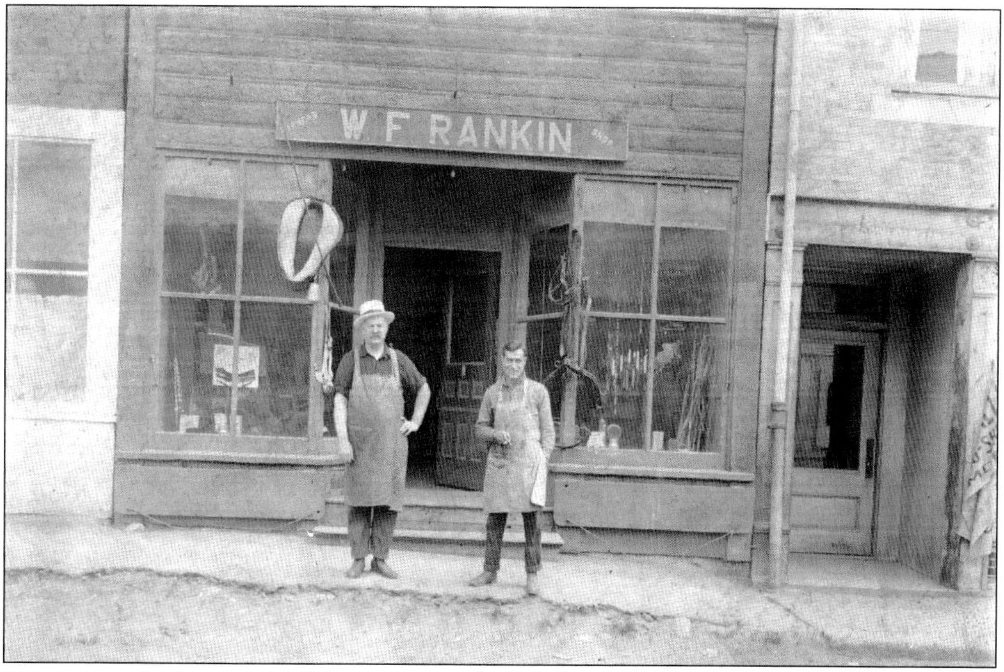

This is an early photograph of the exterior of the W.F. Rankin shop in Camden. William Rankin was a teamster, or one who drove teams of draft animals such as horses and oxen. His harness shop was located at 11 Mechanic Street. By 1952, Rankin's had evolved into selling hardware and home goods on Union Street, where it still operates today.

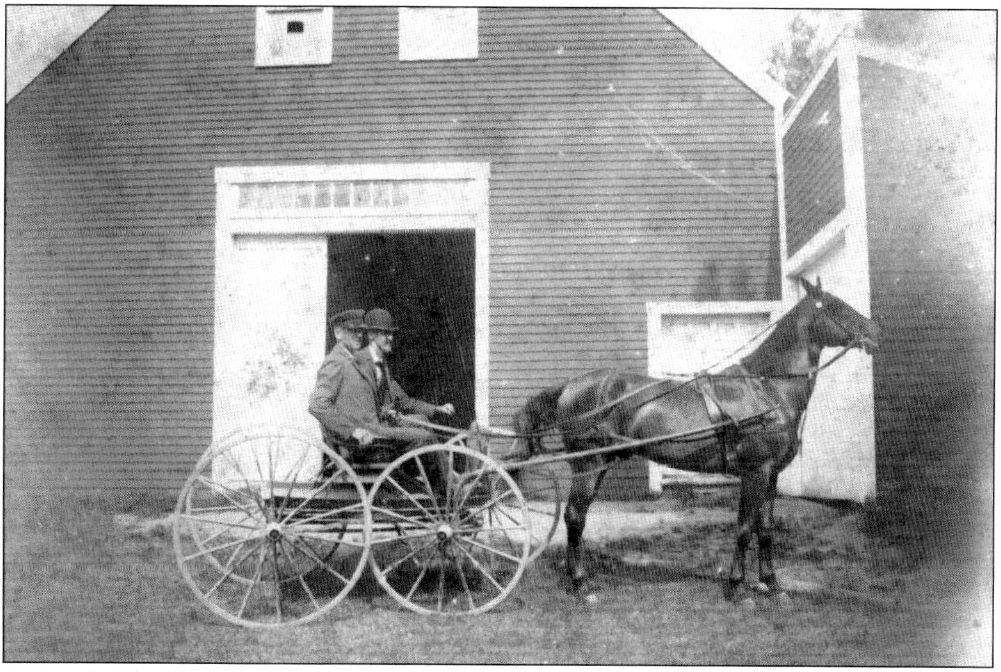

Arthur A. Clark, shown here, was a carriage painter with a shop on Route 90 in West Rockport. The lightweight carriage in this photograph, when combined with a speedy horse, was an efficient means of transportation in the early days before the invention of the automobile.

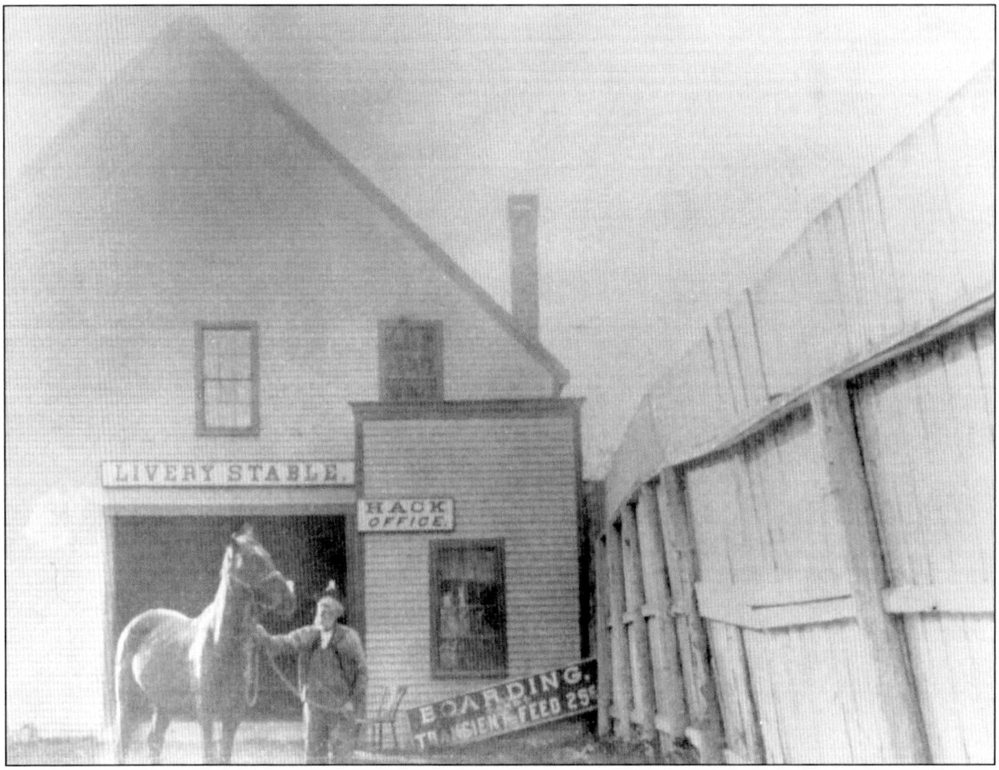

This image is of the Gersham livery stable and hack office as they appeared about 1900. The stable operated on Russell Avenue in Rockport from 1893 to 1907. In 1952, local artists organized as a group called Maine Coast Artists, and held art exhibitions at the site. Over the next half century, the group evolved into the Center for Contemporary Art, one of the nation's most active centers for contemporary art education and exhibitions.

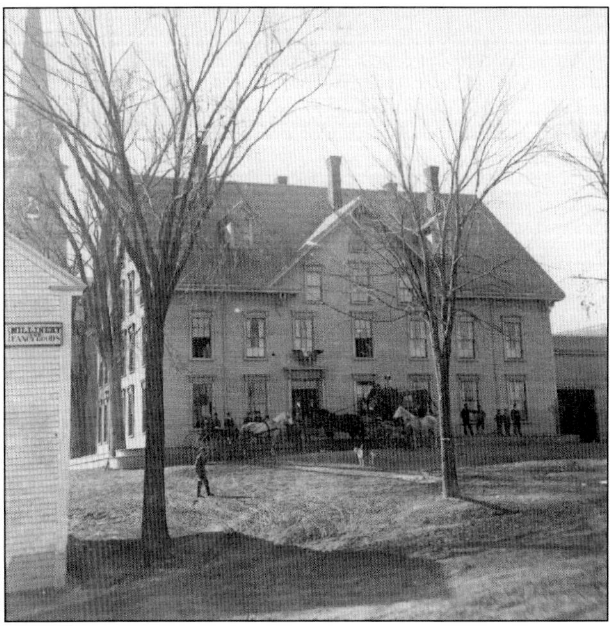

This is part of a stereoscopic view of the Bay View House, located on Elm and Chestnut Streets in Camden. This hotel was a popular destination for visitors, and it was served by several local livery stables. The image was taken around 1885, as the Chestnut Street Baptist Church spire in the background was not removed until 1887 due to decay.

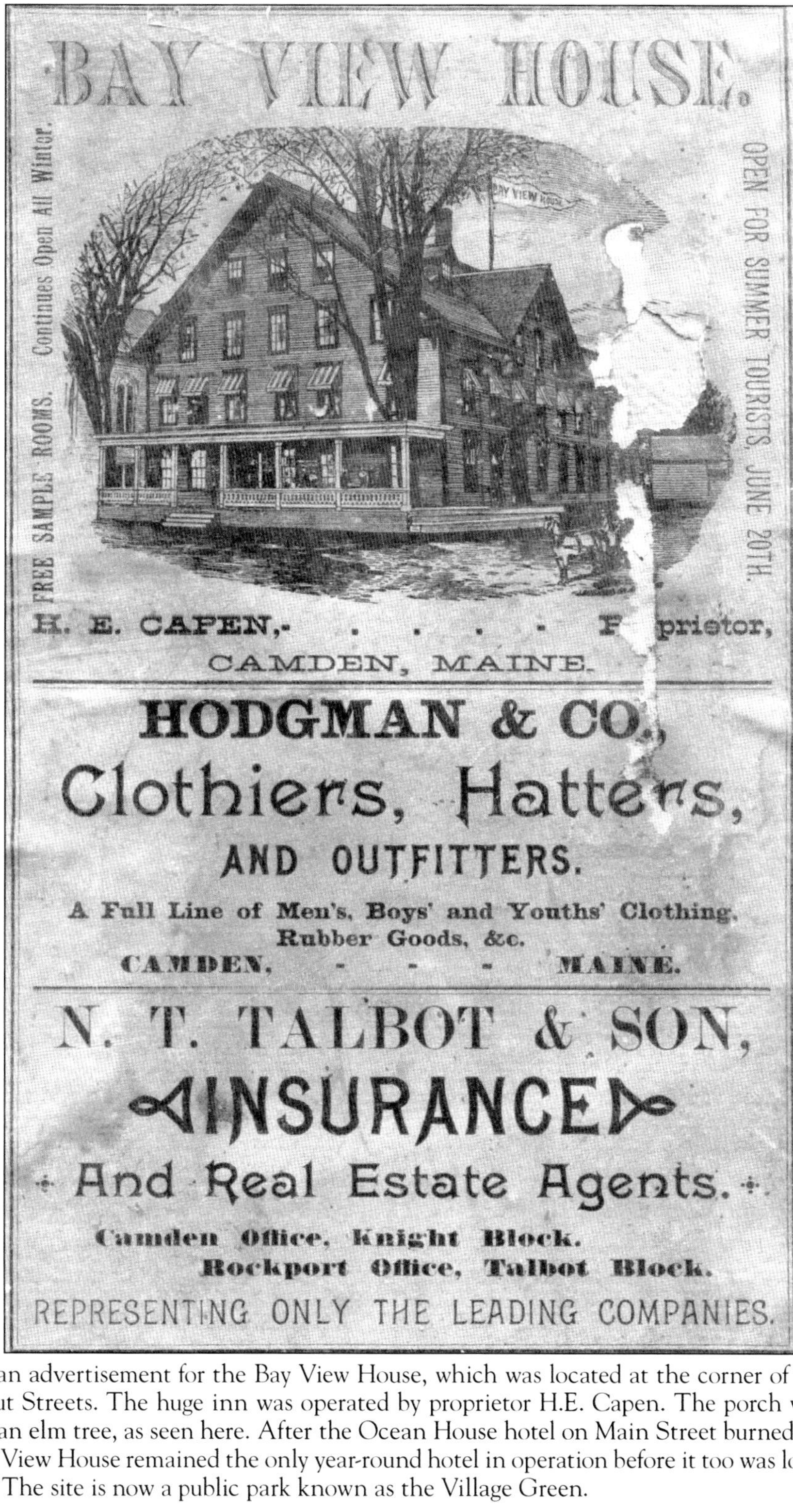

This is an advertisement for the Bay View House, which was located at the corner of Elm and Chestnut Streets. The huge inn was operated by proprietor H.E. Capen. The porch was built around an elm tree, as seen here. After the Ocean House hotel on Main Street burned in 1903, the Bay View House remained the only year-round hotel in operation before it too was lost to fire in 1917. The site is now a public park known as the Village Green.

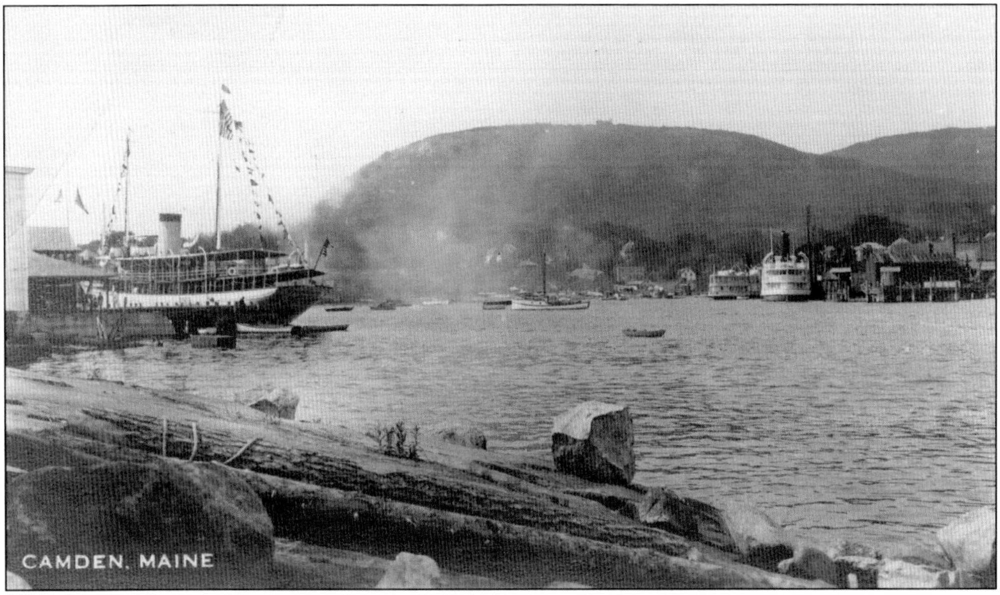

This is a remarkable view of Camden Harbor around 1905. The *Lyndonia*, the large yacht belonging to Cyrus H.K. Curtis, is docked at the Camden Yacht Club. Curtis was owner of the Curtis Publishing Company, which published the *Saturday Evening Post* and the *Ladies' Home Journal*. He and his daughter Mary Louise Curtis Bok were major benefactors to Camden and Rockport. The Boston boats, or steamships, are docked on the opposite side of the harbor near the shipyard.

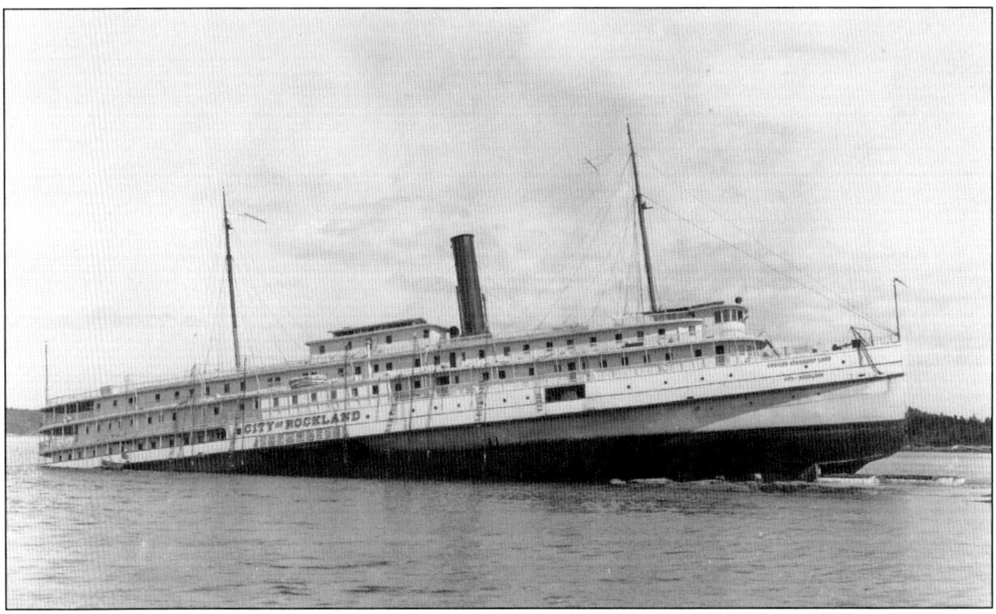

The Eastern Steamship Company operated a series of successful routes between Boston and Bangor. In this image, one of its vessels, the *City of Rockland*, is stranded on Grindstone Ledge off Rockland in 1904. In the photograph, the floats at the bow are in place to move the ship off the ledge. The 1,700-ton ship was repaired and put back in service until 1923 when it was scuttled and burned.

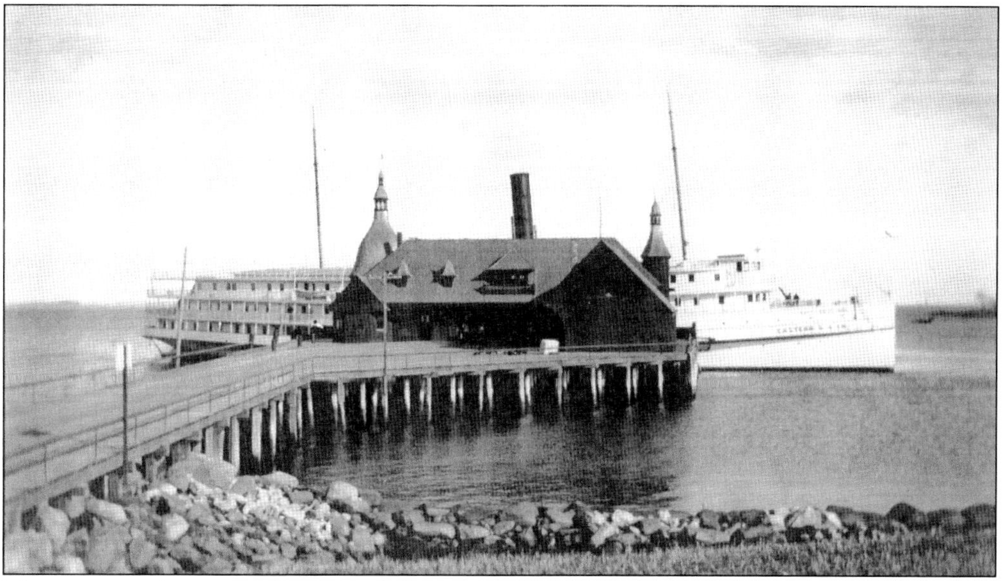

This is a popular postcard image of the steamer *Rockland* docking at the Eastern Steamship Corporation wharf at the end of Sea Street in Camden. The steamers, known locally as the Boston boats, had a regular series of stops up the East Coast from Boston harbor.

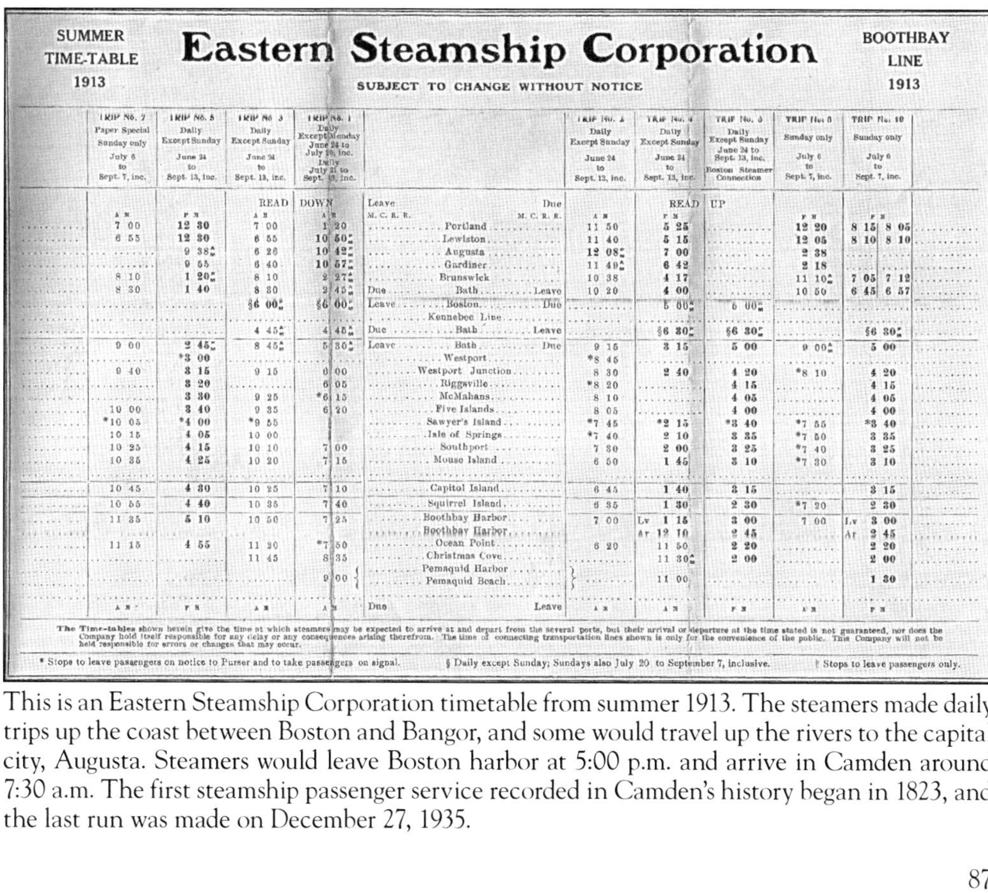

SUMMER TIME-TABLE 1913

Eastern Steamship Corporation

BOOTHBAY LINE 1913

SUBJECT TO CHANGE WITHOUT NOTICE

TRIP No. 7 Paper Special Sunday only July 6 to Sept. 7, inc.	TRIP No. 5 Daily Except Sunday June 24 to Sept. 13, inc.	TRIP No. 3 Daily Except Sunday June 24 to Sept. 13, inc.	TRIP No. 1 Daily Except Monday June 24 to July 20, inc. Daily July 21 to Sept. 13, inc.		TRIP No. 2 Daily Except Sunday June 24 to Sept. 13, inc.	TRIP No. 4 Daily Except Sunday June 24 to Sept. 13, inc.	TRIP No. 6 Daily Except Sunday June 24 to Sept. 13, inc. Boston Steamer Connection	TRIP No. 8 Sunday only July 6 to Sept. 7, inc.	TRIP No. 10 Sunday only July 6 to Sept. 7, inc.
		READ	DOWN	Leave M. C. R. R. — Due M. C. R. R.		READ	UP		
A M	P M	A M	A M		A M	P M		P M	P M
7 00	12 30	7 00	1 20	Portland	11 50	5 25	....	12 20	8 15 8 05
6 55	12 30	6 55	10 50	Lewiston	11 40	5 15	....	12 05	8 10 8 10
....	9 38	6 26	10 42	Augusta	12 08	7 00	....	2 38	....
....	9 55	6 40	10 57	Gardiner	11 49	6 42	....	2 18	....
8 10	1 20	8 10	2 27	Brunswick	10 38	4 17	....	11 10	7 05 7 12
8 30	1 40	8 30	2 45	Due Bath Leave	10 20	4 00	....	10 50	6 45 6 57
....	....	§6 00	§6 00	Leave Boston Due	....	5 00	6 00	....	....
....	....	....	....	Kennebec Line	....	....	....	....	....
....	....	4 45	4 45	Due Bath Leave	....	§6 30	§6 30	....	§6 30
9 00	2 45	8 45	5 30	Leave Bath Due	9 15	3 15	5 00	9 00	5 00
....	*3 00	....	....	Westport	*8 45	....	....	....	....
9 40	3 15	9 15	6 00	Westport Junction	8 30	2 40	4 20	*8 10	4 20
....	3 20	....	6 05	Riggsville	*8 20	....	4 15	....	4 15
....	3 30	9 25	*6 15	McMahans	8 10	....	4 05	....	4 05
10 00	3 40	9 35	6 20	Five Islands	8 05	....	4 00	....	4 00
*10 05	*4 00	*9 55		Sawyer's Island	*7 45	*2 15	*3 40	*7 55	*3 40
10 15	4 05	10 00		Isle of Springs	*7 40	2 10	3 35	*7 50	3 35
10 25	4 15	10 10	7 00	Southport	7 30	2 00	3 25	*7 40	3 25
10 35	4 25	10 20	7 15	Mouse Island	6 50	1 45	3 10	*7 30	3 10
10 45	4 30	10 25	7 10	Capitol Island	6 45	1 40	3 15	....	3 15
10 55	4 40	10 35	7 40	Squirrel Island	6 35	1 30	2 30	*7 20	2 30
11 35	5 10	10 50	7 25	Boothbay Harbor	7 00	Lv 1 15	3 00	7 00	Lv 3 00
				Boothbay Harbor		Ar 12 10	2 45		Ar 2 45
11 15	4 55	11 20	*7 50	Ocean Point	6 20	11 50	2 20	....	2 20
....	....	11 45	8 35	Christmas Cove	....	11 30	2 00	....	2 00
....	....	....	9 00	Pemaquid Harbor / Pemaquid Beach	....	11 00	....	....	1 30
A M	P M	A M	A M	Due — Leave	A M	A M	P M	A M	P M

The Time-tables shown herein give the time at which steamers may be expected to arrive at and depart from the several ports, but their arrival or departure at the time stated is not guaranteed, nor does the Company hold itself responsible for any delay or any consequences arising therefrom. The time of connecting transportation lines shown is only for the convenience of the public. This Company will not be held responsible for errors or changes that may occur.

* Stops to leave passengers on notice to Purser and to take passengers on signal. § Daily except Sunday; Sundays also July 20 to September 7, inclusive. ‖ Stops to leave passengers only.

This is an Eastern Steamship Corporation timetable from summer 1913. The steamers made daily trips up the coast between Boston and Bangor, and some would travel up the rivers to the capital city, Augusta. Steamers would leave Boston harbor at 5:00 p.m. and arrive in Camden around 7:30 a.m. The first steamship passenger service recorded in Camden's history began in 1823, and the last run was made on December 27, 1935.

OCEAN HOUSE

CAMDEN, ME.   FRED K. ALLEN, Prop.

This house is located on elevated ground with large lawn shaded by elms, within a few rods of the sea and half a mile from mountains. Invigorating air, fine sea shore, lake, mountain drives and most charming scenery on the Maine coast.

The Ocean House

is now open under new management.

MODERN IMPROVEMENTS.

RATES REASONABLE.

TRANSIENTS ACCOMMODATED.

Evolution of travel brought an increase of visitors to mid-coast Maine. Formerly known as the John Pendleton House, the Ocean House hotel was Camden's largest hotel and a popular destination for tourists until it was burned to the ground in 1903. The site occupied by the hotel is now the location of the Camden Public Library on Main Street. Here, one of the many carriages is awaiting passengers on the lawn of the hotel. If one looks closely through the trees, the bow of one of the passenger steamers is visible anchored near the shipyard.

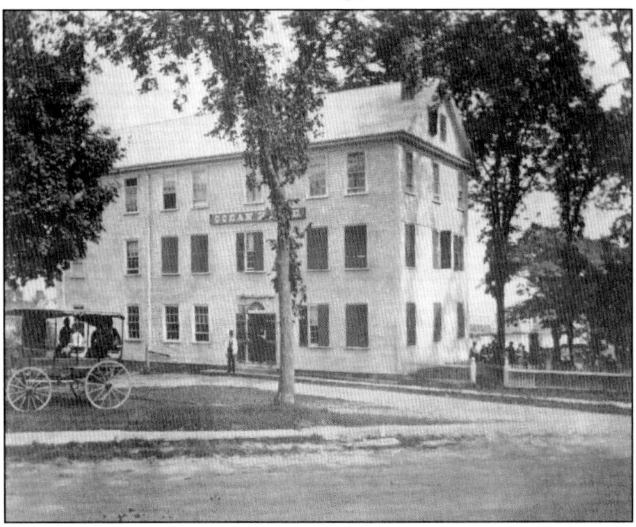

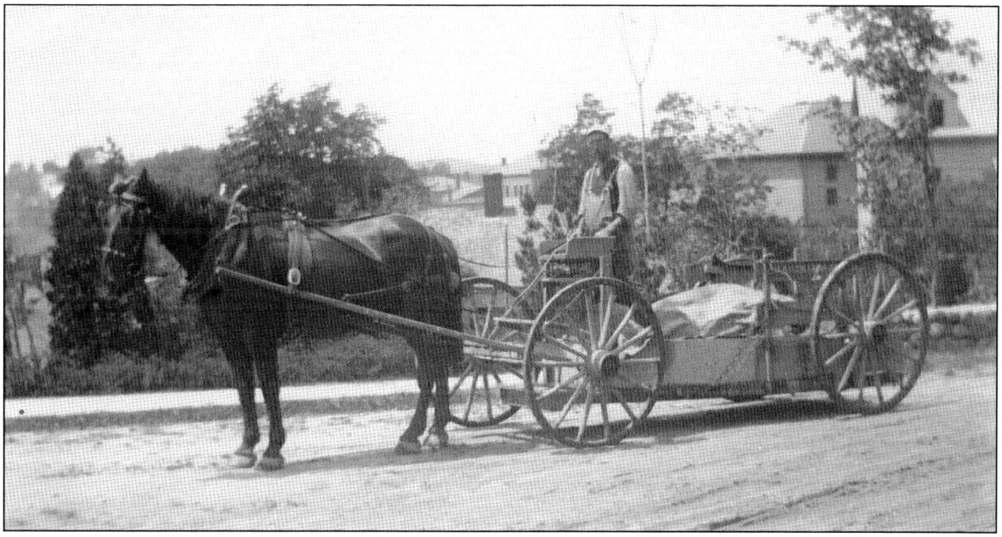

One of the means of delivering goods in late 19th and early 20th centuries was the use of horse-drawn carts like the one in this photograph taken in Rockport. These low-slung wagons made loading and unloading items easier, and the deliveryman could stand up while driving. This vintage advertisement from 1890 for Simonton & Gill grocers is typical of the announcements found in the local town directories. Simonton would have done a thriving business, located as it was across from the Bay View House, one of the largest hotels in Camden.

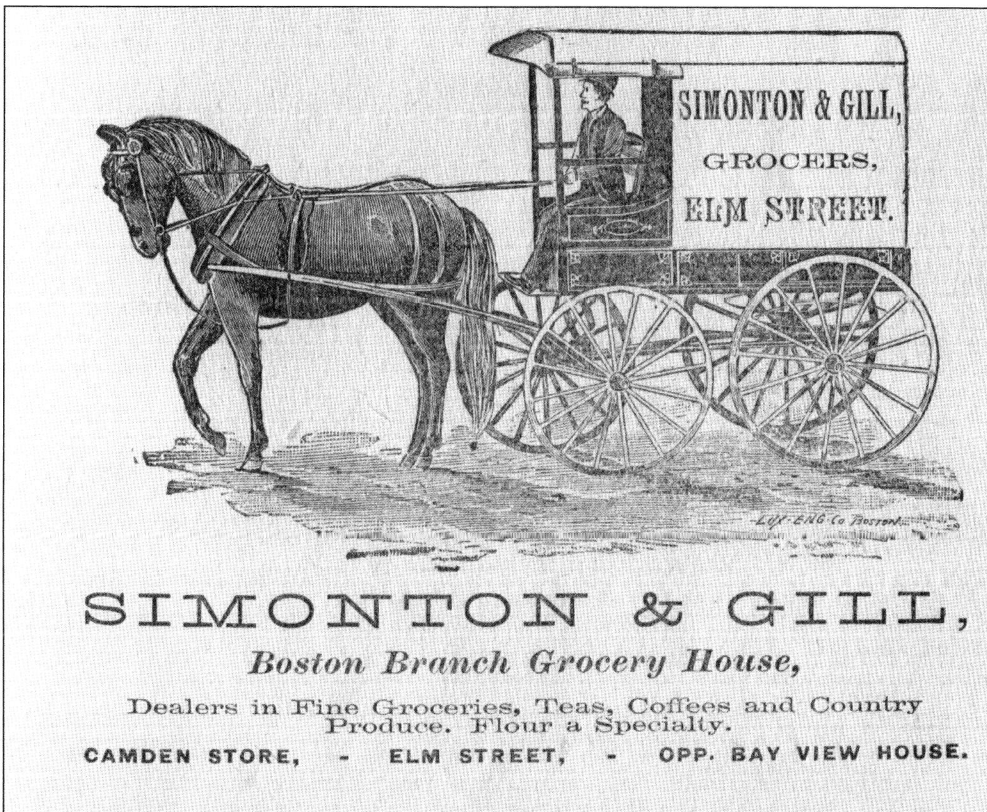

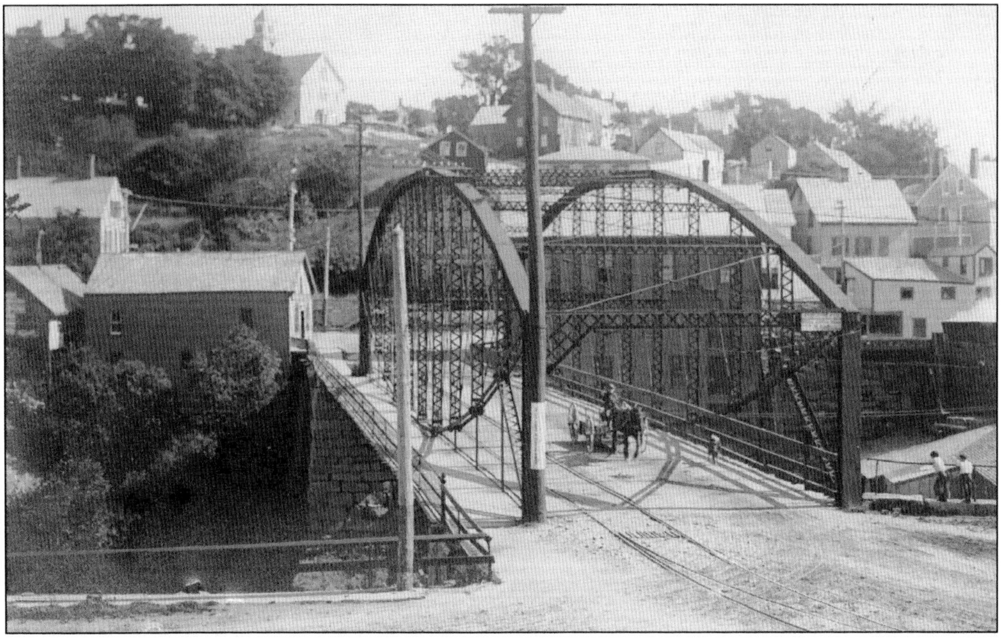

In this vintage postcard, a delivery wagon like the one depicted on the previous page trundles across the old iron bridge over the Goose River. The trolley company ran a line of track along the main thoroughfare through the bustling Rockport village. The schoolhouse with the bell tower was built in 1891 and is visible at the top of the image. The bridge was deemed unsafe and replaced around 1919.

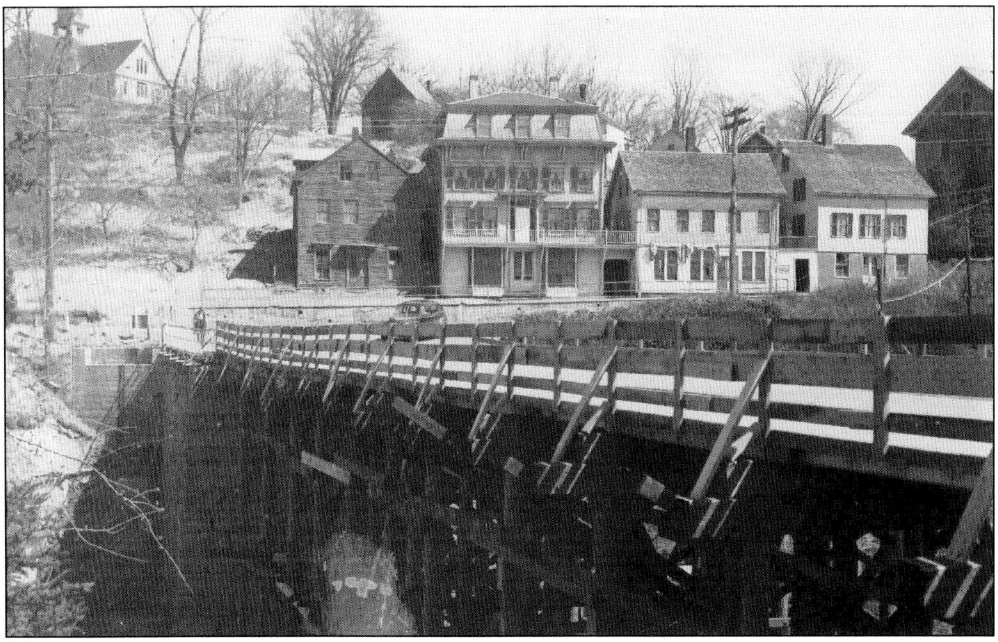

This image shows a portion of the business district of Rockport near the bridge over the Goose River. The Philbrook Building at left is dwarfed by the more flamboyant Piper Building with its raised walkway above the door. This structure once housed the Swan Inn. To the right is the Carver Building, and the Rockport schoolhouse is in the background at far left.

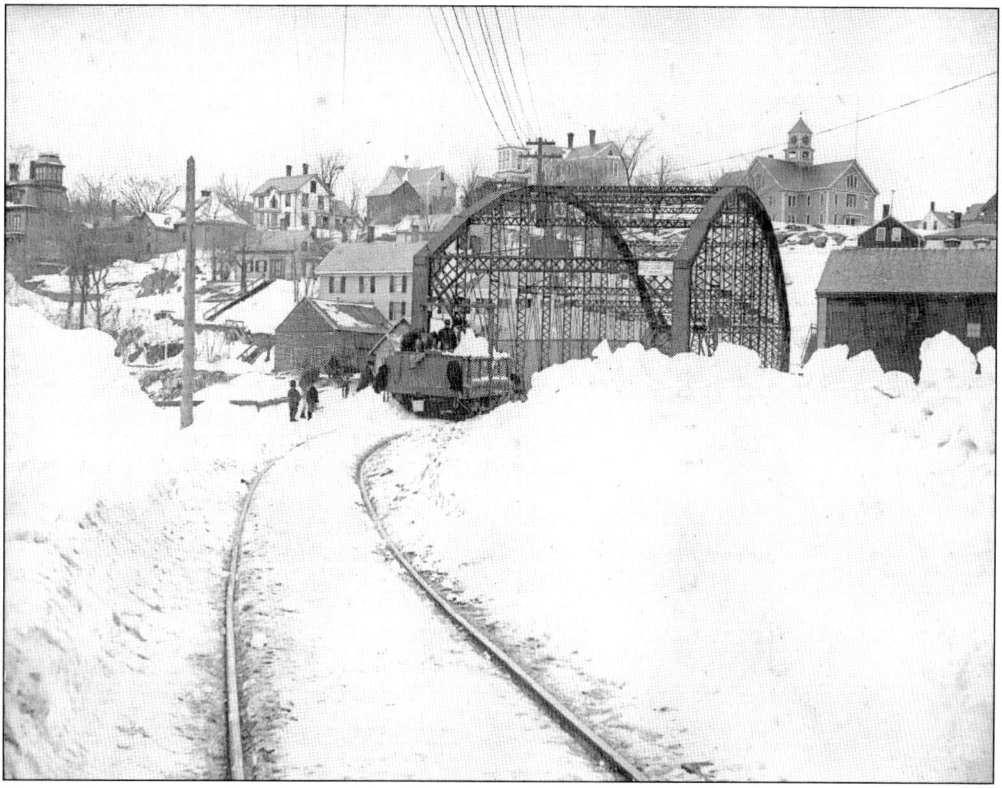

The trolley between Camden and Rockland was a primary mode of transportation in the area from about 1892 to 1931. The trolley barns and powerhouse overlooked Rockport's Glen Cove at a point still known to locals as Powerhouse Hill. In the photograph above, a special car is used to remove ice and snow from the trolley tracks over the old iron bridge in Rockport. In the image below, taken in Camden, the trolley appears outfitted with a special plow, and several men are attempting to shovel a path after heavy snowfall.

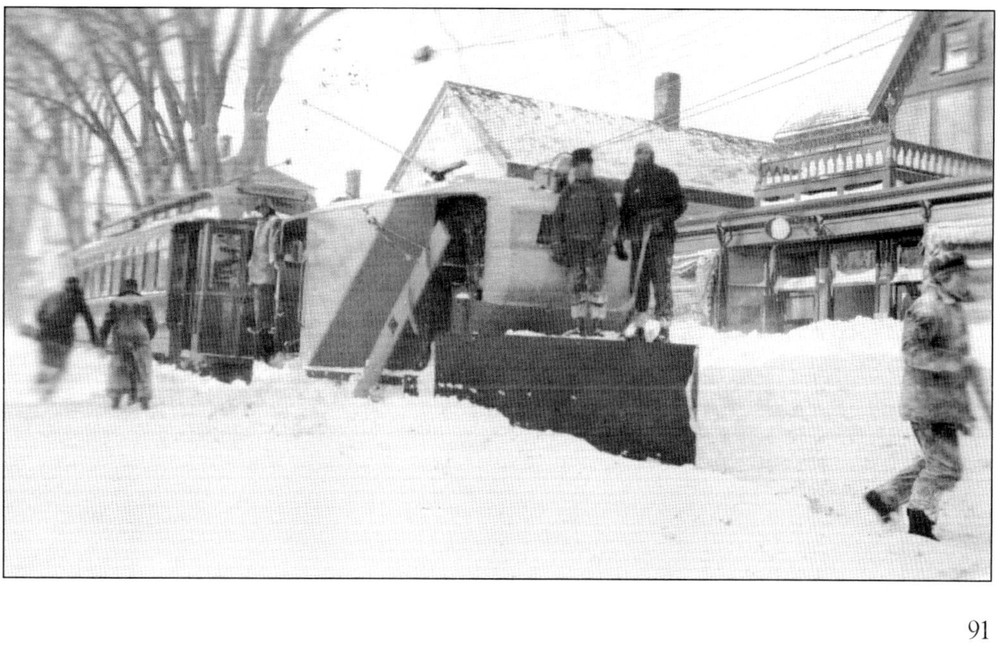

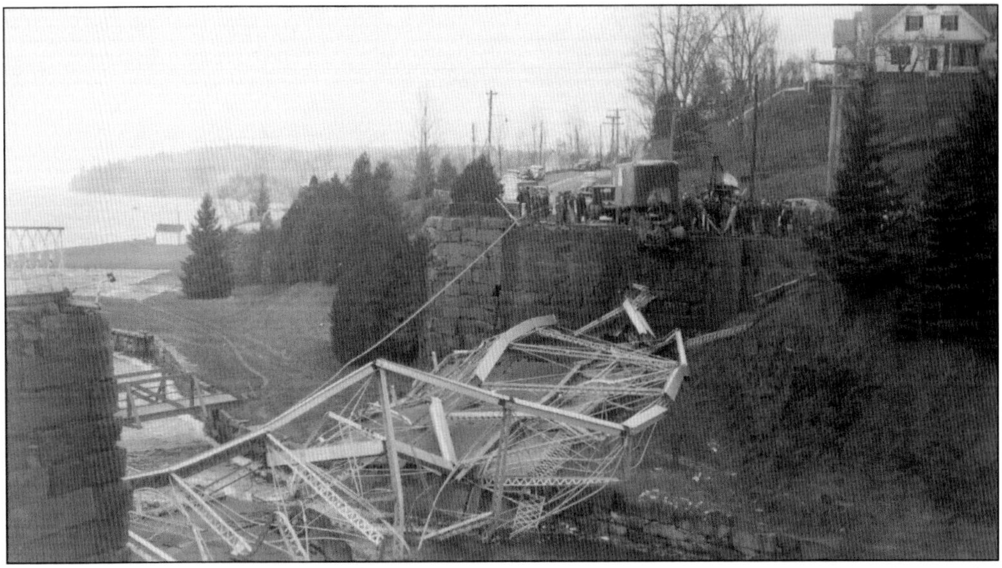

A tragedy struck Rockport in November 1946, when Hubert Craven of Bangor fell asleep at the wheel of his delivery truck and hit one of the northwest posts of the bridge over Goose River. Craven was killed instantly, and the bridge collapsed into the river below. Because of the shortage of steel at the end of World War II, the state temporarily replaced the bridge with a wooden structure.

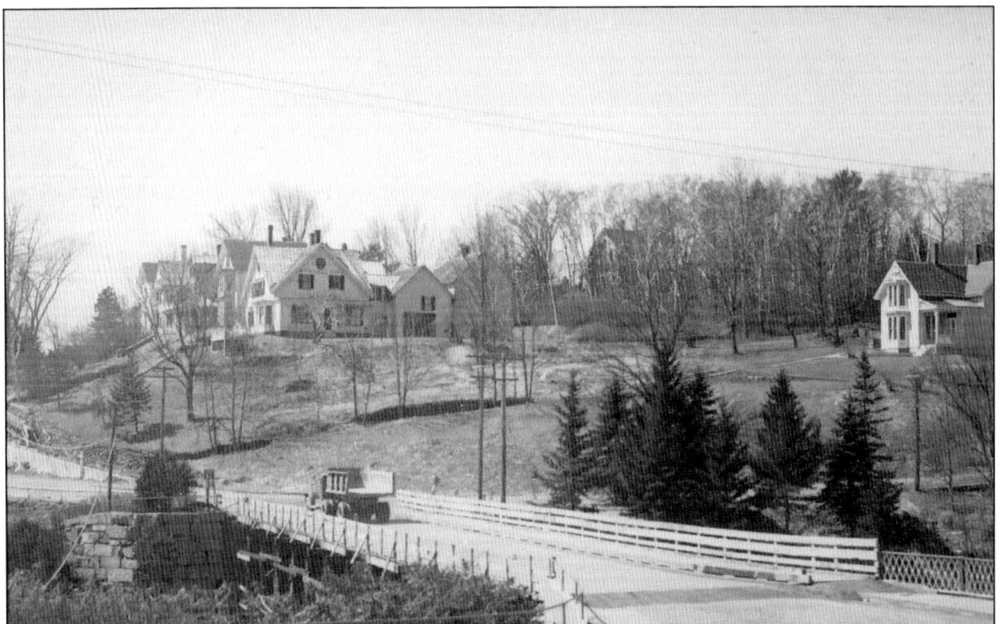

A construction vehicle rumbles along Pascal Avenue headed away from the center of town across the temporary wooden Goose River Bridge in Rockport. The homes on Amesbury Hill are visible in this undated image, and looking at this photograph one can almost feel the cold wind off the harbor.

Eight

INDUSTRIES

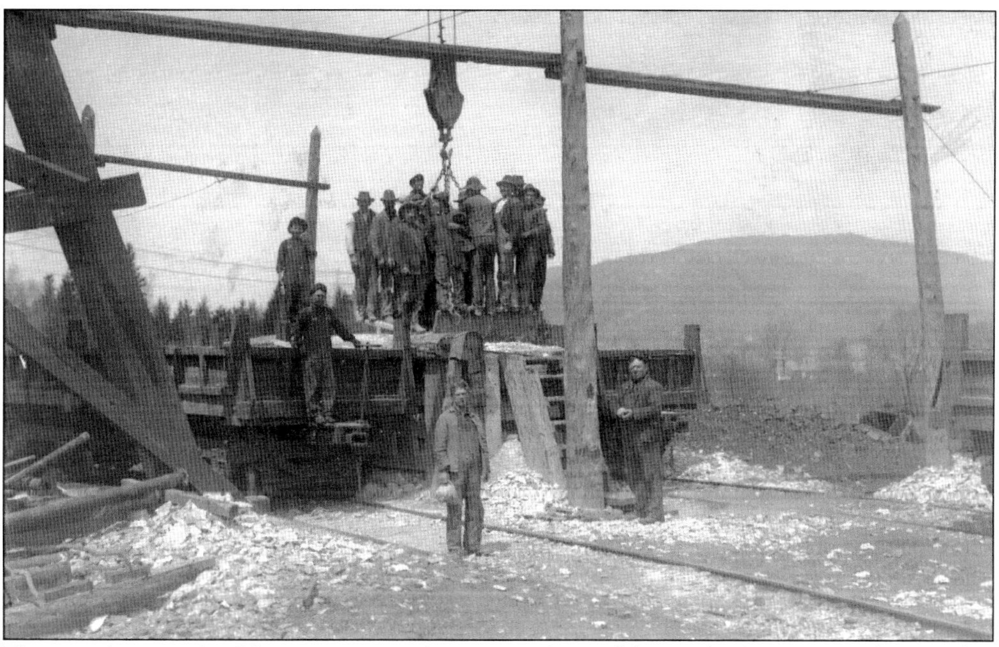

This is a photograph of the quarry train that operated out of the Jacobs Quarry near the Camden and Rockport town line. Mining operations started at the quarry around 1817, and for nearly 100 years it was the most important industry in the mid-coast area. The construction of the Capitol in Washington, DC, was facilitated by 300 casks of lime from Camden. The Jacobs lime was known as the finest lime powder on the market.

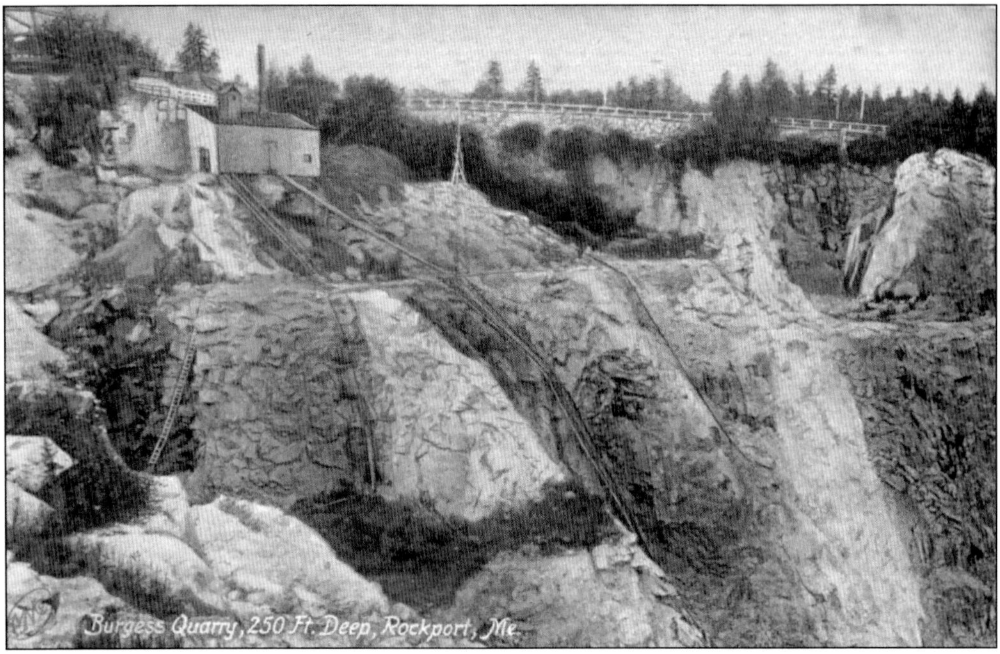

This postcard image is of the Burgess Quarry, located in Rockport, Maine. This quarry was more than 250 feet deep and provided a supply of lime rock that fed the kilns at the head of Rockport Harbor. Once cooked, the lime powder was sealed in casks and loaded onto schooners for transport to major ports along the East Coast, where it sold for approximately $6.50 per ton.

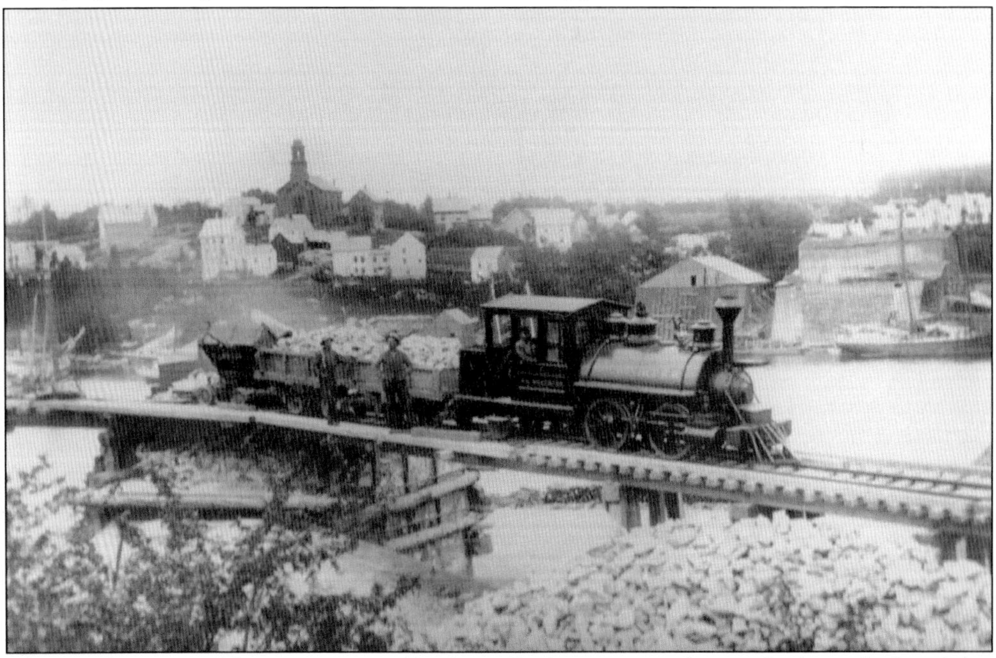

This is a clear view of the narrow-gauge Rockport Railway cars on the trestle above the lime kilns on the west side of the harbor. Loaded with lime rock, they will dump the rock into the top of the kilns where the rock would be burned for many days. Each load required 14 turnings in the kilns, at 12 hours per turn. When it was done, the powder was placed in casks for shipment.

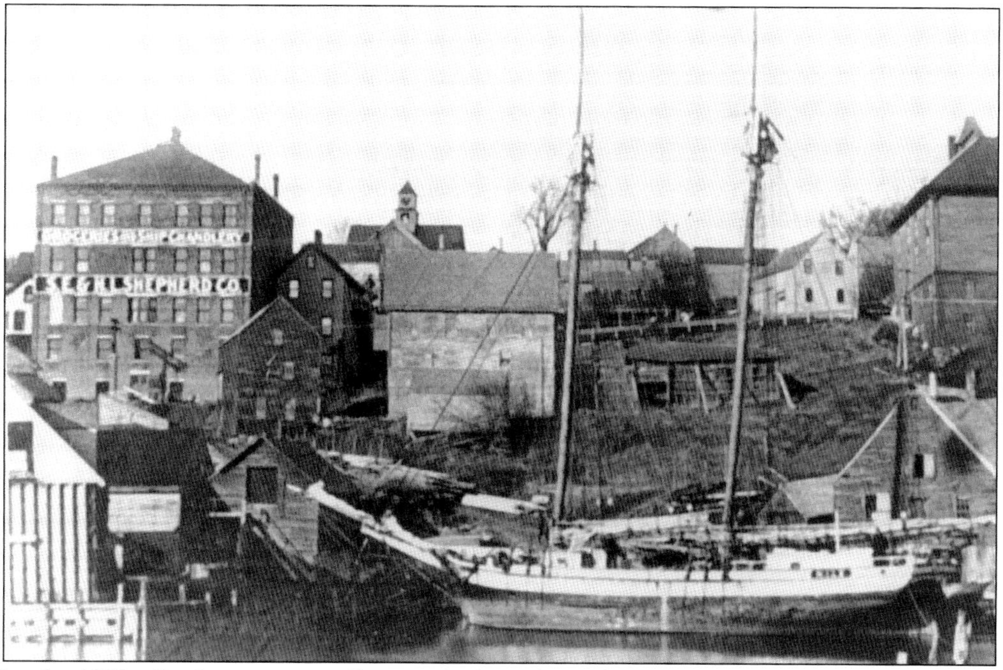

In the 1880s, Rockport was a village tucked up along the waterfront and Goose River. The schooner, or coaster, anchored alongside the wharf is unloading wood brought in from the islands in Penobscot Bay to feed the lime kilns. In the image below, taken around 1895, the quarry train trestle appears at left, and smoke from the kilns partially obscures the kilns and the homes behind them on Amesbury Hill, sometimes known as Smokestack Hill. More wood is being stored in the sheds behind the schooner. The kilns operated 24 hours a day until 1907, when they were destroyed in a massive fire that also made ruin of the icehouses on the opposite shore. It is said that the stacks of ice in the sheds remained steaming for a month after the fire.

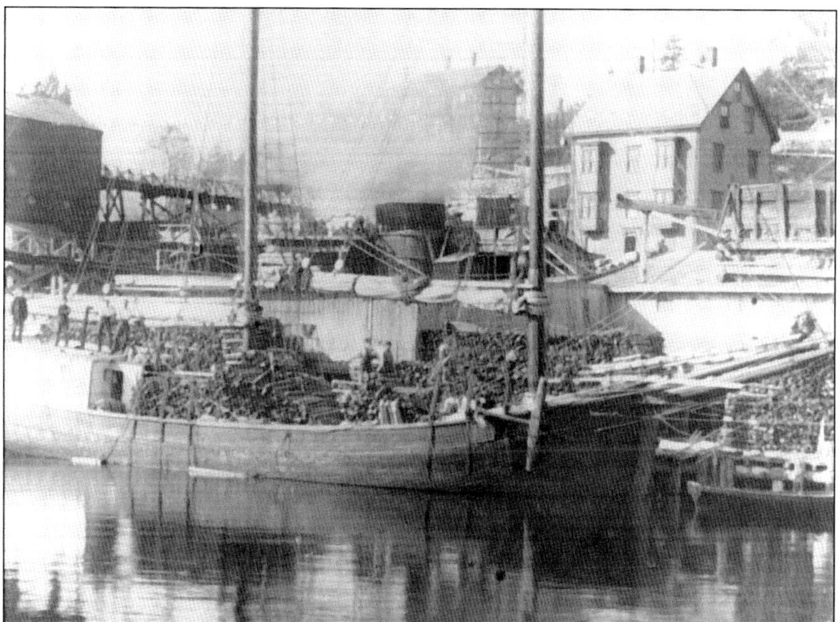

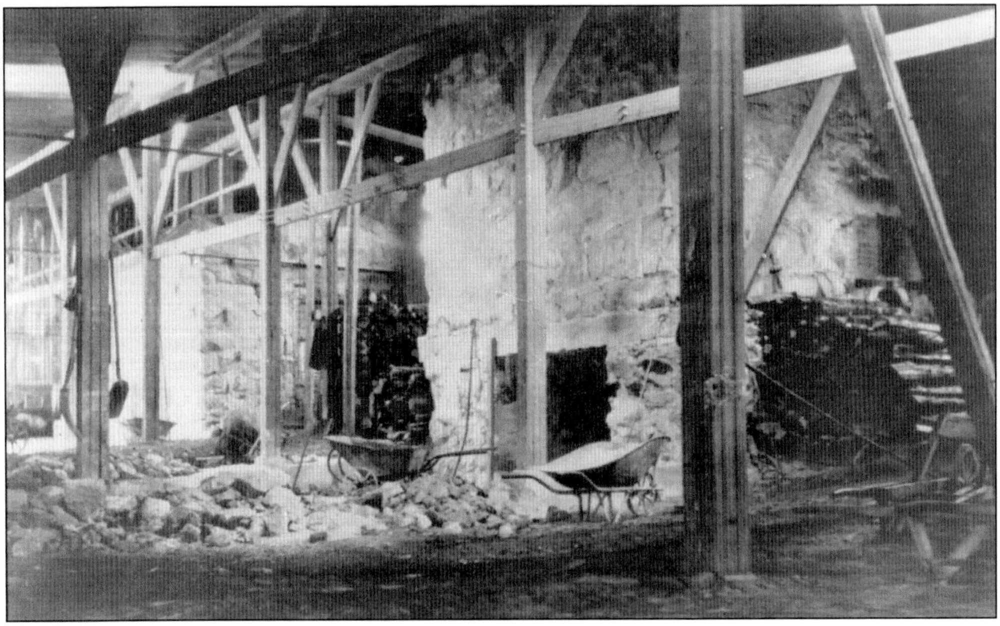

These photographs show rare interior views of the lime kilns at the head of Rockport Harbor as they looked prior to the devastating fire in 1907 that ended both the lime and ice industries in the town. In the above photograph, there is wood stacked at the right of the nearest kiln, which was kept burning all day and night to break down the lime rock into powder. In the image below, barrels of lime powder await shipment via schooner to various ports along the coast. A laborer wheels a full cask of powder into line in the background near the kilns.

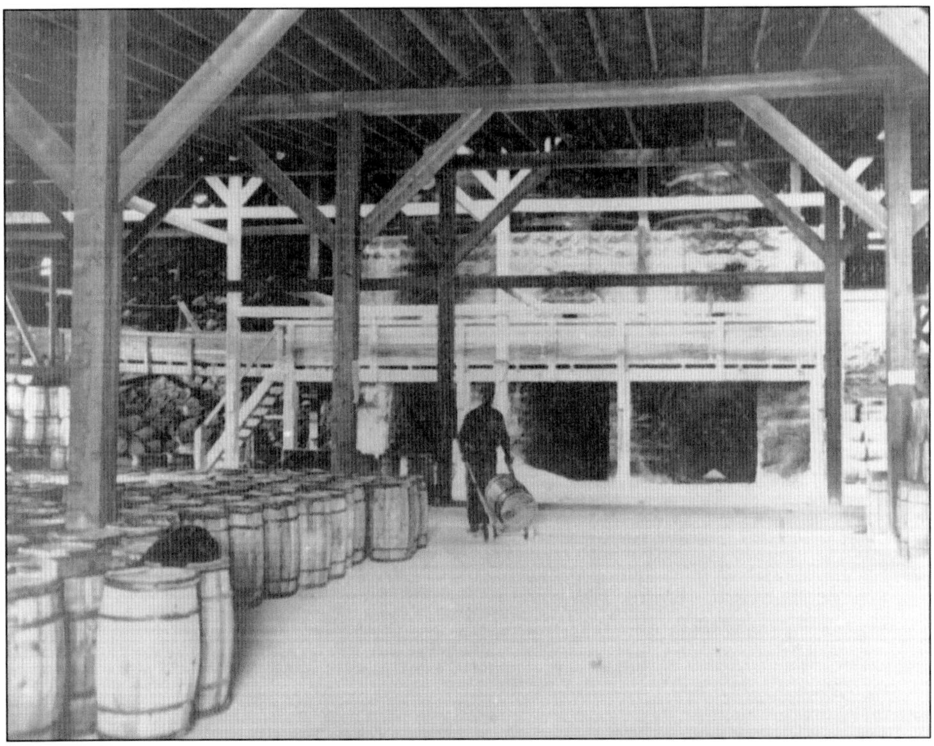

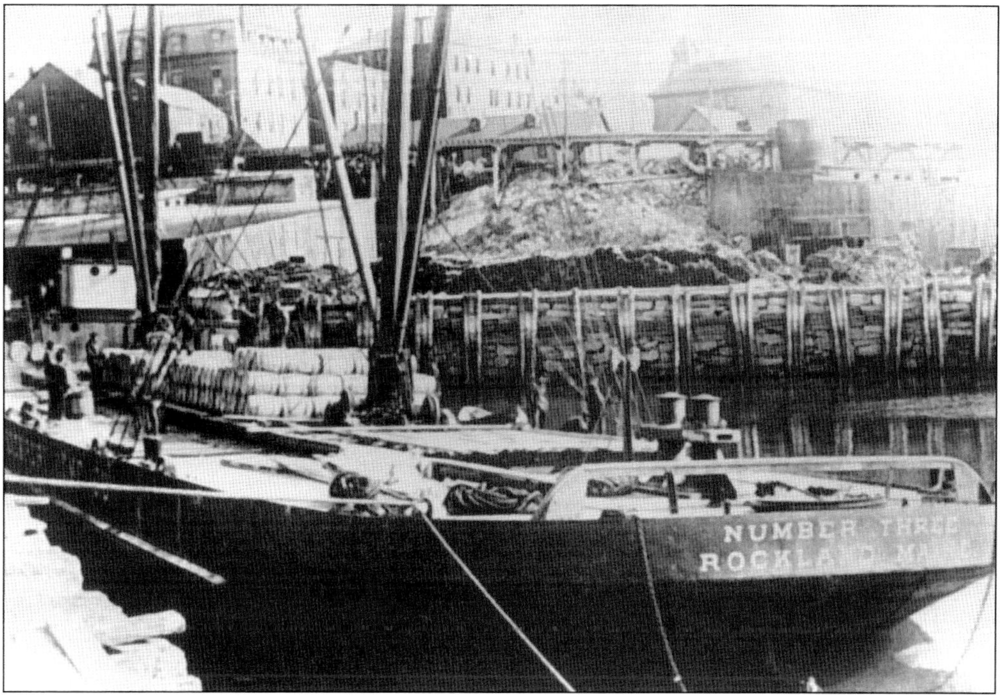

The No. 3 barge based out of Rockland, Maine is shown tied up alongside the dock in Rockport. Barges such as these would transport empty casks to be filled with lime from the kilns, and they can be seen piled up on the deck with the quarry train in the background. The lime powder had numerous uses: mortar for building, toothpaste, and chicken feed. In the image below, a laborer is on a similar vessel loading casks of lime into the hold.

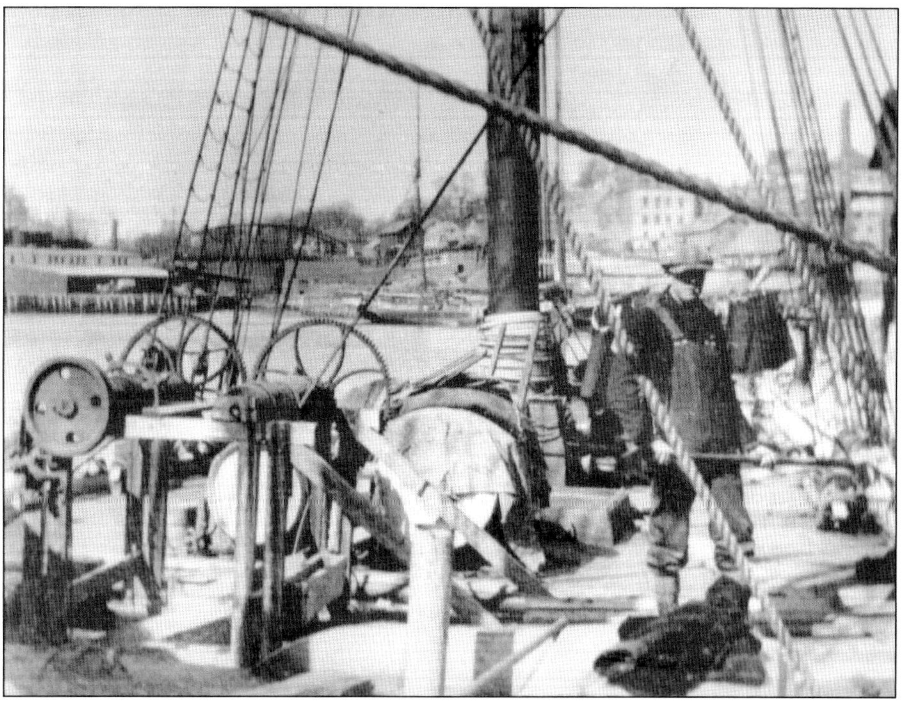

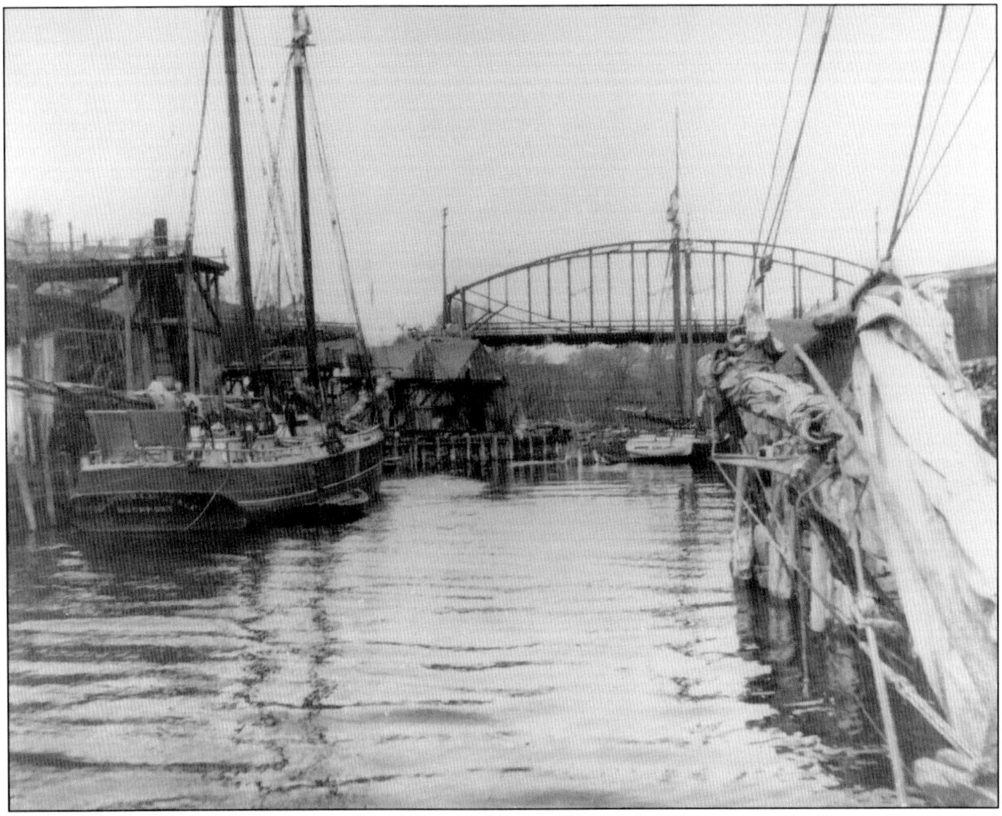

Above, the *Chester Lawrence* is seen tied up near the old iron bridge across the Goose River. The vessel was used to transport lime powder. The bridge over the river was the source of consternation and eventual divorce between Camden and Rockport. The towns had operated under a single government but not without friction. When Rockport wanted to replace the old wooden bridge in 1884, Camden waffled over funding, as Rockport had in a similar decision a century earlier. By 1891, the towns voted to split apart. The view in the photograph below is looking down from the Goose River bridge to the lumber sheds and lime kilns below.

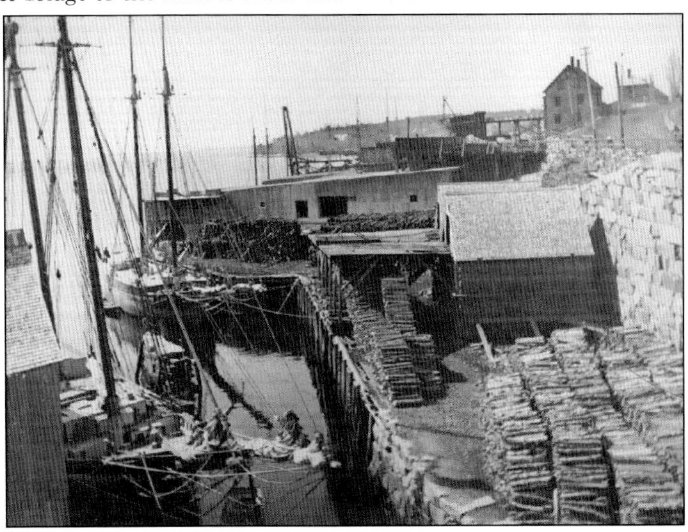

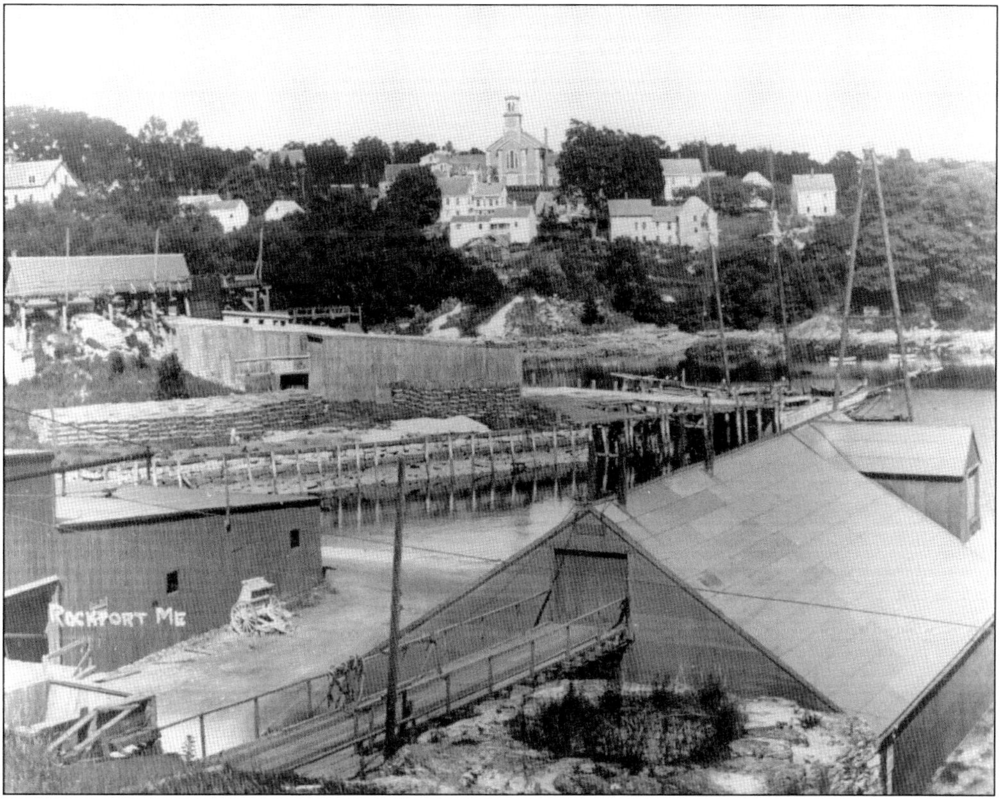

These before and after images of Rockport show the effect of the fire in 1907. In the above image, the waterfront is completely covered in industrial buildings such as the lime kilns and sheds in the foreground. In the postcard image below, the smoking ruins of the kilns are visible through the haze. The 1907 fire completely destroyed both the kilns on one side of the harbor and the icehouses on the opposite shore, spelling an end to both industries in one day's inferno. More than 2,500 cords of wood, three kilns, 7,000 casks of lime, and the ice sheds were destroyed at a cost of more than $75,000.

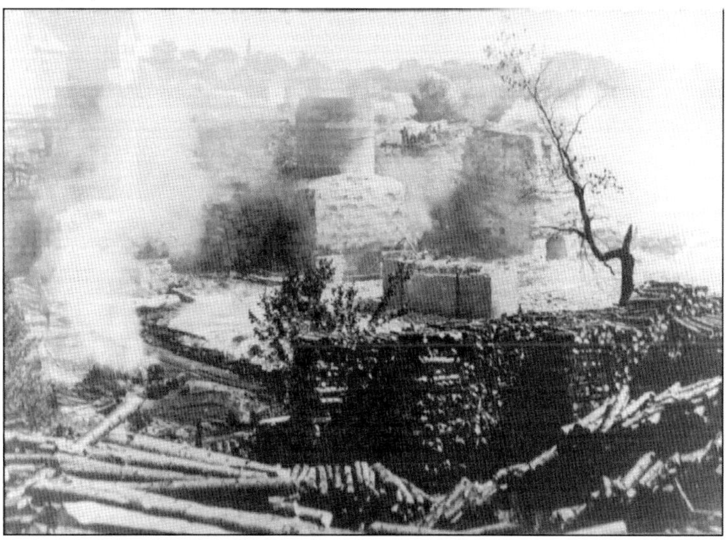

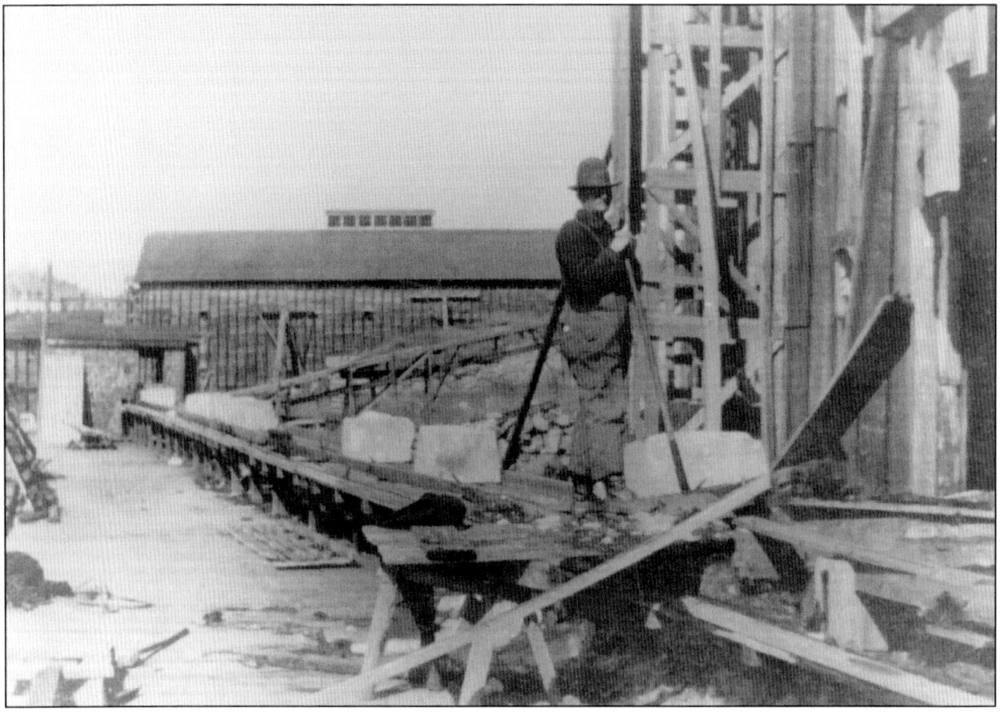

Pictured here is a laborer loading ice into the large storage sheds on the east side of Rockport Harbor. The pure Lily Pond ice was cut by hand using long saws and transported to the sheds at the edge of the harbor. The ice was then loaded onto ships, packed in sawdust, and shipped as far as the Caribbean.

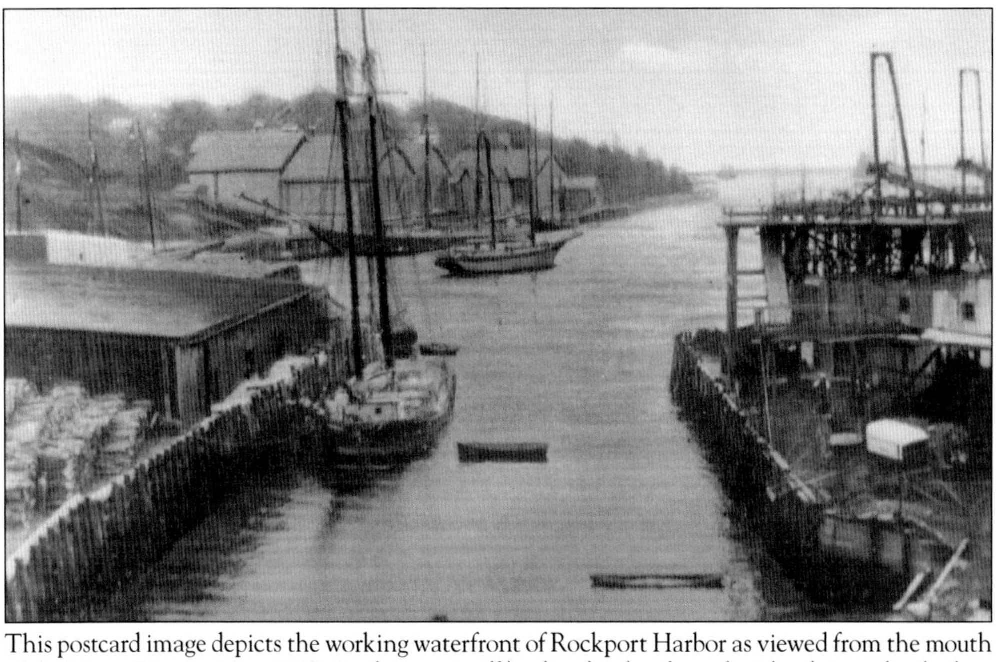

This postcard image depicts the working waterfront of Rockport Harbor as viewed from the mouth of the Goose River prior to 1907. A schooner is off-loading lumber from the islands into the sheds at the left, and a larger vessel is moored by the Rockport Ice Company sheds in the background.

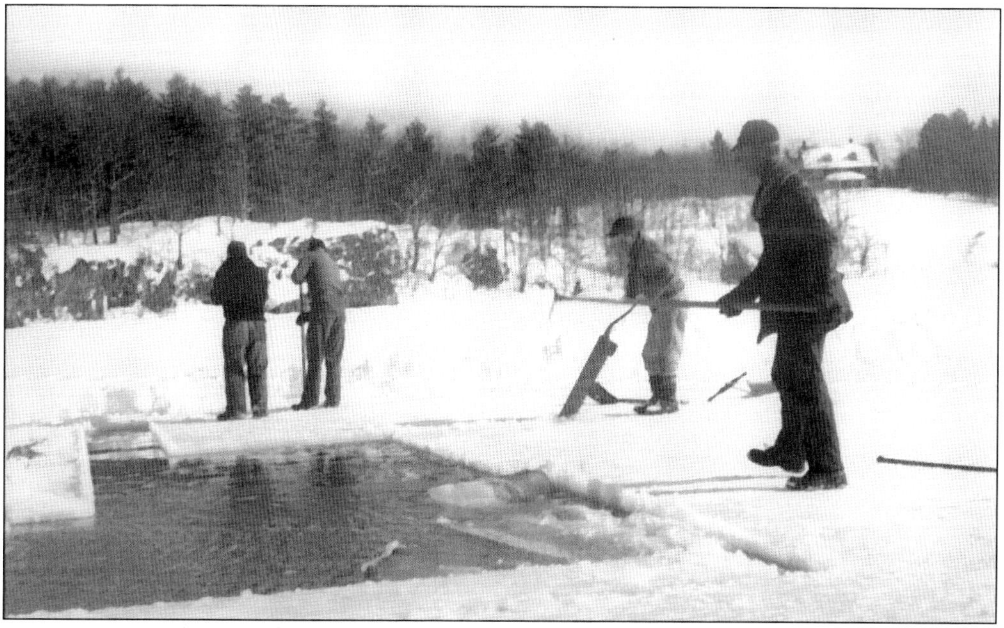

At the height of the ice industry, as many as 50,000 tons of ice were harvested off Lily Pond. After the 1907 fire in Rockport Harbor, cutting ice on Lily Pond in Rockport was no longer the major industry in the area. Instead, it was mainly cut by local farmers for storage of dairy products to keep them fresh for market.

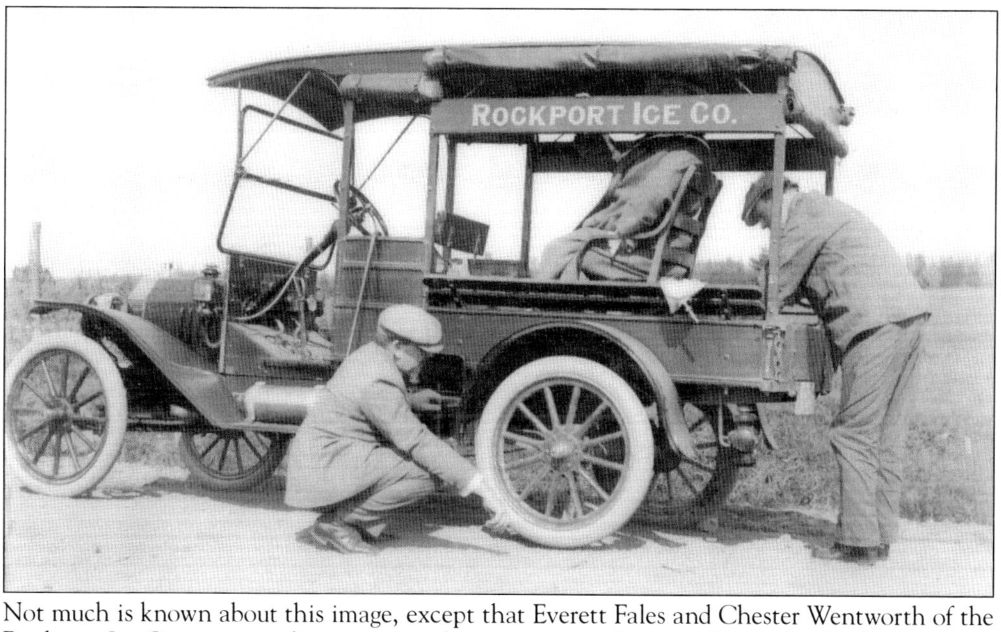

Not much is known about this image, except that Everett Fales and Chester Wentworth of the Rockport Ice Company are having an unpleasant start to their trip. Upon the death of William Carleton Jr. in 1876, the Rockport Ice Company was taken over by his son-in-law Rev. Thomas Brastow, who carried on as treasurer until retiring in 1904.

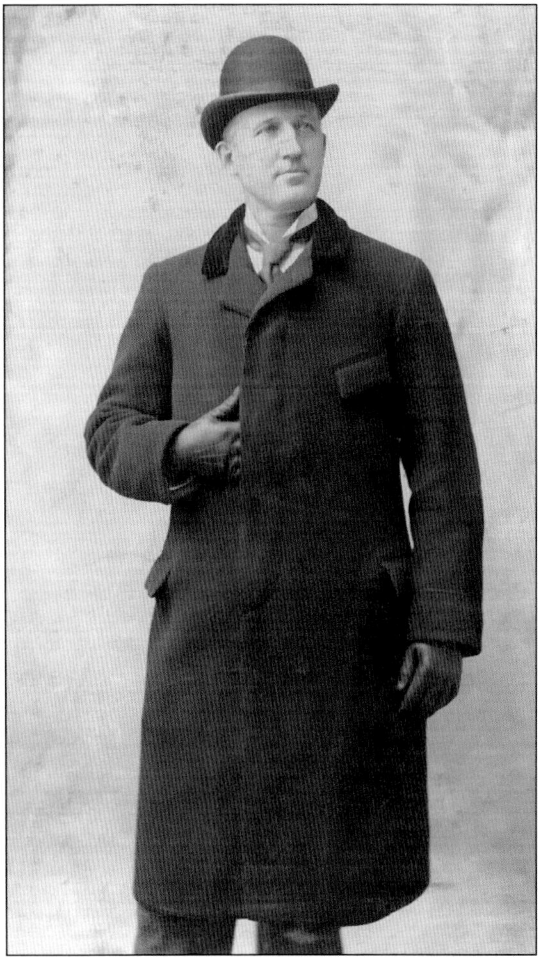

In the left image, the Honorable Herbert L. Shepherd cuts a dashing figure in the clothing of the early 1900s. He was a prominent businessman, and a large brick building in the center of Rockport's business district still bears his name. The image below is a photograph of Herbert L. Shepherd's stately home on Pascal Avenue. The photograph was taken on Memorial Day in 1905. The S.E. & H.L. Shepherd Company was established in 1845 and incorporated in 1892. It was a vast wholesale and retail business shipping and selling groceries, dry goods, coal, wood, lime, and ice. In 1880, Shepherd became collector of customs in Camden, and he helped establish Rockport as a port of delivery by 1890. He was also president of Camden Savings Bank and a state legislator.

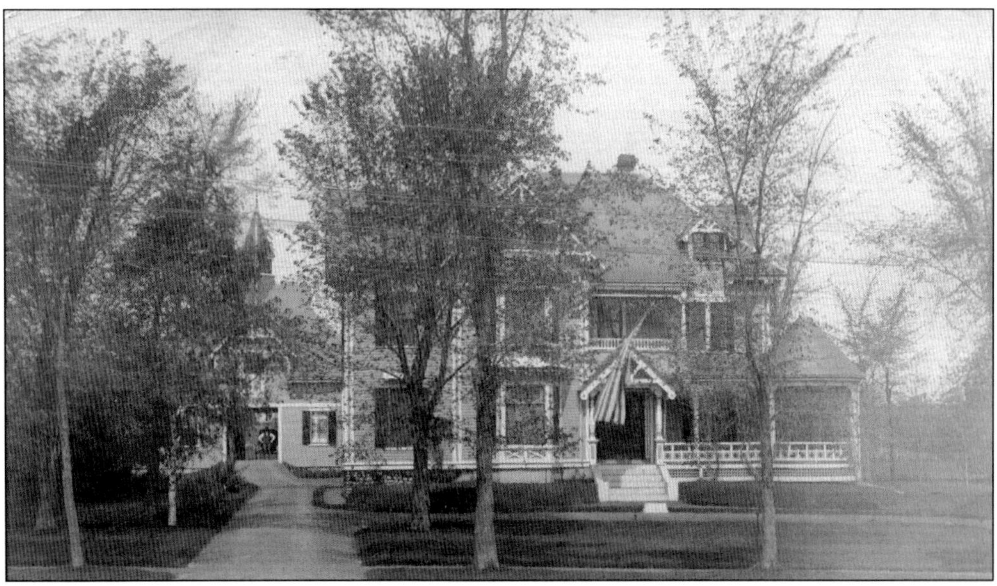

Pictured here around 1900 is the massive brick Shepherd Block in the heart of Rockport's downtown business district. Dealers in coal, wood, lime, ice, and groceries, the Shepherd store was one of the largest and most prosperous retail operations in the mid-coast area.

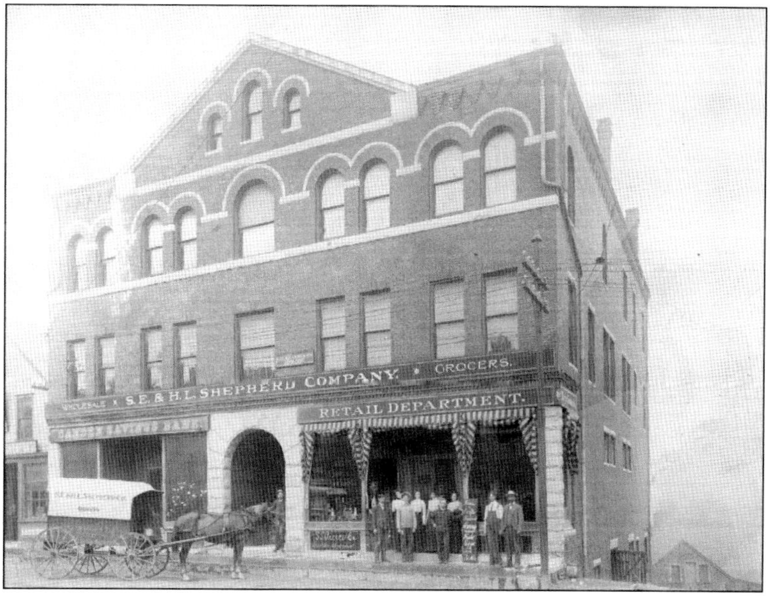

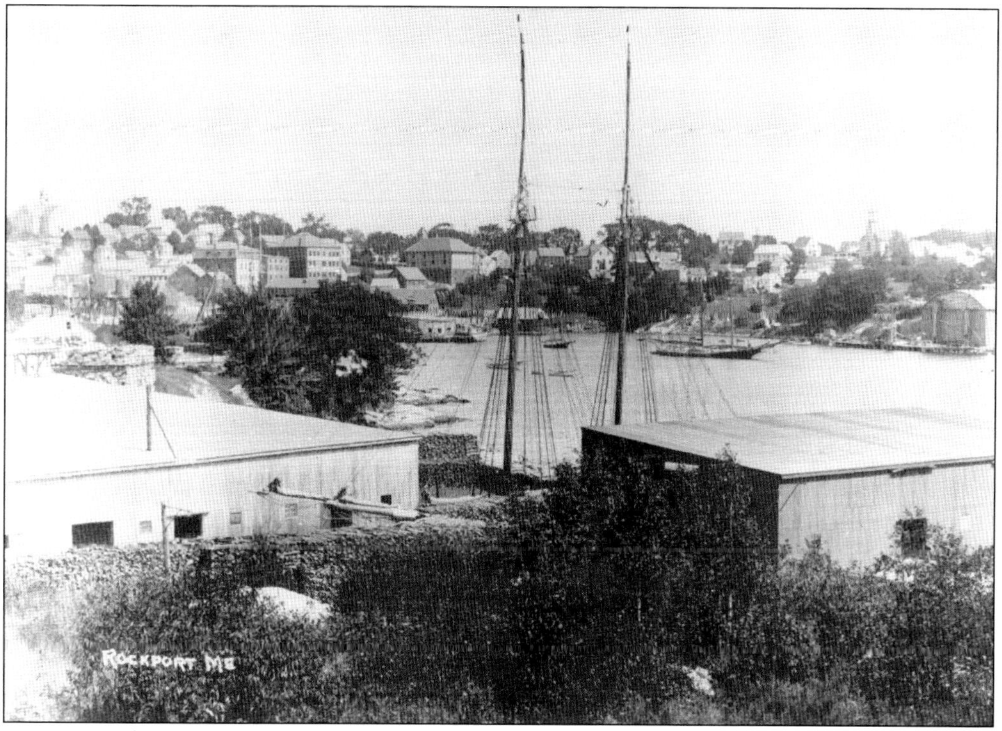

Here is another view of Rockport Harbor around 1905, taken from what is modern-day Walker Park. One of the icehouses is just visible in the far right background, the town's business district is in the background, with the distinctive hipped-roof opera house, and the lumber sheds and kilns are in the foreground with a coaster bringing lumber in from the islands.

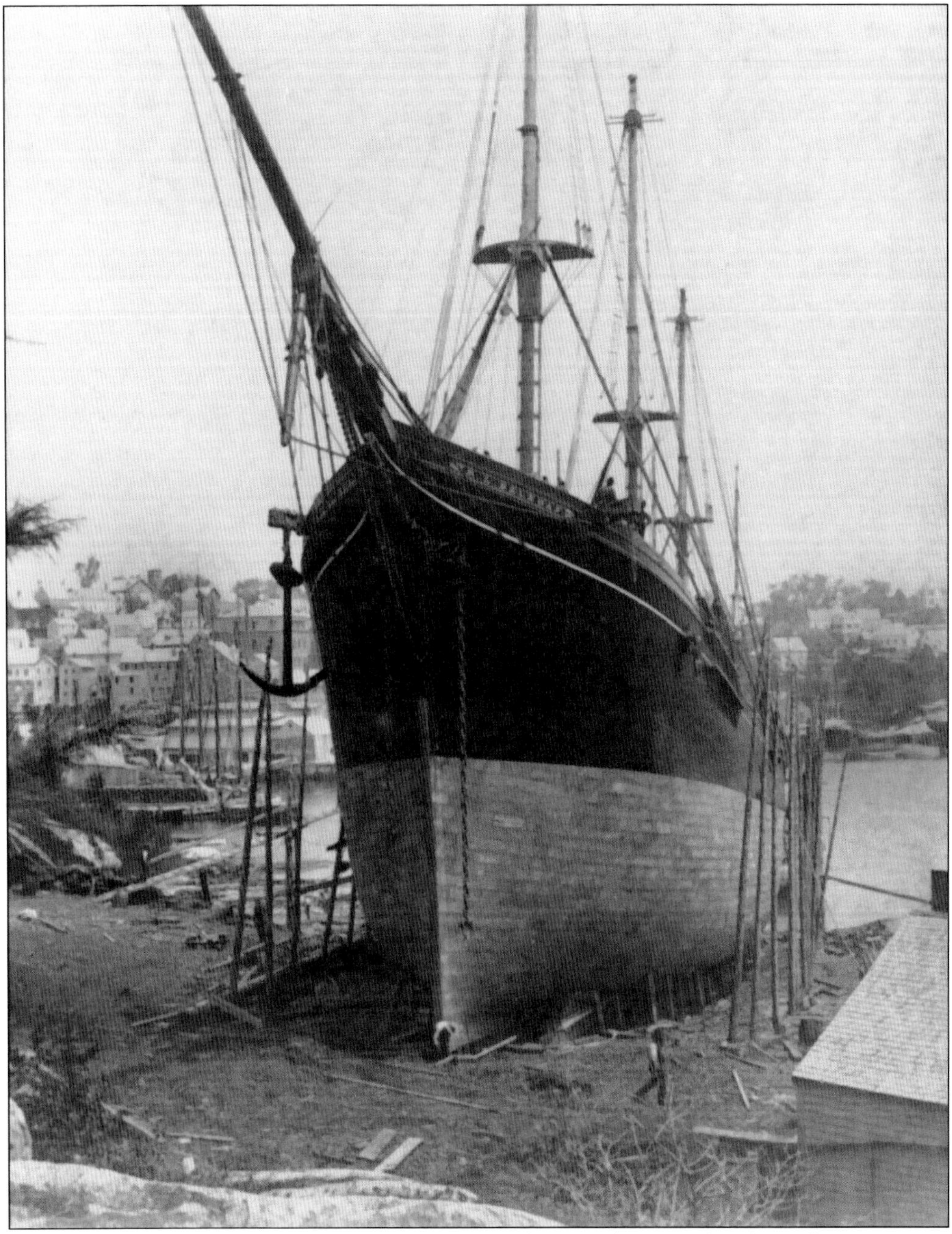

The four-masted schooner *Robert L. Belknap* was built in Rockport and is shown here just prior to launch in 1884. The vessel weighed 2,362 tons and was used for long-distance and deepwater bulk transport. It was captained by shipmaster Everett G. Staples from 1884 to 1896, when it sank in the China Sea.

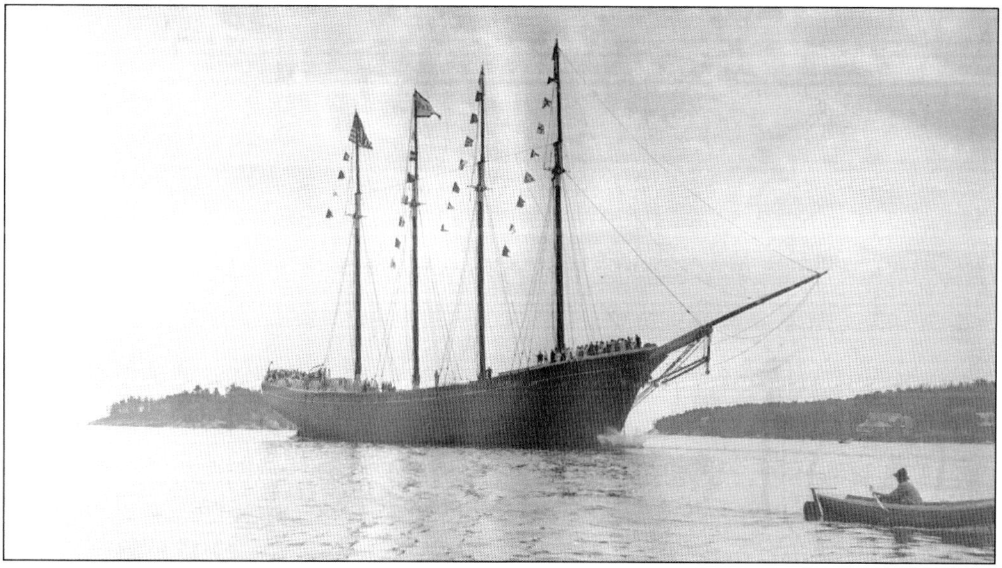

Pictured here is the four-masted schooner *Blue Peter* after sliding down the ways at the Robert Bean shipyard in Camden. Set afloat on August 4, 1917, it was the third vessel launched by Holly M. Bean's son Robert in 13 months. The vessel was 230 feet long and weighed more than 1,200 tons. The two anchors weighed 5,000 pounds each and a 15-horsepower gasoline engine was used to hoist them.

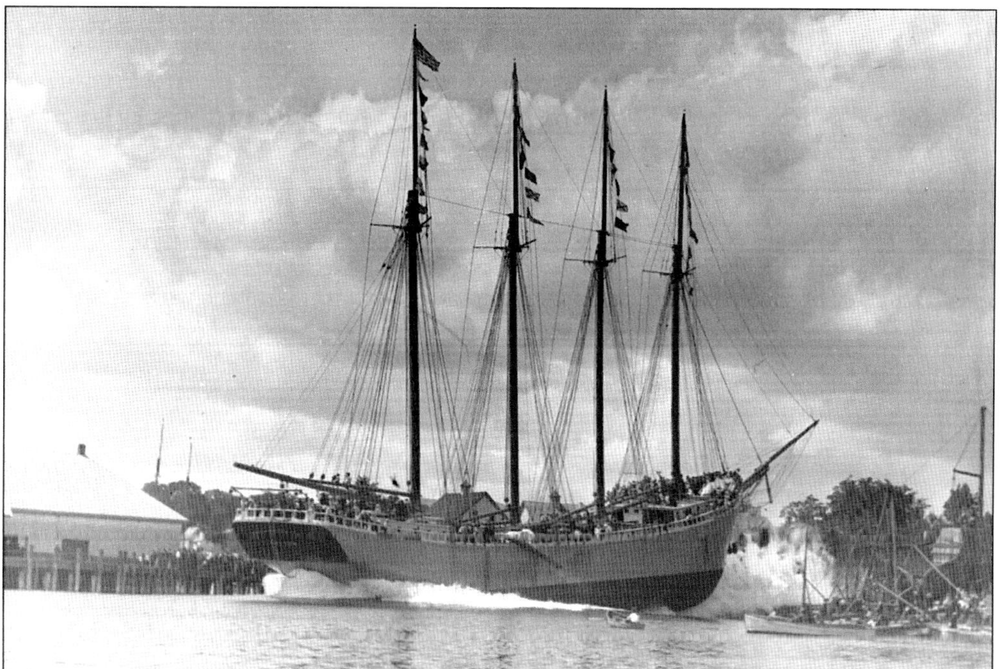

With a massive splash, the four-masted schooner *Helen Barnet Gring* slides down the ways as it is launched from the Camden shipyard on July 29, 1919. The vessel had a keel 190 feet long, weighed 1,250 tons, and cost about $200,000. This is a poignant image, as the era of wind-powered sailing ships was nearing an end as steam power became dominant. Part of the Eastern Steamship Company wharf is visible at the far left of the image.

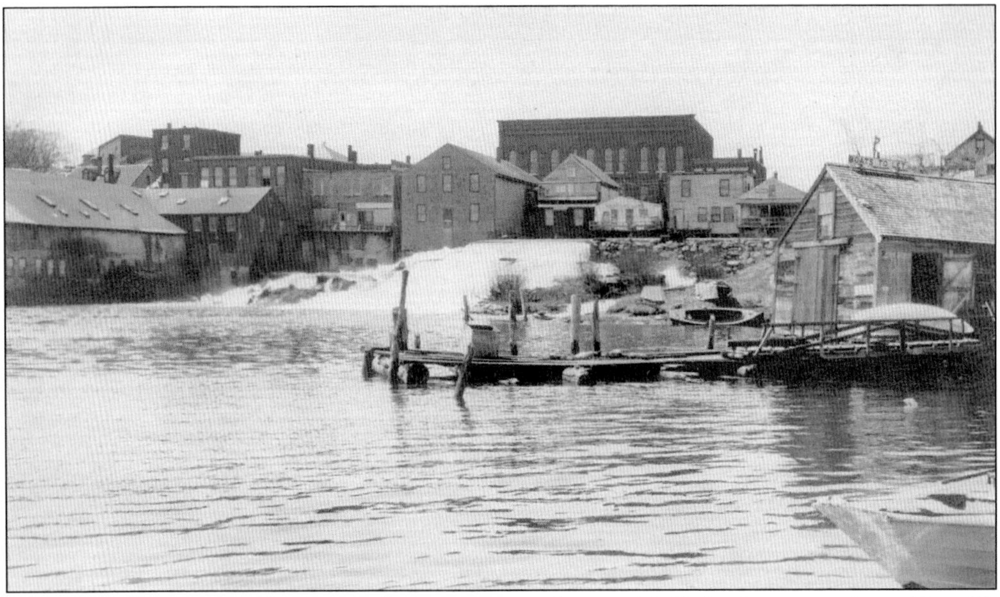

These two images show Camden Harbor as it appeared around 1920. In the image above, Harvill's boat shed is seen near the Megunticook Waterfall in what is now the beautiful Harbor Park. The image below was taken from the top of the falls with a view looking toward the shipyard. The gristmill and anchor factory are at the edge of the frame at right. The falls provided much-needed waterpower to move the mill machinery. Today, the Camden Deli overlooks the sluiceway seen here and is a very popular place for tourists and locals alike.

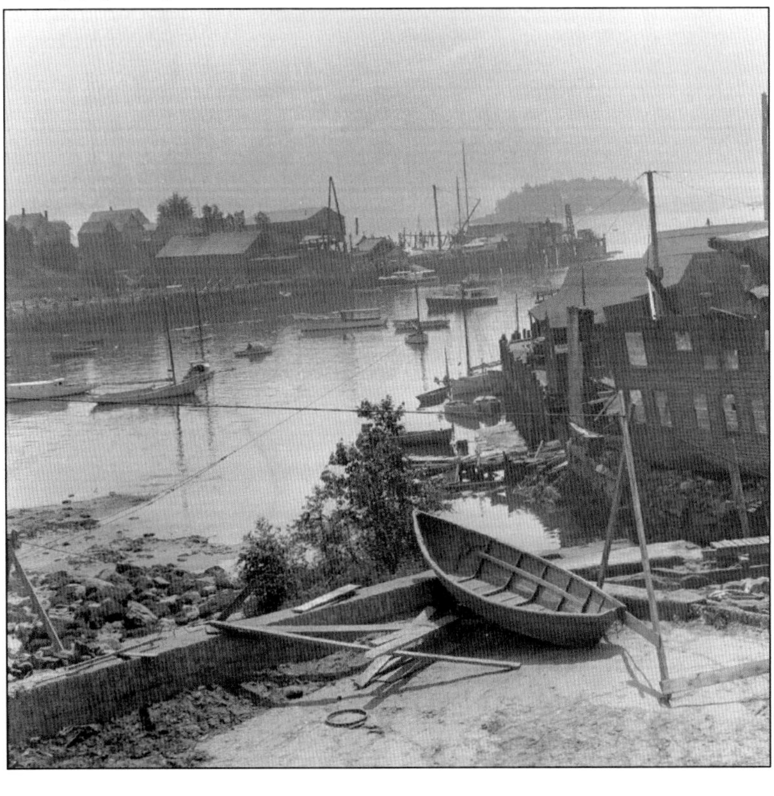

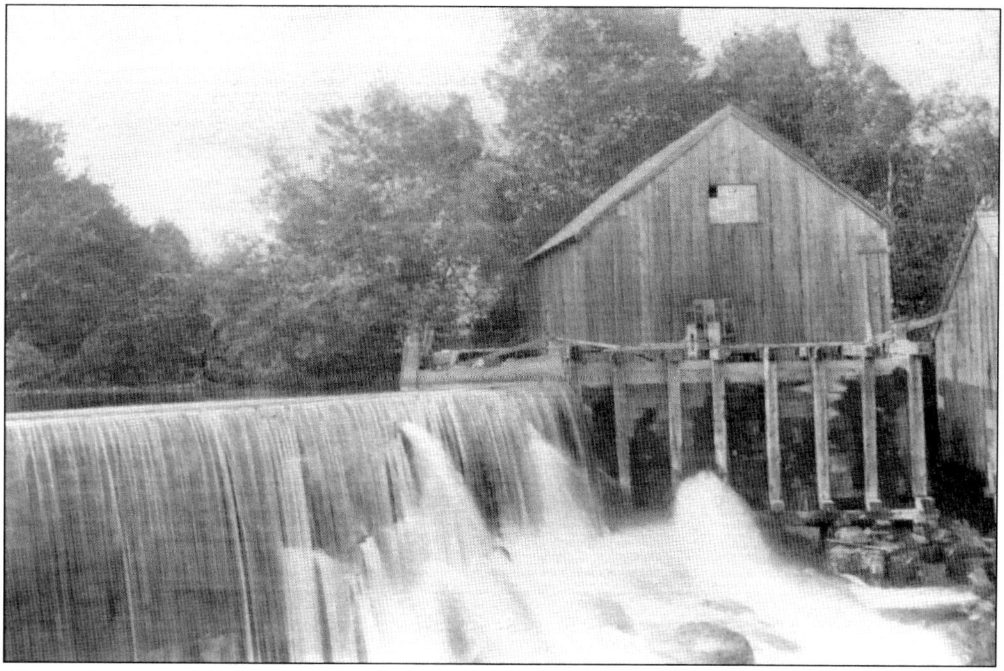

These images are of prominent businessman and gunpowder manufacturer Dr. Deplura Bisbee and the old Bisbee powder mill on the Megunticook River in Camden. Dropping 142 feet to sea level and with up to 10 dams along it, the Megunticook River was a major source of power for the various textile and gristmills in town. The Bisbee powder mill was established in 1853, and it produced up to 50,000 kegs of gunpowder per year, much of which was used in the local lime quarries. It was dangerous work for mill employees, and over the course of its operation, the mill would blow up nine times. One explosion reported in 1853 shook homes, broke windows, and extinguished the light two miles away on Negro (now Curtis) Island. By 1892, the Mt. Battie Woolen Mill was built here, which later became, in succession, the Hughes Mill, a poultry company, Moss tents, and finally a vacant site.

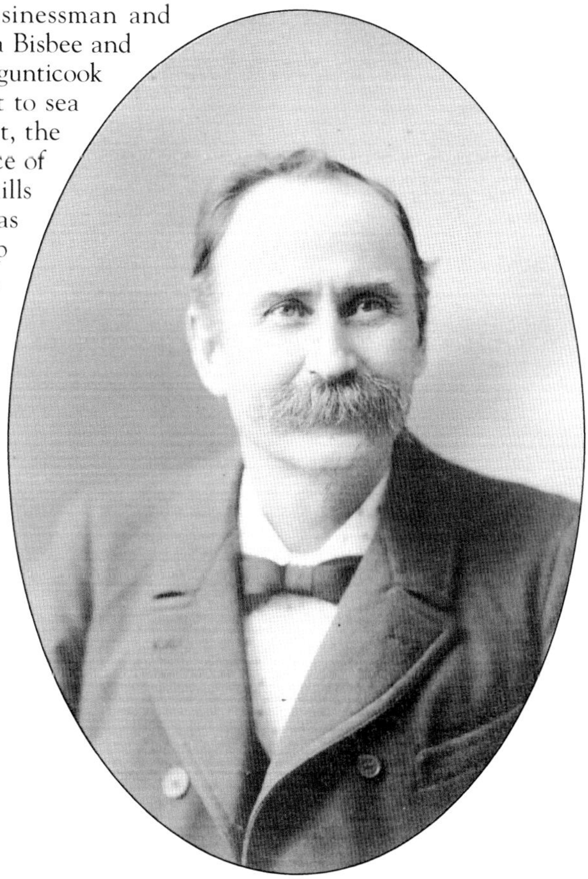

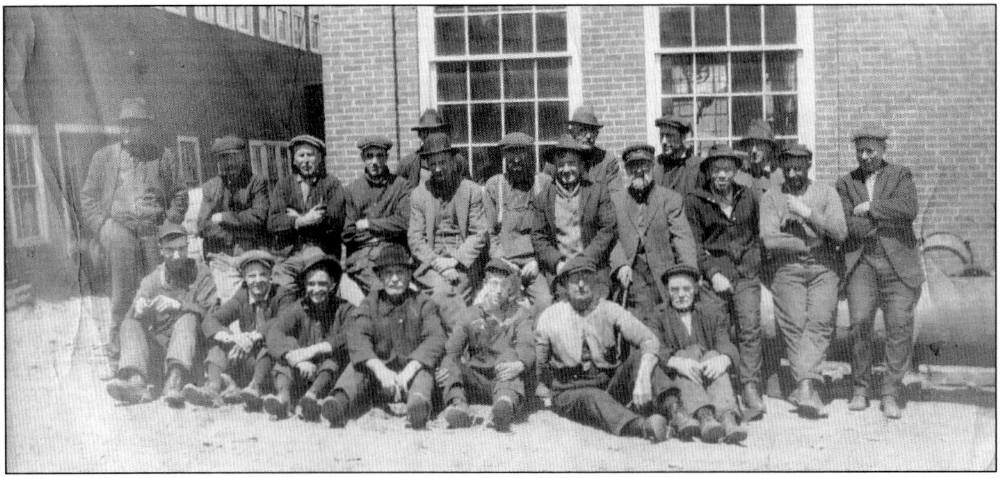

This is a photograph of employees of the Knowlton Brothers Foundry, started by David Knowlton and located on the corner of Mechanic and Knowlton Streets. Knowlton's four sons had joined his business by 1880, and the name refers to the brothers. The foundry made blocks and other supplies such as capstans, windlasses, steering wheels, and deadeyes for the booming shipbuilding industry in the Camden area. By 1900, the foundry employed more than 100 workers at its four-acre property. Later, David Knowlton partnered with Horatio Alden to manufacture machinery to power the oakum factory.

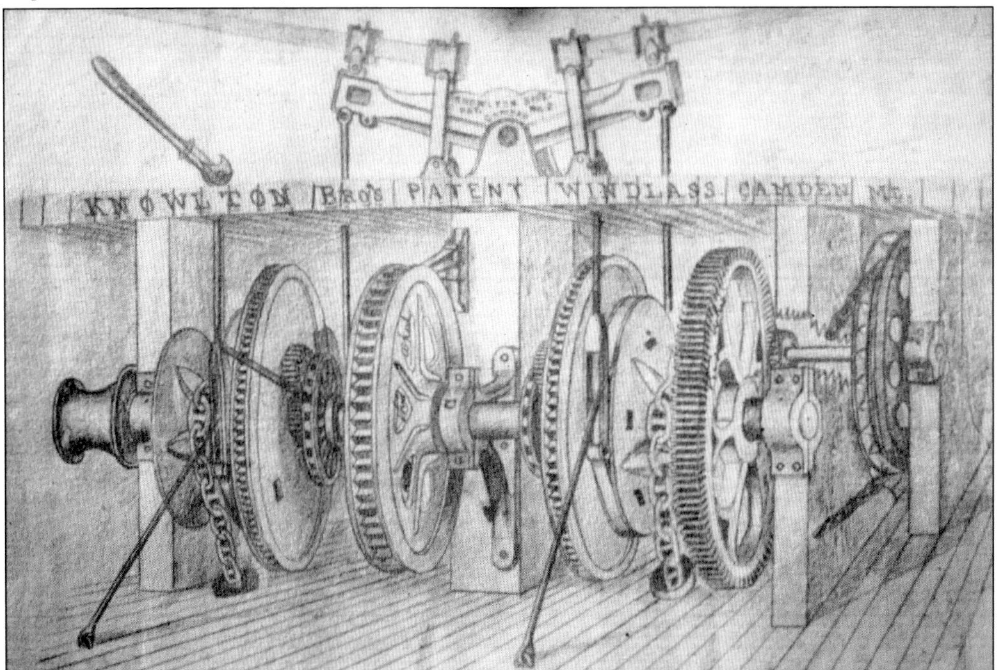

This image is a sketch of the Knowlton Brothers patent windlass. The Knowlton Brothers foundry was started by David Knowlton in 1853, and by 1880 his four sons had joined the business and would continue in operation for more than 60 years. The foundry earned a reputation over the years for unparalleled workmanship and quality. Spread over more than four acres and nine buildings, the foundry was the only block mill east of Boston at that time. It also made the first cars for the North American railroads as well as the local quarry trains.

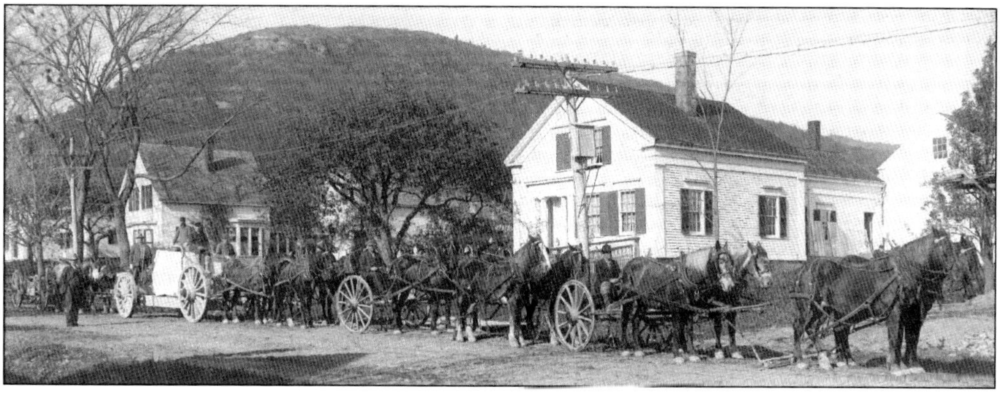

Moving massive blocks of granite in the days before power equipment and engines was an engineering feat. In these two panoramic images, a team of 12 horses moves a block of granite weighing several tons toward the center of Camden, possibly for the construction of the new opera house in 1894. In the image above, the horse team is on Mountain Street. In the image below, the team has proceeded to Washington Street. The Frye & Porter grain and feed mill is at the right of the photograph, next to the bridge. P.H. Thomas's harness shop (behind the granite wagon) advertises horses, carriages, sleighs, whips, and carriage robes.

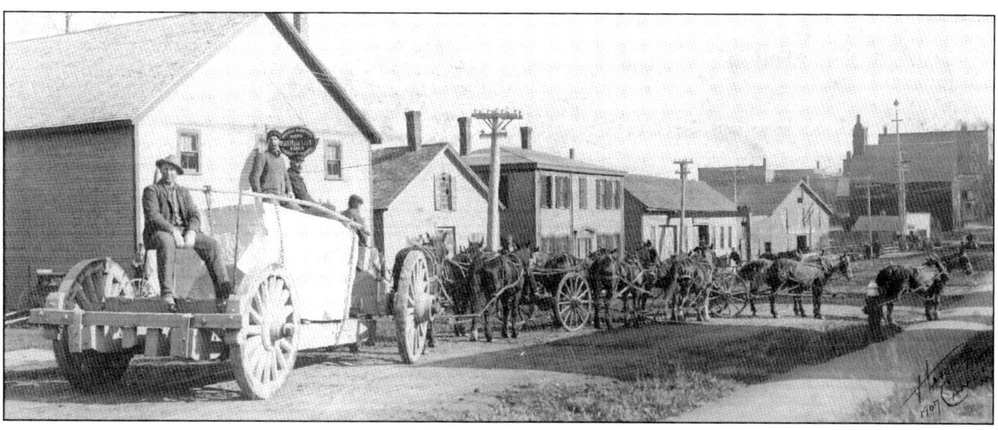

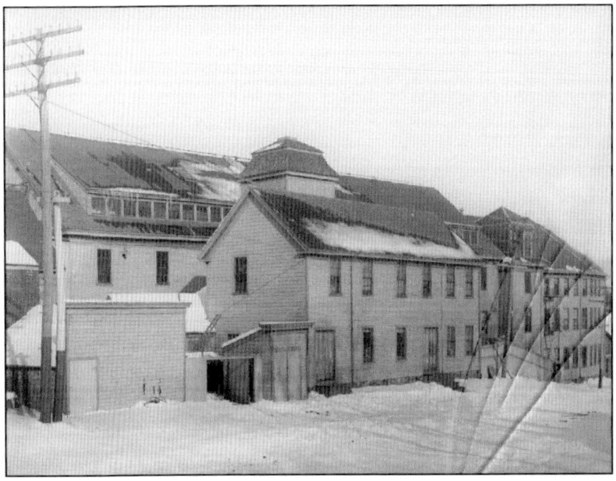

The Knox Woolen Company was incorporated in 1868, and it was the longest-operating textile mill in Camden, where it made "endless" felts for the paper companies. Boasting the largest payroll in Camden, it was a source of employment for generations of families until it ceased operations in 1988. The mill whistle blew four times each day, and many Camden residents used it to keep track of time. This image of the buildings on Mechanic Street shows how the mill looked in the 1930s.

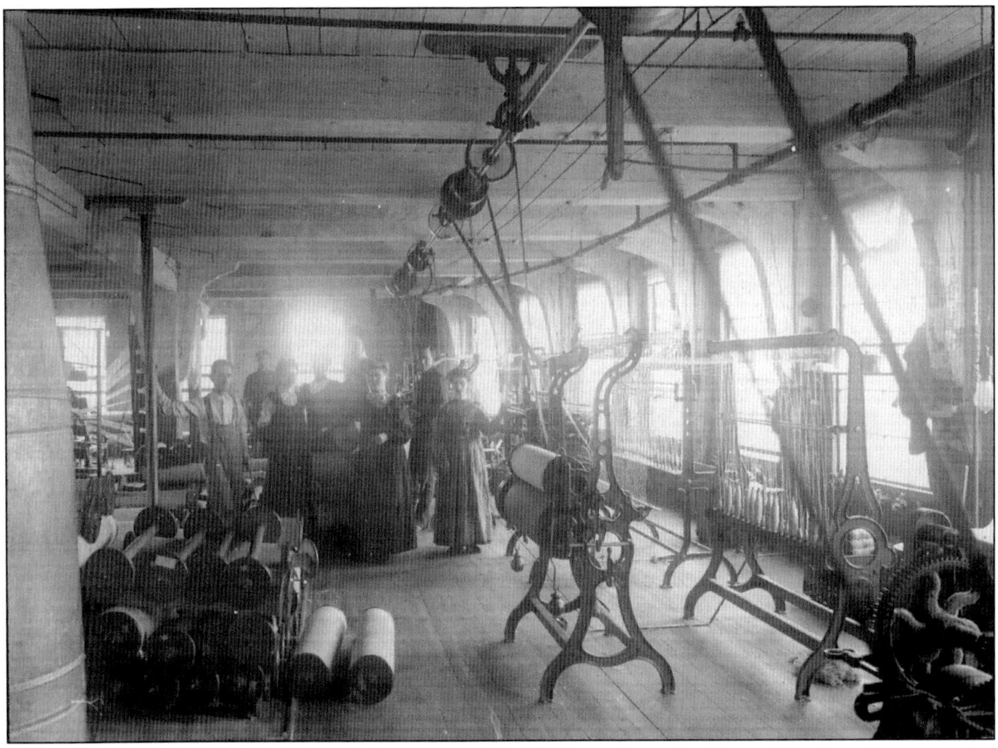

This image shows several employees (both men and women) at the Knox Woolen Company on Mechanic Street in the center of Camden, near machinery used to wind the large bobbins used in weaving the felts.

This aerial view shows the sprawling Knox Woolen Company complex located on Mechanic and Knowlton Streets. The mill was powered by the Megunticook River, which, as it dropped 142 feet to sea level, turned the massive gears under the mill that operated the machinery.

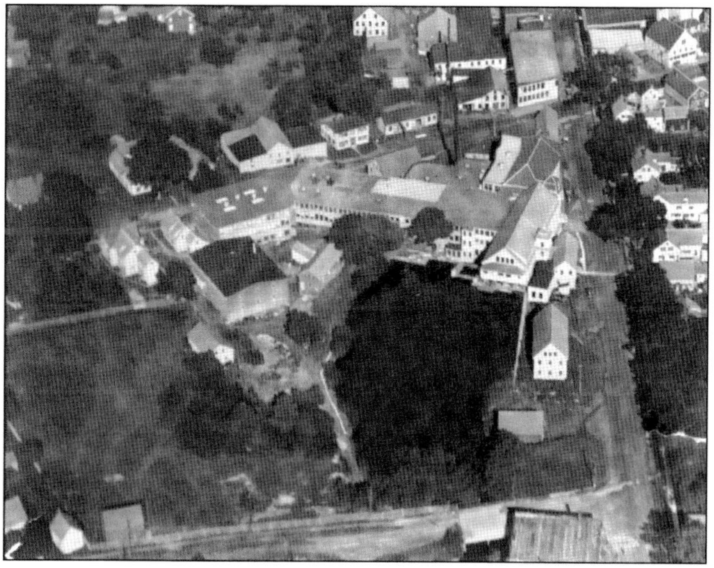

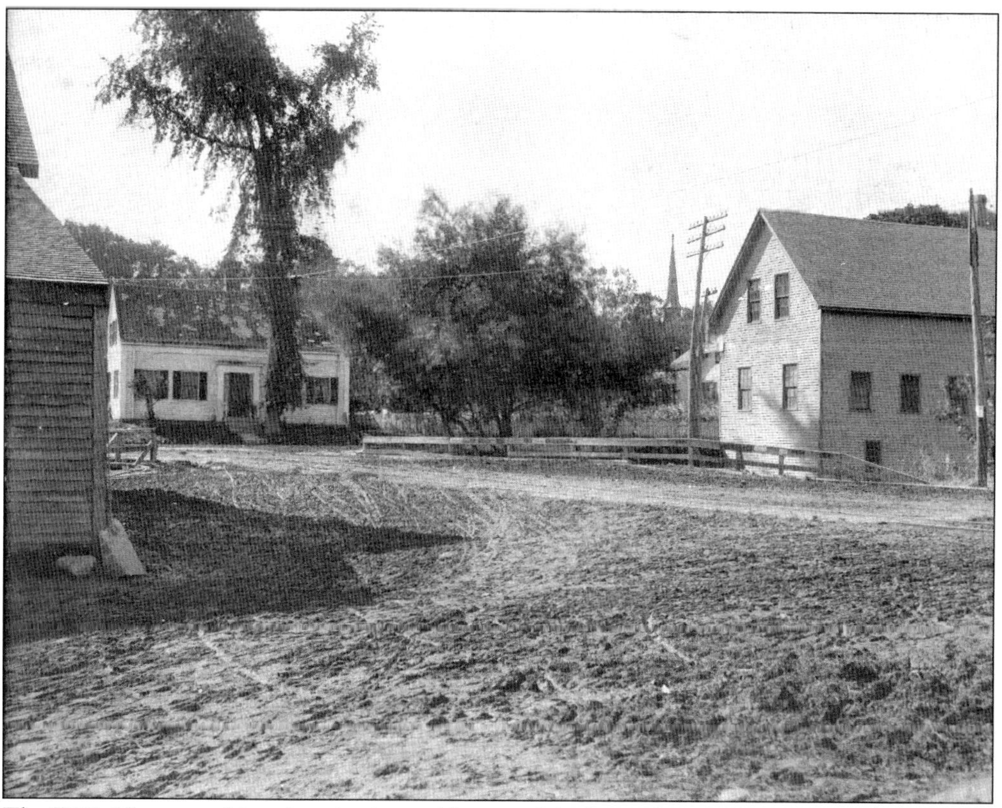

The W.G. Howe machine shop is pictured here on Mechanic Street. Howe repaired all sorts of mechanical equipment, including bicycles, lawn mowers, and guns. He also sold bicycles and cycling supplies at a time when cycling was a popular mode of transport. The safety bike had replaced the high-wheeled early cycles, and pneumatic tires provided a more comfortable ride.

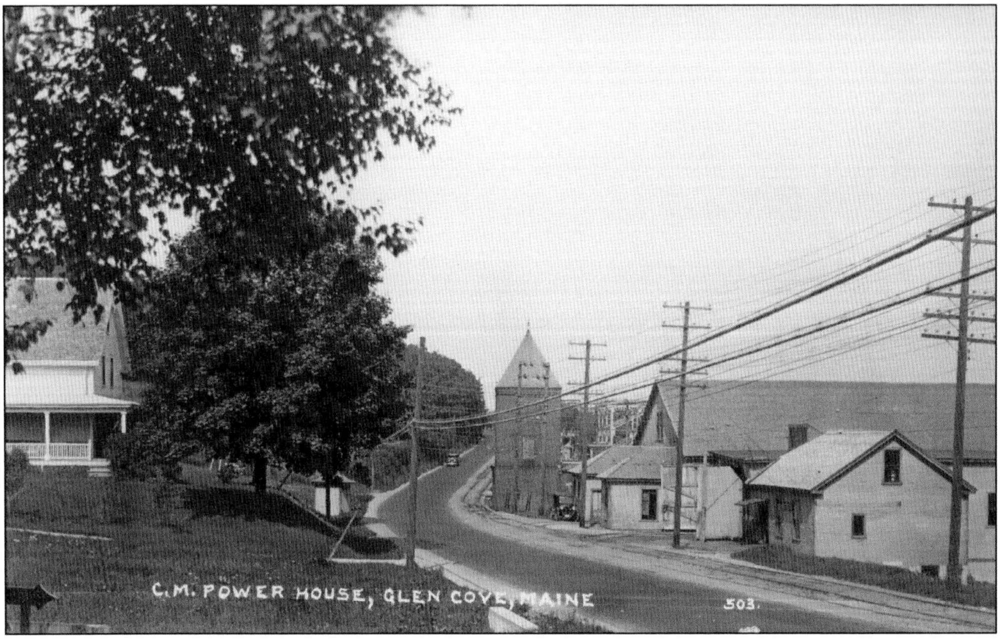

This is a postcard view of the powerhouse and trolley barn on the hill at Glen Cove after it was purchased by the Central Maine Power Company in 1920. According to the local newspaper, the first trolley made its inaugural run at 7:00 p.m. on July 30, 1892. In the early days, there were six cars for good weather and an equal number that were closed for travel in bad weather. In all the years of operation, there were only two serious accidents.

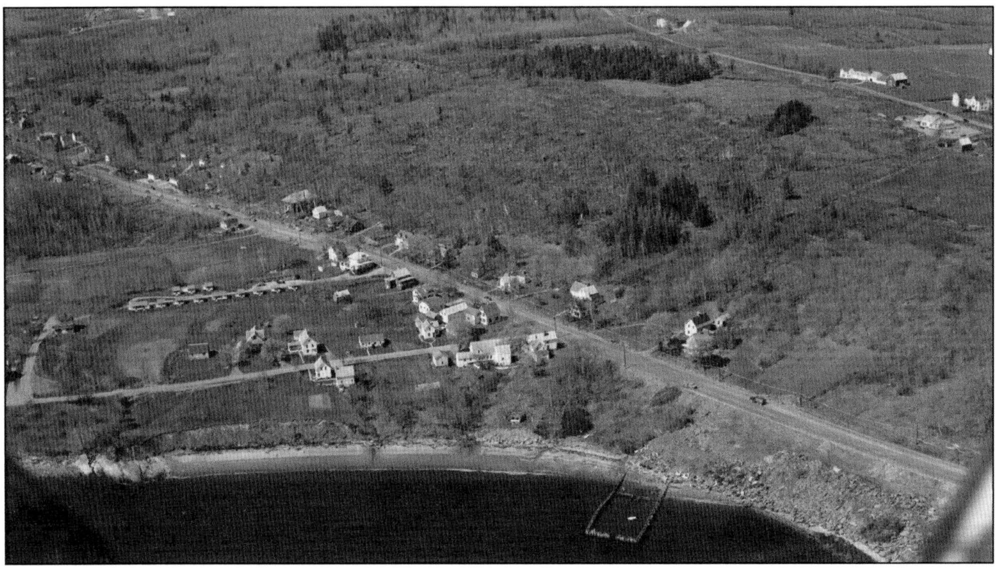

This aerial view shows Route 1 and the area around Glen Cove. Formerly called Clam Cove, this section of Rockport was known as Powerhouse Hill, as it was the location of the trolley barn from 1892 to 1931. The trolley company carried passengers from Thomaston to Camden for 5¢ apiece. The company ran spur lines to the quarries with ever-declining revenue until it was bought out by Central Maine Power Company in 1920. The trolley barns no longer exist, but the name Powerhouse Hill is still used by locals.

Nine

Fires

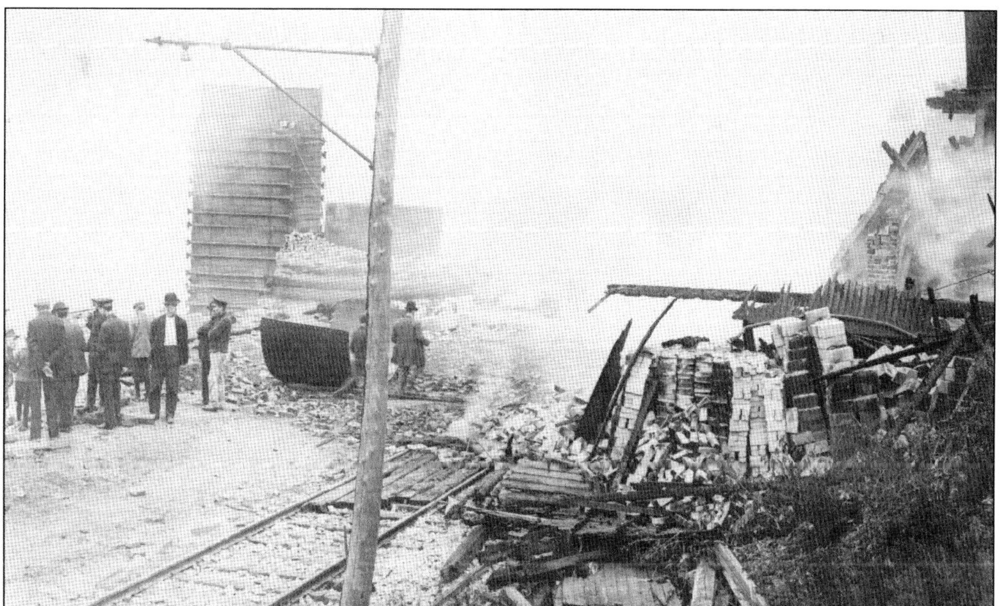

A group of bystanders seems dumbstruck by the devastation at the Rockport lime kilns after the July 1907 fire. The wooden train trestles and shed roofs went up quickly, leaving only the granite and fieldstone kilns remaining. In this image, it appears that some of the trestle timbers have collapsed into the rubble.

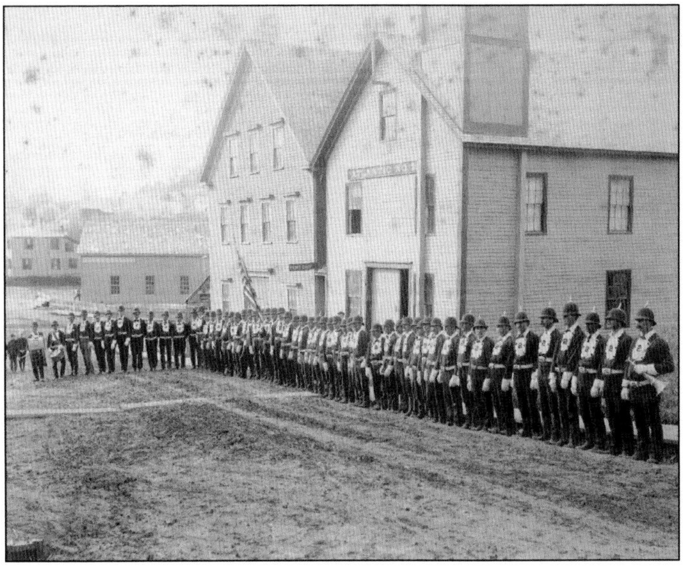

Members of Atlantic Engine No. 2 stand in front of the station on Washington Street around 1880. Organized in 1867, Atlantic Engine No. 2 was originally a private organization that charged money to fight fires. During the great fire of 1892, more than 50 buildings were leveled, as there was not enough water or equipment to go around. After this disaster, the town bought a new steam pumper and made improvements to the water supply lines.

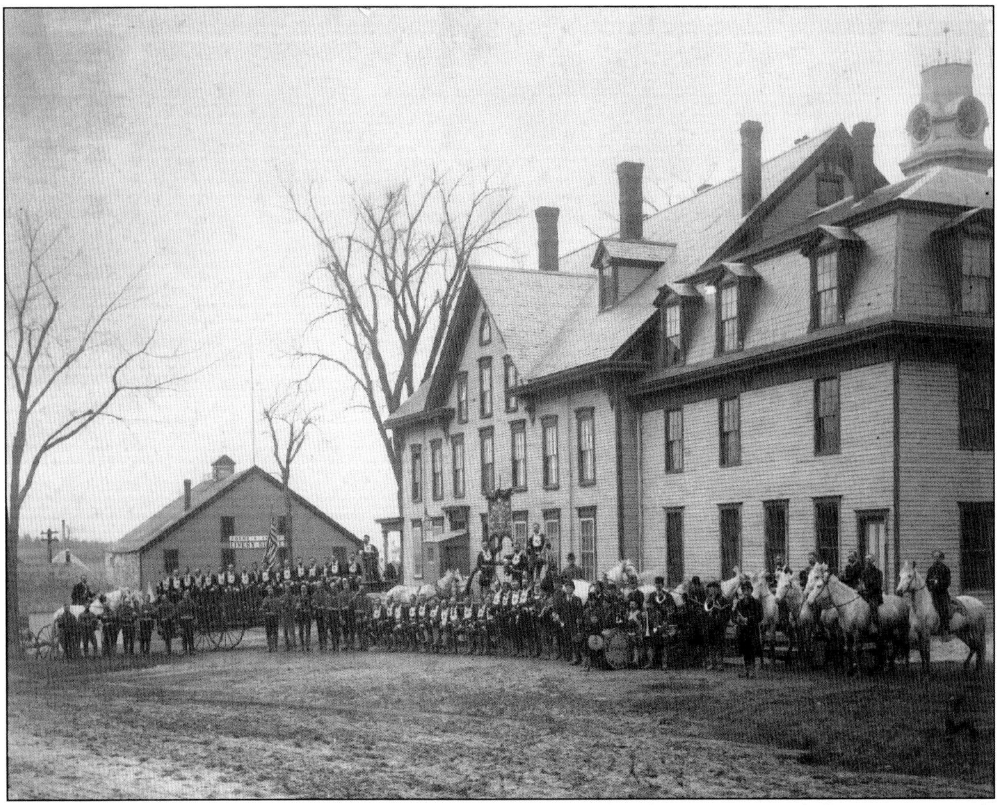

This photograph shows a gathering of the Atlantic No. 2 fire department and the Megunticook Cornet Band in front of the Bay View House. This hotel was a popular destination for visitors, and it was served by several local liveries, including the Rokes & Adams stable directly behind the firemen on Chestnut Street. Operated by H.E. Capen, the grand old hotel burned to the ground in November 1917, and the vacant lot became the site of the Village Green.

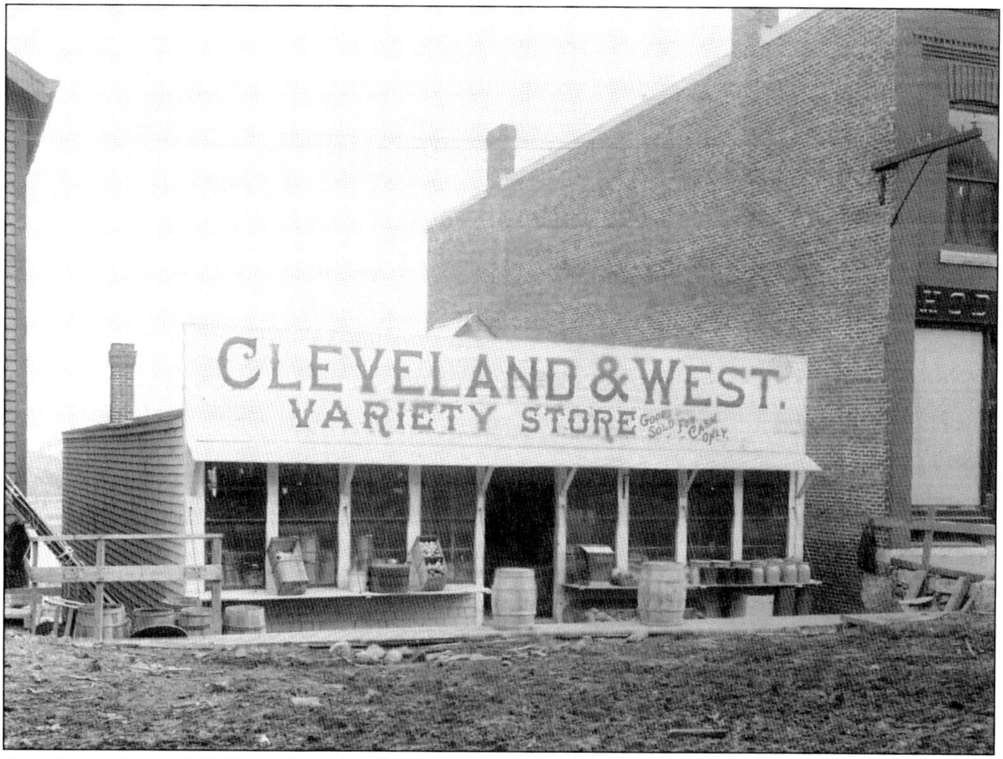

The Great Fire of 1892 in Camden began after midnight in the basement of the Cleveland & West variety store, which at that time was a wooden, multistory building on Main Street. It is believed to have begun in a faulty stove, and the fire was drawn up through an elevator shaft to the roof. Fanned by a gusty east wind, the fire quickly consumed buildings on both sides of Main Street before moving through Mechanic, Washington, and Elm Streets. Thankfully, a snow squall coated the buildings on the west side of the town, which prevented the fire from spreading even farther. More than 50 structures were lost, including the Knight Block and Megunticook Hall, at a cost of several hundred thousand dollars. The image above shows the temporary Cleveland store after the fire, and the image below has a view looking south on Main Street. The large Bay View House on Elm Street is just visible at left in the background.

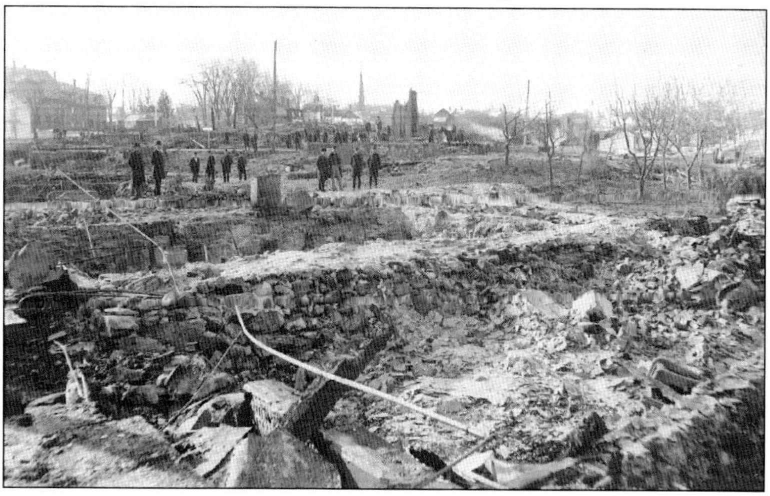

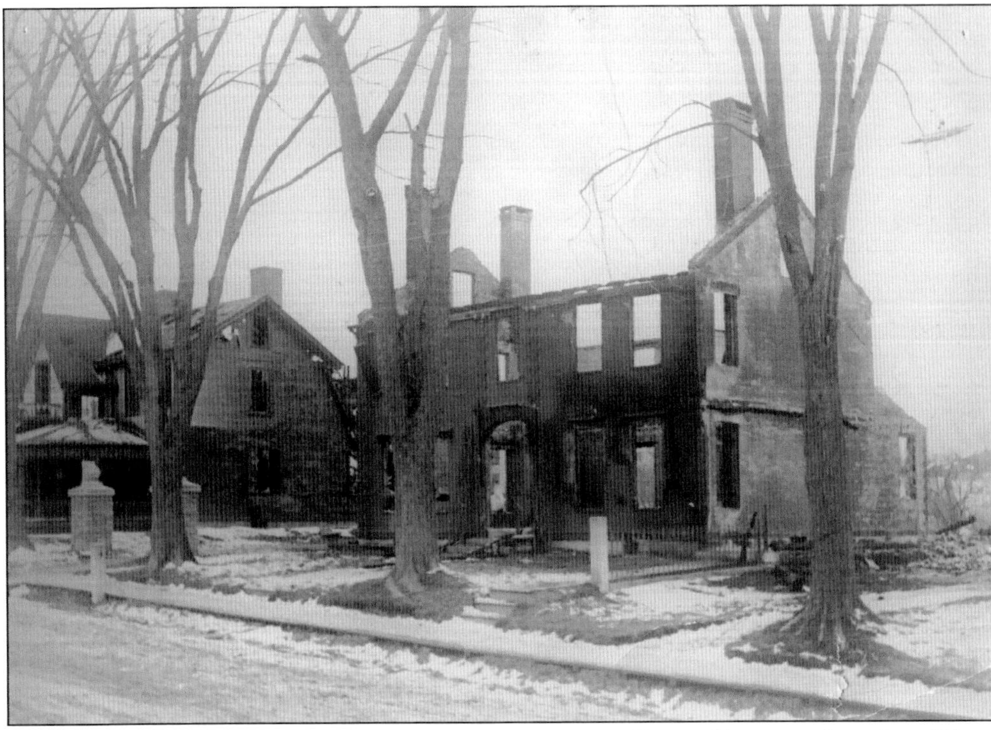

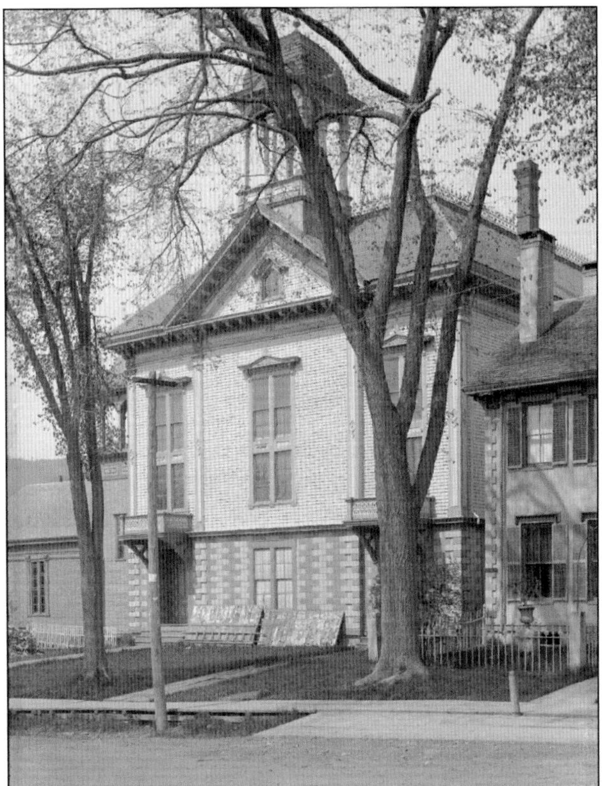

Pictured here are the ruins of Dr. Tibbetts's home (left) at 33 Elm Street and another home on the morning after the fire. Dr. Tibbett resided in what was known as the old Jones House, and it was here that the flames were stopped with the help of one of the steamships. Dr. Tibbetts's home was rebuilt shortly after the fire.

Megunticook Hall (also known as the village hall) was destroyed in Camden's Great Fire, which started in the basement of a shop on Main Street on November 10, 1892. The hall was a large wooden building owned by the Camden Village Corporation and contained a public meeting space, the police station, a courtroom, and the jail.

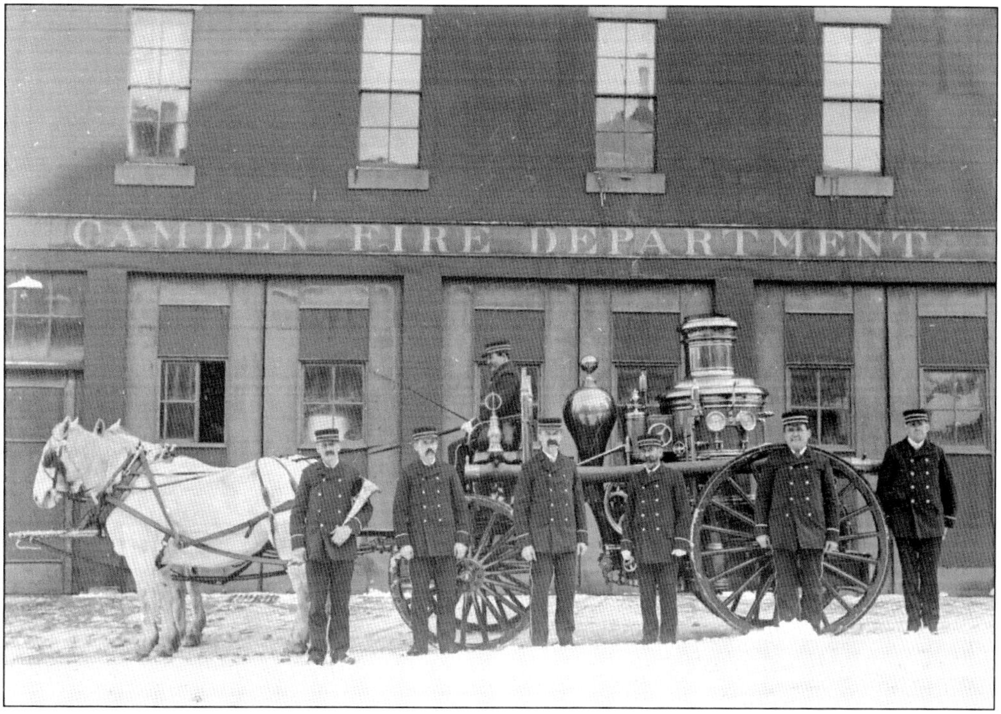

At one point, there were two fire departments in Camden. Atlantic Engine Company No. 2 was formed in 1867 as a private organization. The Camden Fire Department was formed as a town department when the cost for new equipment was greater than AEC No. 2 could afford. Both organizations raised funds for more than 50 years through an annual fireman's ball. In the above image from 1895, members of the Camden Fire Department stand with the new Molyneaux pumper in front of the station on Washington Street. In 1950, the fire department constructed a new brick building near Tannery Lane and named it in honor of beloved chief Allen F. Payson, who led the fire department from 1915 to 1960 and was instrumental in the formation of the ambulance service in 1936. The new ambulance replaced the previous mode of transport for the injured, the Laite Funeral Home hearse.

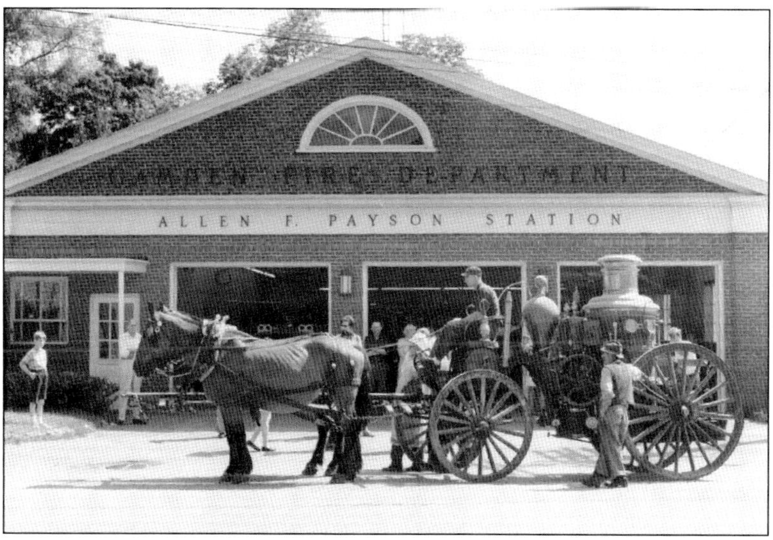

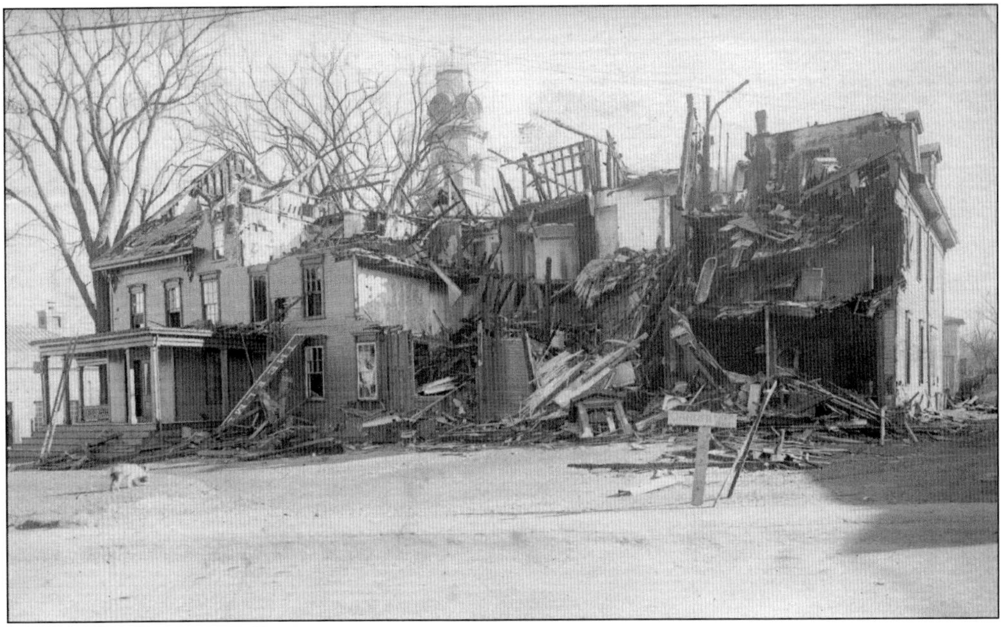

After decades of successful operation as a tourist destination, the grand old Bay View House burned in November 1917. A total loss, the building was torn down, and the vacant lot became the site of a public park known as the Village Green, where the Veteran's Honor Roll is located.

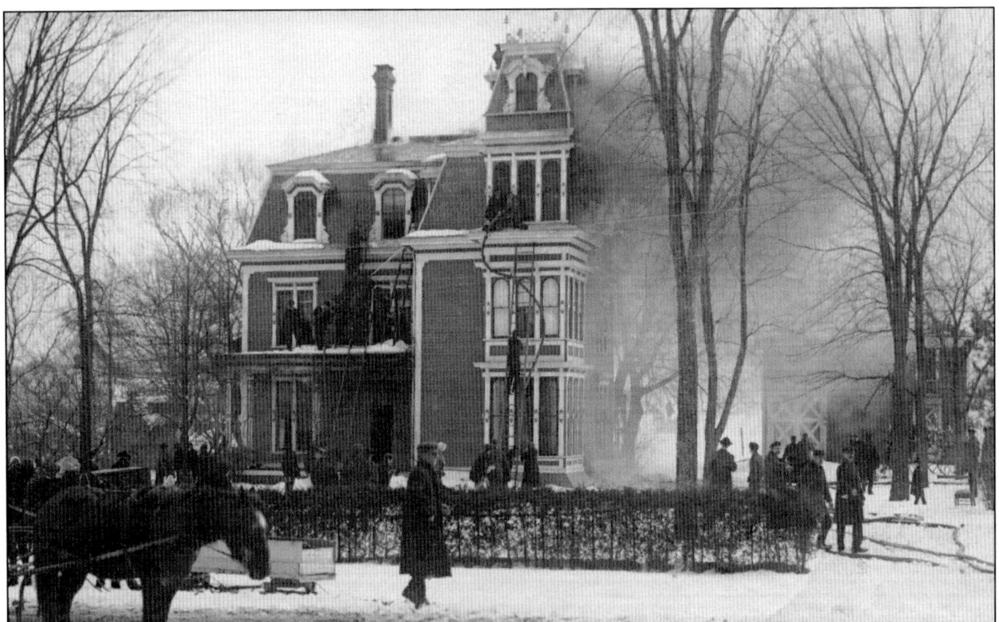

A lovely home belonging to a member of the prominent Shepherd family catches fire on Pascal Avenue in Rockport. The image is undated. In the days before fire trucks were used to fight fires, the townspeople relied on horse-drawn pumper trucks, and many homes and businesses were lost before a fire could be put out.

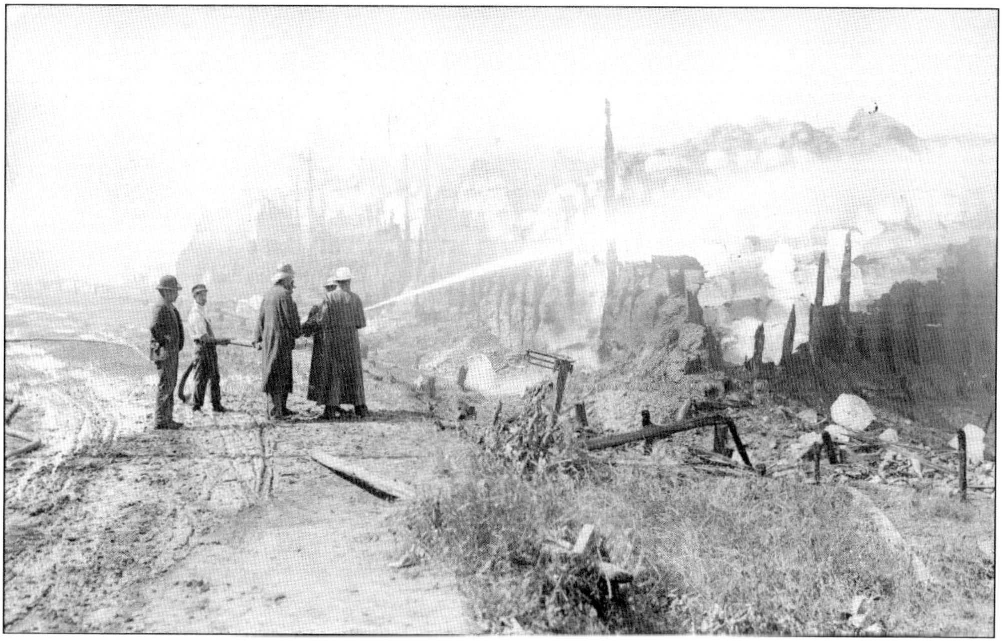

The lime kilns at Rockport Harbor operated 24 hours a day and suffered periodic fires throughout their years of operation. However, 1907 was the year when it all ended for good. Two industries were destroyed in a single day, as a massive fire also made ruin of the icehouses on the opposite shore. In these two images, firemen try to put out the smoking remains of the kilns, while laborers pictured below seem overwhelmed by the destruction.

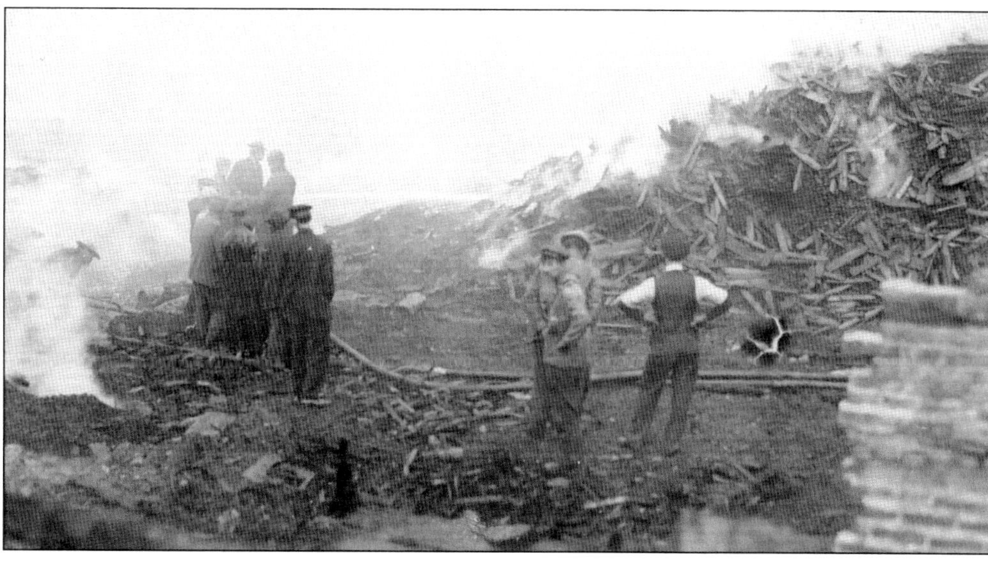

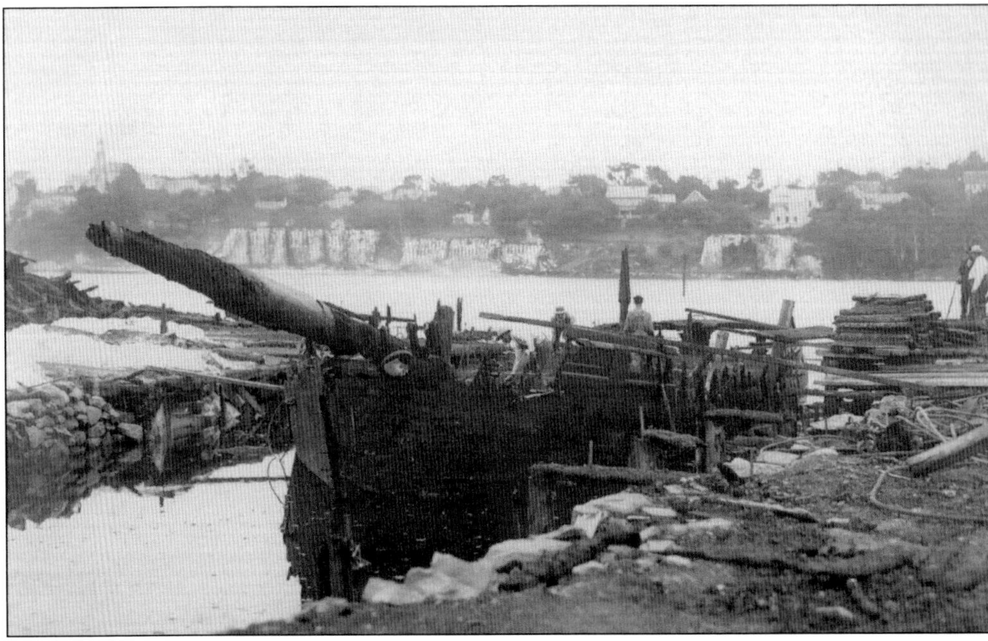

These additional images from the historical society's postcard collection clearly show the ruins of the ice sheds at Rockport Harbor in 1907. Above, a coaster left at the dock has burned to the waterline. The massive blocks of ice from the burned sheds are visible on the opposite shore. Below is a closer view of the ice blocks at the harbor's edge. The fire burned so fast that the sheds were quickly destroyed but the ice was left behind in charred stacks. It is said that the stacks of ice kept steaming for a month after the fire.

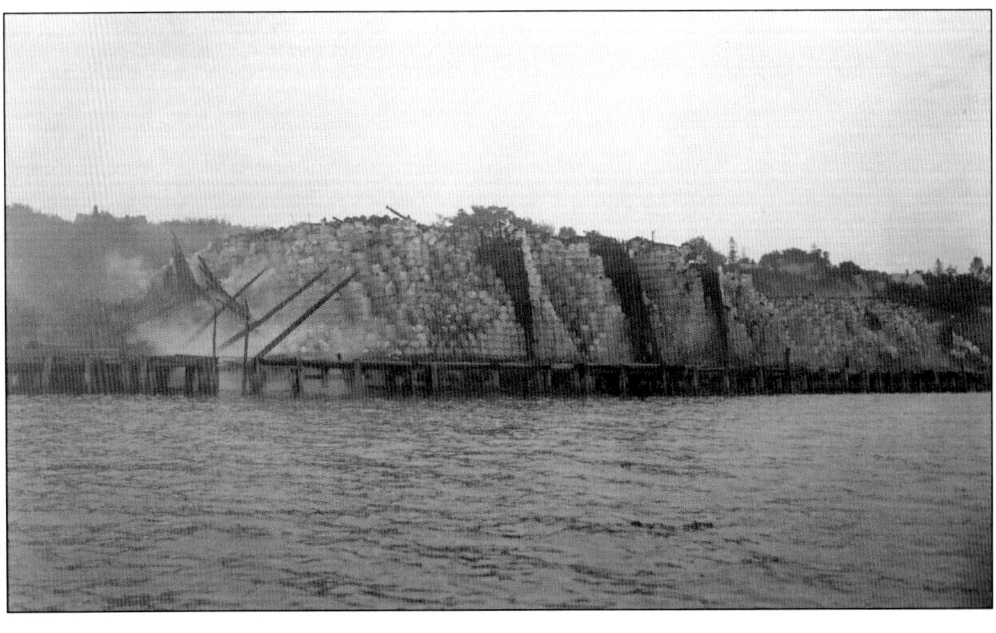

Ten

Local Landmarks

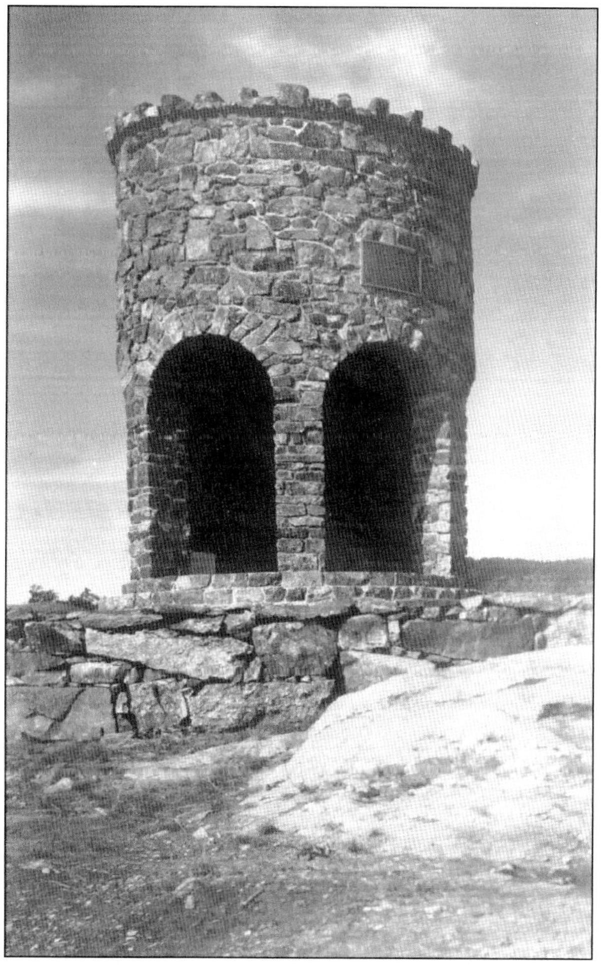

By the end of World War I, the derelict Summit House at the top of Mount Battie was torn down. Camden library architect and summer resident Parker Morse Hooper designed the memorial tower seen here to honor area veterans and their families. He used the stones from the foundation of the Summit House to construct the tower. Every year, a group of dedicated volunteers hangs a wooden star from the tower that lights up the town with 100 bulbs every night from Thanksgiving to New Year's Day.

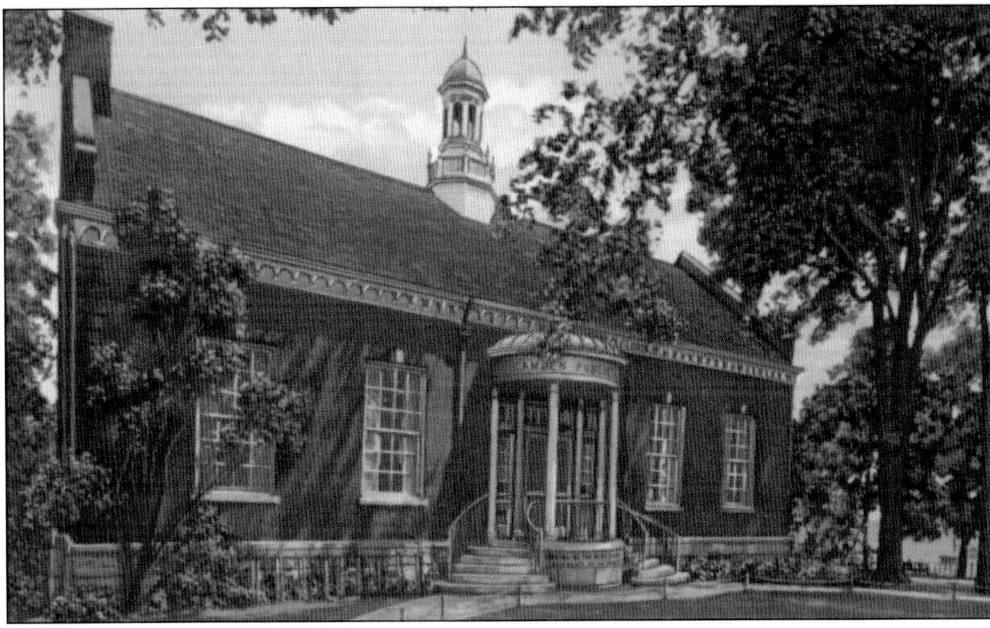

These images of the iconic Camden Public Library and Amphitheatre show the beauty and grace of their design. Parker Morse Hooper, a summer resident of Camden at his estate Hill Acres, designed the library, which was built in 1928 through the fundraising efforts of the local townspeople. The photograph below shows the back of the library as viewed from the Amphitheatre. Designed by noted landscape architect Fletcher Steele, the Amphitheatre is meant to evoke the Maine woods, with birches, pines, and stone terraces. Construction of the Amphitheatre was overseen by Hans Heistad, who also worked on the landscape of Weatherend, John Gribbel's estate on Beauchamp Point in Rockport. The Amphitheatre was opened to the public in 1931, when the Camden High School class of 1931 held its graduation here.

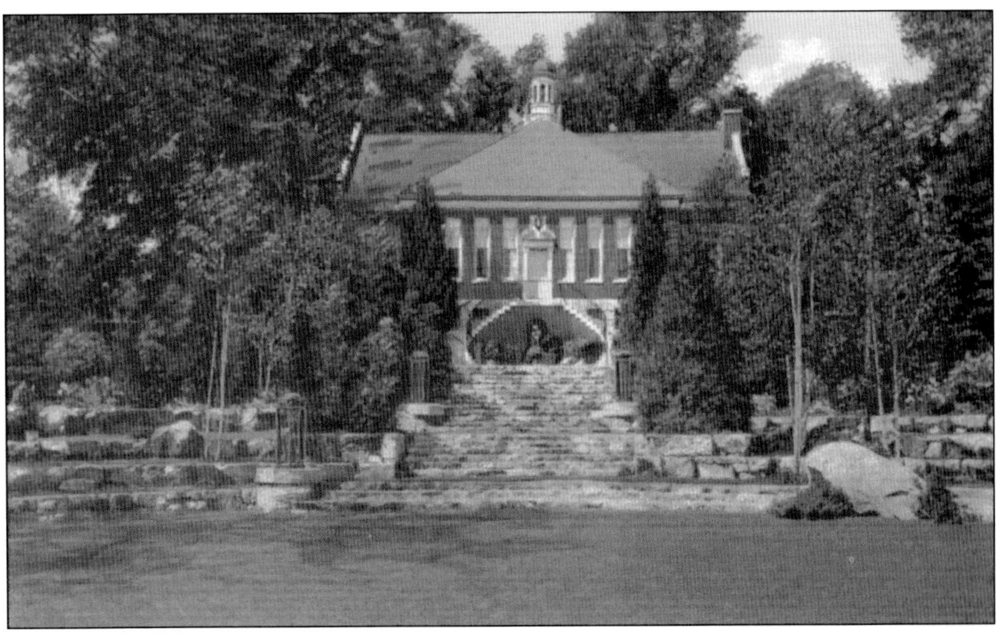

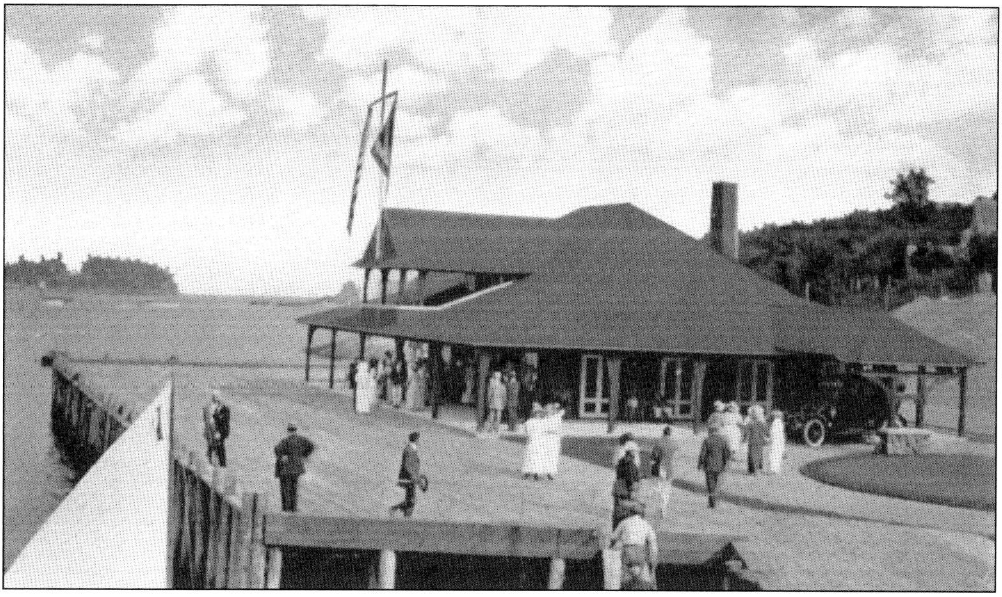

The Camden Yacht Club was formed in 1906 by High Street residents Dr. George Phelps and his neighbor Chauncey Borland. They rented a building near the lime kilns on Bayview Street and put out large floats for dock space. Philadelphia publishing magnate and Rockport summer resident Cyrus H.K. Curtis followed Borland as club commodore in 1910. He bought the lime property, which had gone into decline after the 1907 Rockport fire, and hired architect John Calvin Stevens to design the clubhouse. Constructed by a local builder at a cost of $75,000, the private club opened in 1912. In 1926, Curtis announced that he was gifting the property (worth at that time about $100,000) to the town of Camden to be used by all townspeople as a place of recreation.

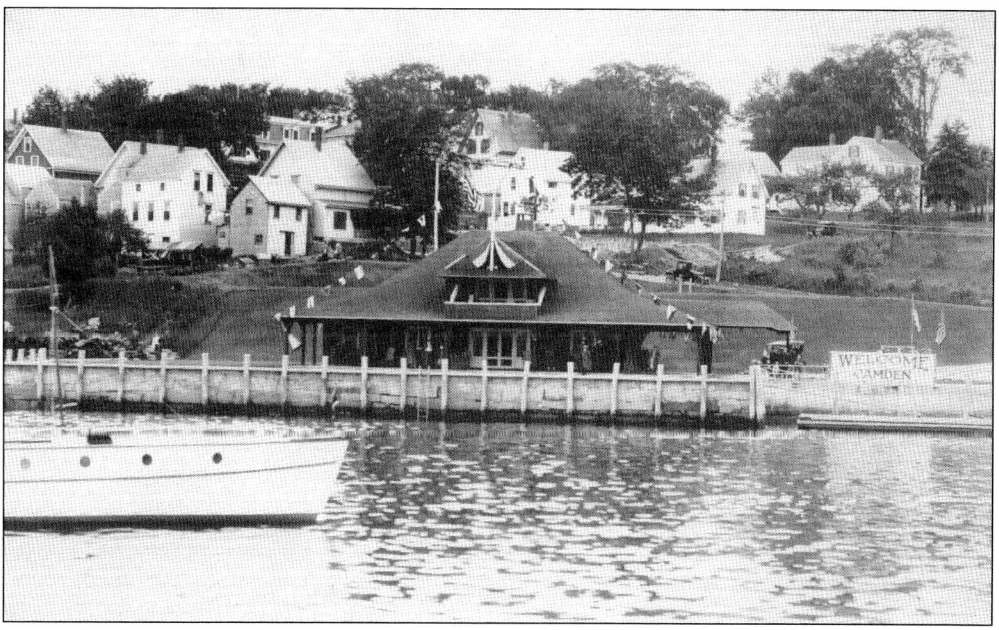

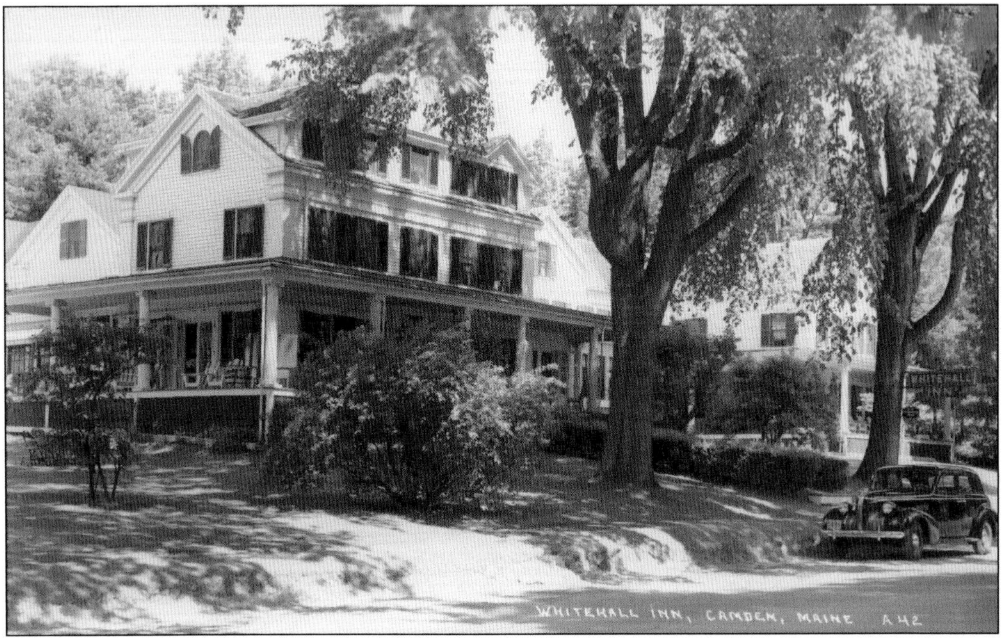

The Whitehall Inn on High Street in Camden has a long history, and it is an iconic part of the town. Once a farmhouse, the property was renovated in 1901 by Ruth Barrett Ordway, a Southern beauty who had married a local sea captain as a mail-order bride. She turned the home into a gracious inn, which earned notoriety as the place of famed poet Edna St. Vincent Millay's discovery. Millay graduated from Camden High School in 1909. It was while attending a party at the Whitehall in the summer of 1912 that she was asked to read some of her poetry. She chose "Renascence," which was published the same year. One of the attendees was so enchanted by her poems that she arranged for Millay's entry into Vassar College. Millay went on to international fame and a bohemian life in New York, and she became the third woman to win the Pulitzer Prize for Poetry.

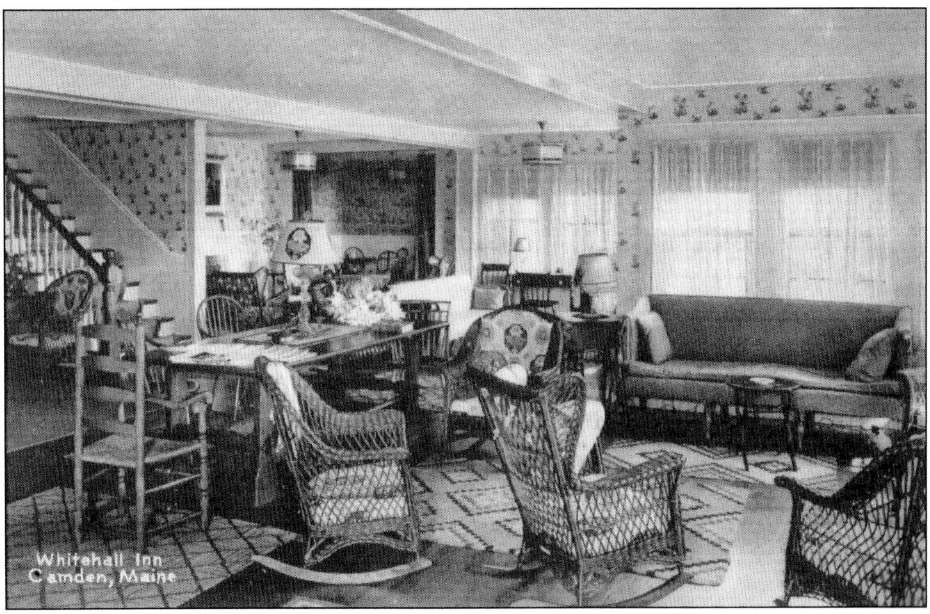

The toboggan chute at the Camden Snow Bowl was built in 1936 as part of the Ragged Mountain ski area. The first winter carnival was held at the base of Ragged Mountain, organized by the Camden Outing Club. There was a hockey rink built on Hosmer Pond, and this was where the toboggan chute had its outlet. At the first carnival in February 1936, more than 5,000 people attended. Community enthusiasm for the sports complex remained high until the onset of World War II. In 1967, the original lodge pictured below was lost to fire after a heater malfunctioned, but it was quickly rebuilt by volunteers. In 1991, the toboggan chute was renovated and dedicated to Jack Williams, the man who organized the effort to revitalize the sport here in Camden. Today, the US National Toboggan Championships are held here every February, bringing in thousands of visitors for a raucous three-day event.

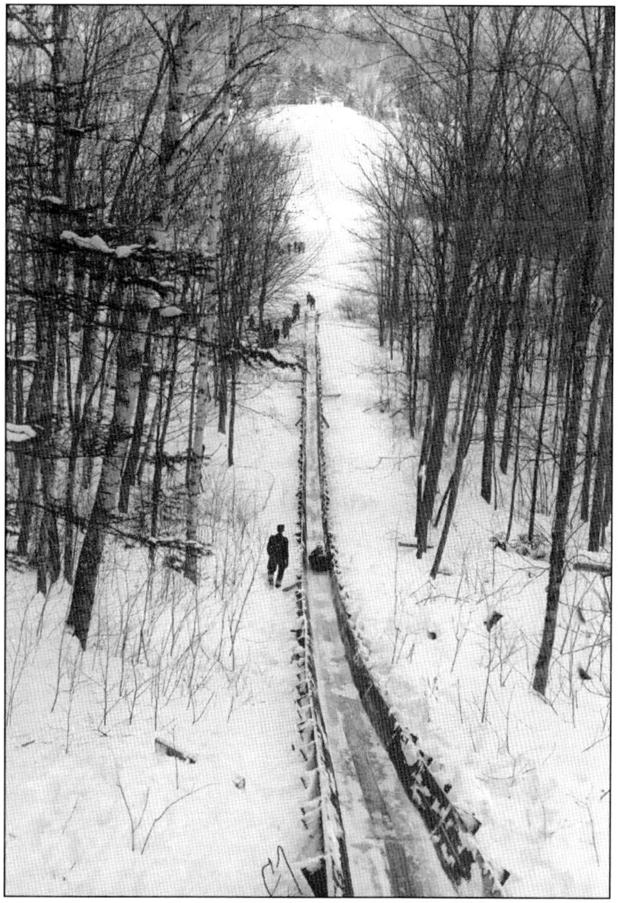

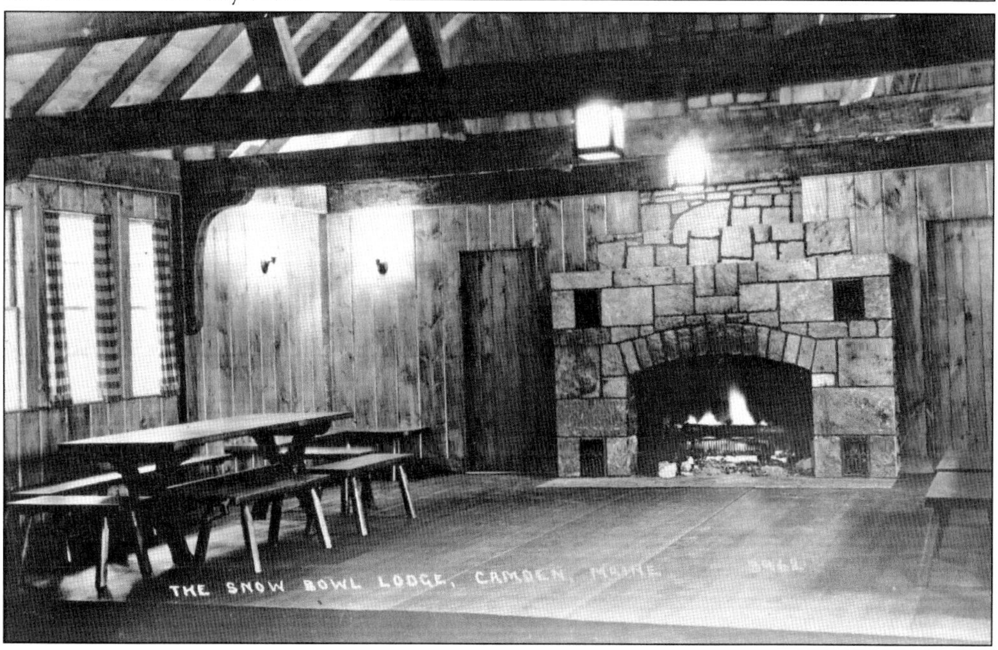

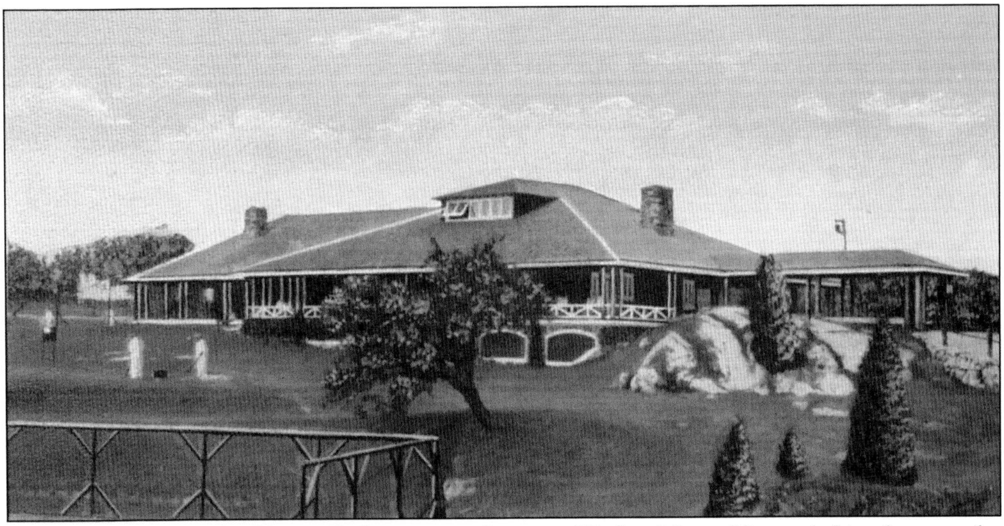

By 1898, the sport of golf was all the rage, and some of Parker Morse Hooper's friends created a six-hole course around his home at Hill Acres. The tiny course proved frustratingly insufficient, so the Megunticook Golf Club was formally organized in 1901 and moved to its present location on Beauchamp Point. Members of the club were owners of the large summer estates in Camden and Rockport—at that time, the lone local member was Judge Reuel Robinson.

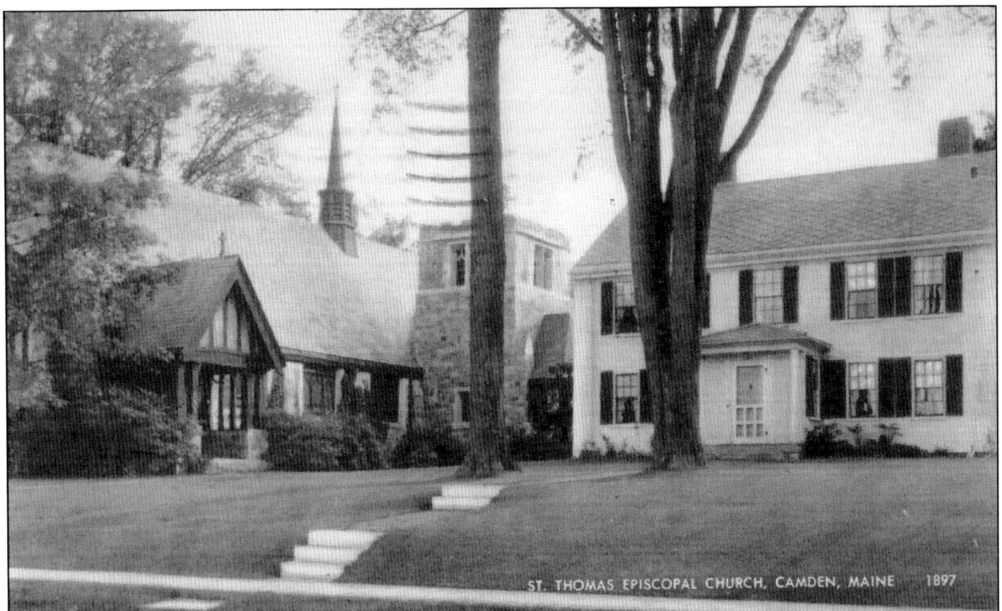

St. Thomas' Episcopal Church was organized in Camden on October 1, 1855. The parish worshipped in the former Universalist meetinghouse on Mountain Street, which became the Farmer's Union for decades and is now a community building called High Mountain Hall. In 1924, St. Thomas' moved to its current English-style stone and timber building on Chestnut Street, which was designed in the 1920s by architect E. Leander Higgins of Portland, Maine. The magnificent stained-glass windows in the church were inspired by those in St. Mark's Chapel at Bishop's University in Quebec where Fr. Ralph Hayden, rector of St. Thomas' from 1919 to 1933, had gone to school.

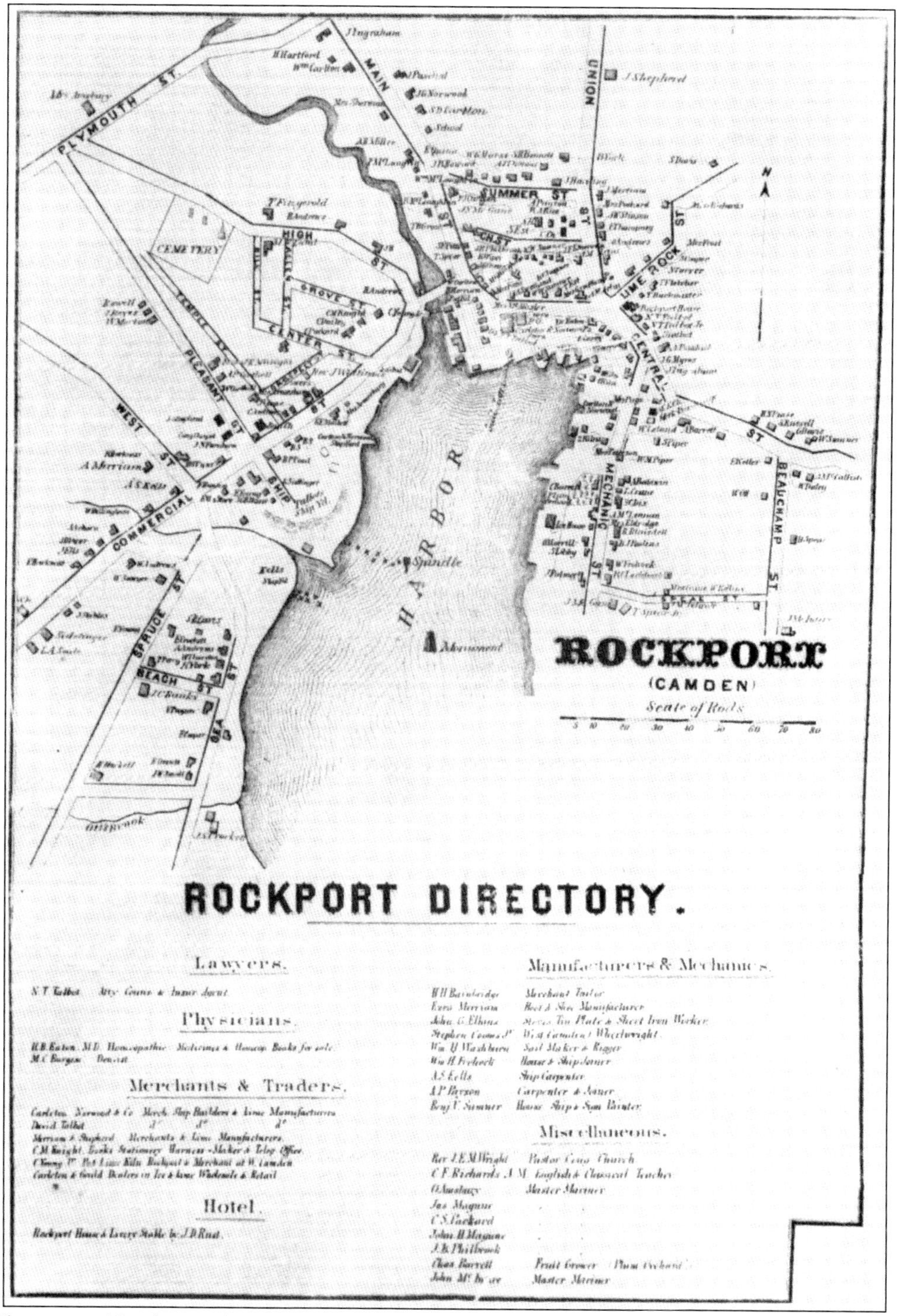

This map of Rockport shows the development around the harbor as it appeared in 1859. The harbor was a hive of activity, with shipbuilders, lime kilns, icehouses, and other industries dotting the shore. Beauchamp Point had not yet been developed, as the wealthy summer rusticators would not begin building their estates until the late 1880s.